Leading from the Front

The War Memoirs of Harry Pope

William Henry Pope, MC

With an Introduction by Dr. David Bercuson

Published by
The Laurier Centre for Military Strategic and D
Studies, Wilfrid Laurier University, Waterloo, O

First published in 2002 by The Laurier Centre for Military Strategic and Disarmament Studies, Wilfrid Laurier University, Waterloo, Ontario, N2L 3C5 CANADA. (519) 884-0710 ext.4594; mbechtho@wlu.ca
www.canadianmilitaryhistory.com

National Library of Canada Cataloguing in Publication

Pope, W. H. (William Henry), 1923-
    Leading from the front: The war memoirs of Harry Pope / William Henry Pope ; with an introduction by David Bercuson.

Includes index.
ISBN 0-9688750-1-7 (bound).—ISBN 0-9688750-2-5 (pbk.)

    1. Pope, W. H. (William Henry), 1923-. 2. Canada. Canadian Armed Forces. Royal Régiment, 22e—Biography. 3. Canada. Canadian Armed Forces—Officers—Biography. 4. World War, 1939-1945—Campaigns—Italy. 5. World War, 1939-1945—Regimental histories—Canada. 6. Korean War, 1950-1953—Regimental histories—Canada. 7. World War, 1939-1945—Personal narratives, Canadian. 8. Korean War, 1950-1953—Personal narratives, Canadian. I. Laurier Centre for Military, Strategic and Disarmament Studies. II. Title.

FC601.P63A3 2002   940.54'215   C2002-902268-1
F1034.3.P67A3 2002

Book & Cover Design: Mike Bechthold
Maps: Mike Bechthold
Printing: Beacon Herald Fine Printing Division, Stratford, Ontario

Printed and Bound in Canada

Contents

Maps and Figures

Photographs follow page xx

Glossary

AAU	Army Administrative Unit
ADC	Aide-de-Camp
AG	Adjutant-General
AHQ	Administrative Headquarters
AWL	Absent Without Leave
CAS	Chief of the Air Staff
CB	Companion of the Order of Bath
CCF	Co-operative Commonwealth Federation
CCS	Casualty Clearing Station
CD	Canadian Forces Decoration
CDS	Chief of the Defence Staff
CF	Canadian Forces
CGH	Canadian General Hospital

CGS	Chief of the General Staff
CIB	Canadian Infantry Brigade
CMHQ	Canadian Military Headquarters
CMM	Commander of the Order of Military Merit
CO	Commanding Officer
COMER	Committee on Monetary and Economic Reform
CP	Command Post
CSM	Company Sergeant-Major
CYR	Carleton and York Regiment
DAAG	Deputy Assistant Adjutant General
DF/SOS	immediate defensive fire
DF	defensive fire
DMI	Directorate of Military Intelligence
DMT	Directorate of Military Training
DSO	Distinguished Service Order
FBI	Federal Bureau of Investigation
FDL	Forward Defensive Line
FOO	Forward Observation Officer
GOC	General Officer Commanding
GOC-in-C	General Officer Commanding-in-Chief
GR	Grenadier Regiment
GSO	General Staff Officer
GSW	Gun Shot Wound
HE	High Explosive
HQ	Headquarters
IO	Intelligence Officer
KR	King's Regulations
LdSH	Lord Strathcona's Horse
LMG	Light Machine Gun
LO	Liaison Officer
LOB	Left Out of Battle
LRDG	Long Range Desert Group
MC	Military Cross
MM	Military Medal
MMG	Medium Machine Gun
MO	Medical Officer

MSC	Militia Staff Course
NAAFI	Navy, Army and Air Force Institute
NATO	North Atlantic Treaty Organization
NCO	Non-Commissioned Officer
NDHQ	National Defence Headquarters
NDP	New Democratic Party
NORAD	North American Air Defence Command
OBE	Order of the British Empire
OC	Officer Commanding
OP	Observation Post
PIAT	Projector Infantry Anti-Tank
PLDG	Princess Louise Dragoon Guards
POW	Prisoner of War
PPCLI	Princess Patricia's Canadian Light Infantry
PSD	*Parti Social Démocratique*
QMG	Quartermaster General
R22eR	Royal 22e Régiment
RAF	Royal Air Force
RAP	Regimental Aid Post
RCIC	Royal Canadian Infantry Corps
RCS of I	Royal Canadian School of Infantry
RCR	Royal Canadian Regiment
RMC	Royal Military College
RMCC	Royal Military College of Canada
ROK	Republic of Korea
ROTP	Regular Officer Training Program
RSM	Regimental Sergeant-Major
RTO	Railroad Transport Officer
RTU	Return to Unit
SMG	Sub-Machine Gun
SP	Self-Propelled (gun)
TEWT	Tactical Exercise Without Troops
UN	United Nations
VCGS	Vice Chief of the General Staff
VE Day	Victory in Europe Day
VJ Day	Victory over Japan Day

Preface

When my copy of *Mémoires du Général Jean V. Allard* arrived in August 1985, I naturally at once looked for any references to me. Having found them, on 30 August 1985 I wrote to the General (in French as always, naturally) as follows (translated):

"My General and my Colonel:

"At last I can address you in this way, as I would have wished to do the day after the death of General Vanier [until then Colonel of the Regiment].

"In the same number of *La Citadelle* [R22eR's regimental journal], that of July, where I learnt that you were now our Colonel, I also learnt that you had published your memoirs. Therefore, I waited until my copy had arrived – which occurred this week – before writing to you.

"But I am greatly humiliated by what I read at page 118 concerning our attack of 19 May 1944 against the Hitler Line

"It is absolutely essential that the facts be re-established. I did not ask my wife to give birth to our son twenty years ago so that in the future he might read that his father was a coward who had surrendered to the enemy. It seems to me that your publishers should be able to stick an 'erratum' page in each copy of your memoirs, clearly stating that after the battle I was made prisoner, unarmed, wearing a Red Cross armband, on re-entering the enemy lines to pick up my wounded. In addition, for those who have already bought your memoirs, truth must be re-established by an article in a forthcoming issue of *La Citadelle* – maybe this letter will do it."

The General was not able to amend his memoirs so I prevailed on the then editor-in-chief of *La Citadelle* to publish two articles in which I detailed the actions of 17 platoon of "D" Company between and 17 and 19 May 1944.

These articles being well received, I ended up producing a total of twenty-six "*Souvenirs de Guerre*" between 1986 and 1993. After a couple of years of this, General Allard wrote me as follows on 9 February 1988 (translated):

"My dear Harry:
"It was with much pleasure that I read your article that appeared *in La Citadelle* of December 1987. I couldn't help smiling when you mentioned your female cousins for I remember very well the occasions when you came to me to ask permission to go visit them.

"I wish you to know that I find your articles truly remarkable. There are not many people that have the ability to transmit their experiences in writing and I believe that those that have this gift must make a present of it to future generations. I do not know if you have ever thought of writing a book with all that you have to tell us. I think it would be really fantastic if you dared attempt the adventure for I know you are able.

"I can only encourage you on this path and I leave to you and your wife my best salutation."

(Signed) "Jean"

After I had translated my twenty-six *Souvenirs de Guerre* into *Memories of War,* Professor Terry Copp of Wilfrid Laurier University, Editor-in-Chief of *Canadian Military History* and Co-Director of The Laurier Centre for Military Strategic and Disarmament Studies, suggested I put them all in book form. In doing so, I have expanded my analyses of the actions of 17 and 18 platoons of "D" Company of R22eR in Italy in 1944 during the time I commanded one or the other, and of "C" Company of 1R22eR and 3R22eR, which I commanded in Korea in 1952-53 for thirteen and a half months. In my analyses I have gone up to company and battalion level whenever I had something to say about actions and decisions made there. Criticizing myself as I do, I have no reason to be shy of criticizing others. My most important criticism – repeated every time we met and defeated the enemy – was our repeated failure to exploit our success.

Moreover, since my mother and my older brother Joe kept all the letters I wrote them during the Second World War, I have been able to add anecdotes that reveal my uncensored thinking.

I have tried to make my memories useful to our soldiers that may yet have to make war. Therefore, I continuously analyse the mistakes I made on the battlefield and show how I could have done better. It does not embarrass me to do this for I know my record in action was not dishonourable.

Harry Pope
Uxbridge, Ontario, 1999

Acknowledgements

Harry Pope completed this manuscript in the summer of 1998. Several trade publishers showed an interest in the book but no satisfactory arrangements could be made and Harry decided to publish through the Laurier Centre for Military Strategic and Disarmament Studies at Wilfrid Laurier University. The original manuscript was edited by John Parry with additional work by Terry Copp and Geoff Hayes. David Bercuson, who had come to admire Harry's contributions in Korea, agreed to write an introduction. Michael Bechthold designed the book and created the maps. Harry Pope died 23 December 2000.

Among the obituaries was this tribute from Mark Lovewell, a colleague at Ryerson:

LIVES LIVED
William Henry (Harry) Pope
Soldier, economist, Canadian nationalist, husband, father.
Born Feb. 22, 1923, in Ottawa. Died Dec. 23, 2000, at Uxbridge, Ont., of cancer, aged 77.

Just after dawn on May 19, 1944, on the Italian front, a 21-year-old Canadian lieutenant discovered that a foray in the early morning darkness had landed him and several comrades in German-controlled territory. For several hours the Canadian soldiers were pinned to the ground, as bullets whistled overhead. A mortar landed nearby and severely wounded two of them, so the lieutenant crawled back to his company and asked for a stretcher and some bearers. This request being granted, he and the stretcher-bearers put aside their weapons and donned Red Cross armbands, then advanced on the open battlefield, only to be taken prisoner.

Once the German captain appeared, Lieutenant Pope strenuously objected: "I come from a military family and cannot accept the dishonour of being made a prisoner," he informed the surprised captain. "So long as I have reason to believe we will all be repatriated, I will not try to escape; but as soon as I come to realize that we won't be, then it will be my duty to escape."

Pope was true to his word. Eleven days later, he jumped off a transport truck, and for the next two months fought behind enemy lines, alongside Italian partisans and British parachutists, before rejoining his own Canadian regiment. For those who knew him later in life, once he'd become an academic economist, these early exploits come as no surprise. Pope had a military demeanor and aristocratic bearing. His mother was a Belgian countess and his father was from a well-known Canadian family that included J.A. Macdonald's private secretary and a father of Confederation.

On graduating with the class of '40 at Royal Military College, Pope enlisted in the Voltigeurs of Quebec and then the Royal 22e - a French Canadian regiment. Besides his Second World War record (twice mentioned in despatches), he was awarded the Military Cross during the Korean War and was promoted to major. In peacetime, he held staff and regimental posts until 1959, when he took strong exception to NATO's defensive strategy of limited nuclear war - a prospect he viewed as suicidal. He publicized his opposition to NATO policy in an article for the Canadian Army Journal, and submitted his resignation from the military soon after.

After his exit from the army, he took on political work, as an assistant to the CCF/NDP federal leaders, Tommy Douglas and Hazen Argue. Later, while a graduate student, first at the University of Ottawa and then the University of Toronto, he ran several times as an NDP candidate.

ACKNOWLEDGEMENTS

In 1967, he began a career as an economics professor at Ryerson University, while publishing widely. His first book, *The Elephant and the Mouse* (McClelland & Stewart, 1971), called for measures to regain control of the Canadian economy. He also co-authored several editions of *Economics*, a widely used principles text. Later publications provided an identifiable perspective of economic policy, combining post-Keynesian theories with a nationalist political stance. Pope gradually lost faith in conventional parliamentary parties. He focussed instead on the Committee on Monetary and Economic Reform (COMER), of which he was a founding member, and was involved in Mel Hurtig's National Party.

Forthright in manner, with a ready wit and a hot temper, Pope was someone who found it difficult to remain idle. After retirement, his economic writings continued with *All You MUST Know About Economics*. And 10 days before he died, the first half of his war memoirs arrived from his editor. With characteristic powers of concentration, Pope worked through the manuscript, to be published this spring. He is survived by his wife Sheila and 21-year-old son Richard. Ryerson is establishing an economics award in Pope's memory.

(from the *Globe and Mail*, 22 February 2001)

Introduction

From the very beginning of his life, William Henry Pope – Harry to his friends – personified the meaning of the word "individualist." For much of his life he was a professional soldier, a career he chose when he sought entry to Royal Military College within a year of the outbreak of the Second World War. For seventeen years thereafter Harry worked at his trade as a soldier of the "active," or regular, army. He fought in Italy and the Netherlands in the Second World War and he fought in Korea. That alone would no doubt have qualified Harry to write an interesting memoir. But Harry's story is not simply the recitation of battle after battle, or army post after army post, because he also fought innumerable battles against the dead weight of military bureaucracy, empty convention, and hidebound army traditionalism.

Militaries are innately conservative institutions. Tradition binds soldiers together before battle, and prepares them as well as anything can for the brutality of it, while the base reality of war – going into danger to kill or be killed – has not changed since the dawn of time. The individualist, the innovator, the soldier who "thinks too much" has historically had a difficult time in the military. But Harry Pope was a soldier who believed that it was a soldier's duty to find new and different ways of achieving effectiveness in his deadly trade. He deliberately chose a hard path in a profession that has historically mistrusted individualism, experimentation, and the application of intellect to the solution of battlefield problems and, almost from the start of his career, balked at simply following army convention. Harry Pope refused to bow to the stultifying conformity of authority that so often and so easily destroys initiative and innovation in armies, so he never achieved high command rank in his profession. Despite his uphill fight against his own superiors, however, Harry Pope eventually emerged as one of the most creative tactical innovators in the Canadian Army.

Harry Pope began his military career in March 1939. He was 16 years old and his father, Colonel Maurice Pope, a Permanent Force officer serving as Director of Military Operations and Intelligence in Ottawa, chose the city's 1st Field Battery as a suitable unit for his son. Harry's first army pay, three days' worth, was for the 1939 Royal Tour. When war broke out in September Harry and his friends were afraid "it was starting a year and a half too soon."

Although Maurice Pope had "little use" for Royal Military College (RMC), he told Harry that if he was going to make a career of the army "you might as well go in by the front door" so in August 1940 William Henry Pope became an officer cadet.

Harry remembered RMC without affection but admitted that the hazing and arbitrary discipline meant that "after RMC nothing could get you and it generated a formidable class spirit. We became," he recalled, "like soldiers that had fought and won a particularly tough campaign." With the wartime course shortened to just two years, Harry graduated as a lieutenant in the Canadian Armoured Corps assigned to a recce regiment. After further training at Dundurn in Saskatchewan he joined the 24th Reconnaisance Regiment, *Les Voltigeurs de Québec.*

Harry Pope was fluently bilingual, proud of his Belgian-born mother and his paternal grandmother, a member of Quebec's prominent Taschereau family. Many of his friends were young, bilingual French Canadians, the children of families with long military traditions. Harry was proud of the *Voltigeurs,* writing hours to his parents to describe "a very good regiment" with "great esprit de corps." Unfortunately the *Voltigeurs* were understrength and according to Harry couldn't get enough men, especially men suitable for recce squadrons, from the recruiting depots.

In early 1943 the *Voltigeurs* were reconfigured as a motorized infantry battalion slated to serve with 4th Armoured Division. Harry welcomed the change as he was now old enough to go overseas and believed that the *Voltigeurs* would be brought up to strength and sent to where the action was. The regiment was sent to train at Sussex in New Brunswick but there was little to do beyond route marches and simple tactical schemes. There was ample time and energy to get into trouble and Harry and his men were soon involved in what the press called the battle of Sussex - a clash between the *Voltigeurs* and the Dufferin and Haldimand Rifles.

The *Voltigeurs* reached England in July 1943 demoralized by rumours that they would be one of a number of battalions broken up to provide reinforcements for Italy. Harry, impatient for action, asked his father for advice and went up to London to see what could be done. In one weekend he saw Brigadier Beament, a senior staff officer at Canadian Military Headquarters (CMHQ) in London, Lieutenant-General Nye, the Vice Chief of the Imperial General Staff and General Georges Vanier. Harry followed this up with a letter to the senior officer at CMHQ asking to be placed on the next reinforcement draft, preferably to an armoured regiment. The transfer was arranged but the armoured corps insisted he needed three months further training before he could be sent into action. Harry was frantic and did his cause further harm by protesting his fate to anyone, of any rank, who might help. Relations with his father were strained and Maurice Pope, now a Major-General, reported sadly that "Harry I am sorry to say is growing increasingly difficult." No doubt Harry Pope was difficult but all he wanted was to serve in action and the army bureaucracy seemed determined to block his efforts.

The best part of his enforced stay in England came when he was transferred back to the infantry and sent to a replacement unit as an instructor at the battle school. Harry recalled that,

> The course was designed to be rough. The time of year for my two courses - late November 1943 to March 1944 - made it a little rougher: if you must wade across rivers, shoulder-deep, try to avoid a winter battle drill course. But those that could not take the course would have been worse than useless as platoon commanders in action: their cowardice would have been a constant menace to their platoons. It need hardly be stressed that rough as the battle drill course was, it was still trivial compared to the fighting then going on around Ortona - or

practically anywhere else for that matter. Moreover, at Findon Manor, no one was soaked for more than a few hours at a time, all could dry out at night, sleep in warm beds, get three hot meals a day, and know no one was trying to kill them - not even their instructors.

Characteristically Harry quickly developed strong opinions about the role of an infantry platoon commander in battle. He reflected on the battle drill doctrine, which called for the platoon commander and his headquarters to co-ordinate the lead sections from behind. He insisted that, "the platoon commander must *never* have anyone ahead of him." The platoon sergeant was able to take charge of the HQ and mortar section while the officer led from the front. Harry always insisted "that if a higher proportion of corporals are killed than lieutenants the lieutenants are not doing their job."

Harry's memoirs show that once in Italy with the "Van Doos," he adapted quickly and applied his ideas to the brutal realities of combat and just as quickly began to think systematically of the deadly craft he had started to practise. He saw that many soldiers on both sides failed to adapt and thus did not survive and he was determined to do both. He saw, and wrote about, how his men responded under fire, failed to use their weapons properly, if at all, tended to be too cautious in the advance and too quick to dig in, and often did not use sufficient force or firepower to win through to their objectives. He wrote about the consequences of platoon or company commanders following stupid orders issued by men who were far from the battle front. He vowed to learn from the mistakes he saw all around him and to take as few risks as possible with the lives of his men so as not to waste those lives when battle was inevitable.

As commander of what was purported to be one of the toughest platoons in his Regiment, Pope soon earned the reputation of being the toughest "bandit" or warrior of them all. But the very first time in combat, when Pope's platoon encountered a German patrol led by a sergeant armed with a submachine gun Pope was the only one to fire; he killed and wounded several of the Germans and the rest surrendered. It was a sobering experience since, as he wrote, "it should hardly have been necessary for the platoon commander to give a fire order!" Thus he found how difficult it was to get even the "toughest characters" to shoot.

INTRODUCTION

On 19 May 1944, Pope led a small party of unarmed infantry acting as stretcher bearers into the forward German positions of the Hitler Line to recover wounded members of his platoon. They wore red cross arm bands but they were not bona fide "medics" and Pope did not try to arrange a local parley under a white flag to get his men out. He and the others were taken prisoner, though he strongly objected, and he did not rejoin his regiment for more than two months. That did not mean he was idle in a prison camp. Like the hero of a feature film, and the more fantastic for being true, he escaped from the back of a truck carrying him into captivity and joined an anti-fascist partisan band fighting Germans and Italian Fascists behind enemy lines. When his group stumbled on a British Parachute officer leading a Long Range Desert Group (LRDG) reconnaissance party, he went with them. During his two months behind the lines he had occasion to witness, and record, the terrible brutality of the German occupiers on Italian civilians in reprisal for losses suffered at the hands of both the partisans and the LRDG. He concluded that it was grossly irresponsible to conduct such warfare behind enemy lines without regard to the fate of the civilian victims of German retaliation.

Pope's memoirs of his time in Italy are filled with gripping accounts of battle from the platoon level. As a platoon leader he saw the bravery, the foolhardiness and the heartbreak of war close up. He wrote copious letters to his family and friends back home and those letters form the core of what eventually became his memoirs. But the memoirs also contain cogent and pointed remarks and observations on the pitfalls of patrolling without proper preparation, the correct and incorrect way to organize a defensive position and when and how to reinforce success. These observations may strike some as the minutiae of combat, but in fact they are the essence of battle. And this is what makes Harry Pope's memoirs not merely a good read, but an important document for those who would study and understand modern war.

No army is ever prepared for war by peacetime training. War cannot be simulated, even by today's computer-driven, laser-firing, battle simulation systems. In real war people suffer gruesome death while soldiers and their commanders try to make decisions that, in non-war, would be simple to make and carry out. "In war everything is simple," Clausewitz wrote, "but the simplest things are very difficult." They are difficult because of the very high stakes involved and the intense fear and overwhelming confusion that are a consequence of those stakes. That is why peacetime training at its very best can only prepare an army to learn real war when real war begins. It is the capability to learn under fire that is the measure of an army. Armies and their commanders are victorious only if they learn more quickly than their antagonists.

Learning in the field has been much studied lately. Canadian military historians Terry Copp and Jack English have examined how the Canadian Army learned lessons in the Second World War while Bill Rawling, Tim Cook and Shane Schreiber have looked at the "lessons-learned" process in the Canadian Corps in the First World War. A whole crop of books have recently emerged on the manner in which the US Army learned lessons in the Second World War and so also with other armed forces. Military historians have gone beyond the ground first ploughed by John Keegan's *The Face of Battle* not only to learn what battle was, but how armies learned, or failed to learn, the lessons of battle so as to do better the next time. Although explaining higher command decisions will always remain a focus of military history, most of these latest works have concentrated on platoons, companies and battalions and how they adapted to modern war. Harry Pope's memoirs show how the lessons learned process inevitably began. An astute observer, Pope shows in detail why field level operations failed and offers up suggestions as to how they might have gone better. The conclusions he reached are an integral part of his story, adding tactical interest to what is, in any case, a good war story.

Pope rejoined his regiment at the end of July 1944 and fought his way through the rest of the Italian campaign until wounded on New Year's Day, 1945. After two months in hospital, he was back with the Van Doos in western Holland, when the 1st Canadian Corps finally joined the rest of First Canadian Army in the closing months of the campaign. Though his battalion commander had sought to have him considered for the Military Cross, his capture delayed the inevitable bureaucratic process and the medal got lost in the cracks. He did receive two mentions-in-dispatch, however, one that came only in April, 1946.

Pope stayed in the army in the five years between VE Day and the outbreak of the Korean War, acting as *aide-de-camp* to the Chief of the General Staff in Ottawa, and to the Governor General. Young, intelligent and sure of himself (even his father called him conceited), Harry lost his job working for the Governor General when he sent a letter to the Vancouver Club complaining of poor service. His superiors thought the letter insulting to the club and asked him to apologize, which he would not do. As a result he was transferred to duties at the cold weather testing facility at Fort Churchill where he again ran into trouble. At his farewell party at the end of 1948, Harry attacked Canadian defence policy as too accepting of US demands in the Canadian north and declared that in peacetime he would just as soon see Russian troops in the north as American. He was fast gaining a reputation as an officer who could not hold his tongue. His private life was, to say the least, no less complicated. At one point in December 1949 his father wrote him: "As for your love affairs you will, I am sure, understand me when I say I can't keep up with them."

Harry's fascination with women delayed his departure for the front after the outbreak of the Korean War. Attached to the newly created 2nd Battalion of the Van Doos (created for the specific purpose of service in Korea) Pope accompanied the regiment to Fort Lewis, Washington, for training with the rest of the Canadian Army Special Force (later referred to as 25th Canadian Infantry Brigade). At an off-base hotel, Harry wandered into an anti-Korean war meeting being held by the Trotskyite Socialist Workers Party and became enamoured with a young blonde activist. Harry pursued her, unsuccessfully, but in the process ended up attending several other Trotskyite functions and fell afoul of the Federal Bureau of Investigation (FBI). Since Harry's moderate left-wing sympathies were already well-known (he had met CCF leader M.J. Coldwell on a visit to his father in Berlin and became a social democrat), the

FBI's suspicions were enough for Army Headquarters to pull his name from the 2nd R22eR's active list and order him back to Ottawa. Desperate to get to Korea, Harry fought the army bureaucracy for almost two years to clear himself.

Harry's superiors did not think him disloyal, only lacking in judgment and tact, which was surely true. But good platoon and company commanders were desperately needed in Korea and the fact that he had acquitted himself so well in combat as a platoon leader in Italy ought to have far outweighed his minor indiscretions. For two years, however, his combat record seemed to avail him little and Harry languished, denied promotion, increasingly determined to force the issue. He finally decided that if he was not to be allowed service in Korea, he would either seek prolonged unpaid leave for educational purposes or permanently resign from the Active Army. He had no need to carry out his threat, however, because the army eventually saw that Harry's indiscretions were minor and in mid-August 1952, Harry reached the front lines in Korea as Officer Commanding "C" Company of the Van Doos. He was an outstanding company commander; he never lost a man forward of the Canadian lines.

When Harry arrived in Korea, the war had long since degenerated into a stalemate. Talks aimed at armistice dragged on even though both sides had agreed that the current front lines would become the demarcation lines whenever the shooting actually stopped. The US and the UN had decided in the late spring of 1951 that they would not pursue victory in Korea – a wise choice – but they also ordered their commanders to cease all unduly aggressive action along the front lines as long as the talks went on. From November 1951 until the end of the war, the initiative passed to the Communists. The UN's refusal to launch large scale spoiling attacks on Chinese positions led to a defensive mentality. Night after night Chinese troops dominated no-man's-land and used that domination to make hit and run attacks against UN troops. Along the Canadian lines, a lack of expertise in night patrolling and ambushes, and badly laid out defensive positions, hampered the soldiers' fighting ability. Harry saw this almost as soon as he arrived and set out to do what he could.

The ultimate solution to the problem lay at divisional level; that was where defensive doctrine ought to have been coordinated and patrolling schools established. But in the meantime Pope made certain that his own company's positions were as secure as they could be through correct layout of trenches and bunkers, effective siting of machine guns and mortars, and close cooperation with the heavier arms. He also treated the art of patrolling with deadly seriousness, knowing that simply choosing an infantry section neither equipped nor trained for night interdiction was a recipe for unnecessary casualties. Eventually, when Jean-Victor Allard, Harry's old battalion commander, was appointed to command the Canadian brigade in early 1953, Harry was asked to establish a brigade patrolling school to teach the required skills. In March 1953 Harry finally received his promotion to acting Major, soon confirmed as a permanent appointment. He also learned that he and the Military Cross, which had eluded him in Italy, were finally going to meet up. He received the award in early June 1953.

In his numerous reports from the field on the state of the Canadian defence lines, Pope tried to convince his superiors to improve the Canadian positions. He criticized the practice of placing defensive localities atop every hill in the line. This thinned the defenses and rendered supporting fire difficult. The localities themselves were poorly designed, he believed, because once the Chinese penetrated the outermost defensive trench, they were right into the Canadian positions. And, of course, he constantly harped on the need for more aggressive and effective night patrolling.

Although Allard took up his cause, not many others in the Canadian Army hierarchy were willing to listen to Pope's criticisms either during the war or after it. When Pope tried in the late 1950s to publish articles in *Canadian Army Journal* on lessons that ought to have been learned from Korea on defence and patrolling, he was turned down because the articles were too critical. The Canadian Army of the post-Korea era was interested only in how to meet

Russian tank forces on the North German Plain, not in how to prepare itself for limited wars of the Korea type.

Harry Pope left the army for good in August 1959 and began a new career working for the CCF's national headquarters in Ottawa. He became a professor of economics and published works on the subject, including a basic economics text. He also wrote a series of articles on his combat experiences in the Second World War and Korea for *La Citadelle*, the Van Doos journal, which are especially marked for his cogent observations on field level operations. Much of the material in those articles is incorporated in this book.

Harry Pope was a major when he departed military life and even that promotion had been long delayed by commanders who thought there was no place for his sometimes erratic brilliance in the Canadian Army. The Canadian Army today would do well not only to incorporate some of the wisdom Harry Pope learned in the field, under fire, into its fighting doctrine, but to recognize in the future that some of the best commanders in history have been no less stormy petrels than Harry Pope.

David Bercuson
University of Calgary

Chapter One

Italy At Last

I arrived from England at the beginning of April 1944 reporting to the Canadian infantry reinforcement centre in Avellino. A couple of days later I joined "D" Company of the 22nd at Ortona. The company, commanded by Major Oliva Garceau, was in reserve. Two days after I arrived, one of my new colleagues was under close arrest, something to do with insulting a major in the officers' mess. Nothing serious, except, I suppose, from the point of view of the major concerned. Since officers were not kept in the clink (not even awkward lieutenants), the bad lad was guarded by another lieutenant in the large room shared by all the lieutenants.

The lieutenant on guard duty told me he had business in town and asked if I would replace him as guard that evening. Having arrived in Avellino that very day, I had nothing planned, so I accepted.

My prisoner was not an idiot: he had immediately understood that I did not judge it necessary (neither then, nor at any time) to discuss everything with my superiors before acting as I thought best. So he said to me: "Harry, nobody told you that you had to keep me in this room. Provided you wear your Smith & Wesson loaded with its six bullets and that I remain bare-headed and without a belt, there's nothing to stop us taking a turn in Avellino."

Perfectly sensible! Five minutes later we were having our first glass of wine of the evening in a small café. But we had to see more of the town. While we were strolling in a nondescript alley, a young woman waved to us from a second floor balcony. We were up stairs in nothing flat. The whole family was there and we were very kindly received with spaghetti and red wine.

My prisoner was proud to be under close arrest while being received like a prince by the family. "Take your revolver out of its holster, Harry," he said, which I did. I had to open the cylinder of my Smith & Wesson to show that it was all properly loaded with its six bullets, all ready to shoot down my prisoner if he jumped out the window. Cries of horror came from the whole family, who all sought refuge in the farthest corner of the room. Nothing for it but to take the bullets out of the cylinder and put them in my pocket, where they remained. It would have been a discourtesy towards my prisoner to have put them back in the cylinder once we found ourselves back on the street, something that happened quite suddenly. Apparently we got back to the barracks without meeting the insulted major for no one asked me embarrassing questions the next day.

Still, I was glad to go up to the front to join the 22nd at Ortona a couple of days later. Commanding a platoon in the line, one has other things to do than get into trouble.

Two days after I arrived, Garceau summoned me to his command post. "Harry," he said to me, "you will take one of your sections and you will conduct it along the path that leads to 'A' Company" (a forward company). I'm thinking: "He's setting out the route for my first fighting patrol, my first action against the enemy!"

Garceau continues: "There you will find four dead cows. Go and bury them."

Getting close to my cows, I realized the major was mistaken. There were not four dead cows: there were six and they had surely been there since the battles of December 1943. I looked around me and noted that my six cows were at the foot of a very steep monticule. During my last six weeks in England I was a battle drill instructor at Findon Manor and in consequence I considered myself an expert on explosives. Also, happily, CSM Irené Roy was a walking depository of all that was needed to blow up a mountain. When we found him, he at once placed all his munitions at our disposal.

Arriving at the top of the monticule, and being careful not to fall into the slaughter-house fifty feet below, we set ourselves to dig a trench three feet deep and about ten feet long. I placed in it everything that Roy had given us and then I set off the finest explosion of my career. The whole top of the monticule came down on my six cows, which no one has seen since.

On 23 April 1944, the regiment quit the Ortona front to prepare for the attacks on the Gustav and Hitler Lines that started on 17 May. Major Garceau decided to have "D" Company quit the front in two phases. We were in very hilly country: vehicles could not reach our positions; all our heavy equipment was carried by mules. The day before we quit the front, Garceau had the mules carry out our field kitchen. On the 23rd, we had a late lunch: it was not until 1530 hours that Sergeant Careau and I had finished cooking the men's steaks, two by two, in our mess-tins over the small fire in our dugout. But the delay paid off after dark. "D" Company left the front quietly. The other companies, with their braying mules, were caught by enemy shelling and suffered losses.

When the company had marched back far enough, we were picked up by 3-ton trucks, a platoon to each truck, the men in back, the platoon commander in front next to the Service Corps driver. I asked mine: "Which do you prefer: transporting, troops, ammunition and rations, or Ordnance stores?" "Ordnance stores," he replied. "Say I'm bringing twenty boxes of boots forward. It's easy to make one disappear and then sell its contents on the black market." I knew that half my men had holes in the soles of their boots. If this driver nicked a box of boots whenever he could, how many of his fellows did the same? And were his officers, equally comfortably out of range of enemy fire, unaware of these thefts? Did no one in authority count the boots at the beginning of the trip and at the end? Or were they all, officers and men, happily engaged in these cowardly thefts from the troops that were doing the fighting? I was silent the rest of the trip.

I wrote my mother on 30 April 1944: "Recently General Vanier came to inspect the Regiment. He made a very fine speech and then dined with the officers in a tent improvised for the evening. Since I was the junior lieutenant, I acted as mess vice-president. The general spoke very kindly and asked about you. He told me he would write to you, probably to tell you he had seen me and had found me in good health and satisfied with my lot." As for the troops, "My platoon is beginning to work as I wish it and I'm most eager to go back into action with it." Our company second-in-command was Captain Lawrence Cannon, son of a judge. He was a distant cousin of mine through the Taschereaus. He was killed in action by an enemy shell the following month.

On 10 May 1944, Colonel Allard allowed five officers, the RSM, and 74 other ranks to go in a couple of trucks to spend a day in Naples. We were to rendez-vous at 1800 hours to return from Naples. At the hour set for our return, there were 74 soldiers in more or less proper state, one lieutenant who wasn't at all, and Lieutenant Fred Letarte, sober and worried that I was a hell of an example for the troops. I am conscious of having got on to the truck and that Fred got me off. What I did during the next nine hours, I haven't the faintest idea. When I came to at 0300 hours, I saw the big boots of an American military policeman and behind him the bars of the clink. I was on all fours, and apparently had just begun to show signs of life, for suddenly I heard Fred: "Look, he's not drunk: he can move."

On that, they kicked us out: what a magnificent lawyer Fred would have made!

After a trip in the back of a truck loaded with oil, we found the regiment and I collapsed under my mosquito net, where I still was when Garceau found me at the hour of the first parade in the morning. With genuine concern, the major asked: "Harry, do you do this often? The next time you want to go on a drunk like that, let me know ahead of time and I will give you a forty-eight-hour pass."

In leading "D" Company to the start line at dawn on 17 May 1944, Major Garceau temporarily took the wrong road. Along this road I found a rifle that I used that day and the next. But we arrived on the start line at H-Hour in single file. I was tight up against the flank of "A" Company and at precisely H-Hour, that company's Lieutenant Fred Letarte and I shook hands, wishing each other good luck. I was to have more than Fred.

We had no time to get our platoons in line for the attack and to establish clearly each platoon's objectives. However, in the early-morning mist and the smoke of our exploding shells, I saw before me a hill with farm houses on the top. Since our barrage was moving in 100-yard steps towards this hill and as no other platoon was in sight, I decided that No.17 would take the hill. Placing Corporal Colas's section on one side of me and Corporal Lachance's on the other, I began to follow the moving barrage as closely as possible, that is, within a hundred yards of where our shells were landing. As soon as I saw that the barrage had lifted and that the shells were exploding a hundred yards closer to the enemy, I galloped forward to jump into a shell-hole made thirty seconds earlier and still warm from the explosion.

Unless there were enemy shells mixed in with our own, nobody bothered us during our advance. Therefore, during the one-minute rests between my hundred-yard dashes, I had the time to feel proud of myself leading my platoon in my first attack against the enemy. It was then that I noticed that one of my boot-laces was undone.

After a few minutes, we were almost at the top of the hill, about a hundred yards from the houses, when I arrived in a shell-hole already occupied by the first German soldier I had ever seen in my life. Since he was very still, I took him for dead. To make sure, I pushed him with the muzzle of my rifle. At this, the German, very much alive, indicated that he wished to surrender by presenting me with his pistol, still in its holster. I accepted the weapon, very happy to have already captured my Luger before we had even fired a shot, and told him to go to the rear by crawling through my platoon.

If my lad was supposed to be there to ambush us, he did a hell of a poor job. (Moreover, when later I had the time to open the holster, I found that it contained the German equivalent of a Very (flare) pistol! The bastard!)

An instant or two later, a German soldier rose fifty yards in front of me to run as fast as he could from one shelter to another. On one knee, I fired at the centre of the target and the German, apparently a sergeant and commander of the position, fell dead, a bullet in his head. At this, we completed our, until then, entirely peaceful assault. There was not a German in sight: all were hiding in their dug-outs. Here was the advantage of following our barrage so closely: we were on the objective before the enemy realized it.

We had to get the Germans out of their dug-outs. So I teamed up with Corporal Lachance. My mother being Belgian (Walloon) I had learned that the Flemish for "out" was "uit," and thinking that "uit" would work for Germans also, I went from dug-out to dug-out yelling "uit." Unfortunately, the Germans were not bilingual in Flemish, so Lachance was obliged to throw a 36 grenade into each dug-out. At one dug-out our grenade did not explode. I told the corporal to try another and we both leaned over the entrance to see how this one would work. There was an enormous explosion at our feet and I did a back somersault. Less lucky, Lachance fell, wounded gravely in his right shoulder. At the moment, I thought that a shell had landed between us. Now, I'm not so sure: it could have been our two grenades going off together. In any case, not having a stretcher, we had Corporal Lachance carried on a door by five of the prisoners.

British tanks had now come up about a hundred or so yards on our left. Since it was "A" Company and not "D" that was supposed to have tanks in support, I said to myself: "Here we are on the wrong objective; worse, maybe ours is ahead of where we are now." My signaller, who had accompanied Careau and the reserve section during the assault, had rejoined me. I therefore tried to contact Garceau by wireless. The fact that I was not able to do so confirmed to me that we were in the wrong place: clearly we were detached from the company.

We therefore set off for another farm a few hundred yards in front, the British tanks keeping pace in more open ground on our left. We reached this second objective without incident.

We were now on an elevated plateau, with the British tanks a couple of hundred yards away on our left. Leaving Careau in charge, I went alone to make contact with our allies for the first time. Arriving close to a tank (commanded, I believe, by a lieutenant), I almost stepped into a slit trench that contained a couple of German soldiers, both very pale and quiet. Seeing me, one of them, very painfully and slowly, raised his arm towards me so that I might help him out of the trench. I took his arm and then noticed that he and his companion were covered with blood, mortally wounded in the stomach. Furious, I asked the tank lieutenant: "What happened to these two? Did you drop a grenade in on them?" When the British officer replied that he had, I doubt that I was able to hide my anger. The tank lieutenant could easily, pistol in hand, have ordered the two German soldiers to surrender, which they would eagerly have done. And 17 platoon was close by and able to set the new prisoners off in the right direction. At any rate, when I then asked the tank lieutenant to use his wireless set, much more powerful than mine, to tell his squadron commander where 17 platoon was so that the latter could then pass the happy news on to Major Garceau, the tank lieutenant flatly refused to do so.

Maybe he was also in a bad temper because my two men on the Projector Infantry Anti-Tank (PIAT), who had been with Careau during the assault, on seeing a tank in the mist and smoke, and knowing that we were not supposed to have tanks with us, fired on it. Happily, the bomb did not penetrate the turret, but I suppose that the tankers saw enough stars to be utterly fed up with 17 platoon and determined to have as little as possible to do with us from here on in.

Back with my platoon past noon, I decided that it was time for lunch, probably bully beef to complement our breakfast of beans on toast seven or eight hours earlier. During this meal, I heard Private Trudel say to the platoon, in a voice loud enough for all to hear: "Our lieutenant is a bandit: he likes to kill." This was not true; but he meant it as a compliment, and I took it as such.

With lunch over, and having no orders to the contrary, I decided to continue the advance. After several hundred yards, we were along a hedge, facing towards the enemy, when I decided to call a halt. I was at last confident that we had gone beyond our objective (wherever it was!) and we were alone, without support, for the British tanks had not followed us. After some time, a platoon of the West Novies appeared, commanded by a lieutenant whom I knew. Happy after all these hours at having found Allied troops with whom my platoon could co-operate, I started my platoon up alongside the West Novies' one. But after a few moments of thinking about it, I realized that the West Novies being there must mean that the 22nd was now in reserve and that 17 platoon should perhaps take a rest also in readiness for the morrow.

I explained this to the West Novies' lieutenant and then turned my platoon about to retrace our steps. Back in our own lines, Careau and I were marching side by side when the sergeant drew his fingers in a line above his left breast pocket – indicating his belief that I had earned the Military Cross that day. In time for supper, we found Garceau, who told me that he was pleased with us.

On 17 May 1944, I first experienced the slowness of our army to reinforce a tactical success. 17 platoon had quickly and efficiently taken an enemy hill-top position, the last defended locality before the Hitler Line. We did not close with the Hitler Line for another 36 hours. We should have been there the afternoon of 17 May. Of course, this would have exposed us to counter-attack backed by tanks, possibly to encirclement of the forward elements. Therefore our tanks should have been required to give continuous close support and the battalion anti-tank guns should have moved forward along with the HQs of the assaulting companies. In other words, when 17 platoon saw an opportunity to exploit success, backing by support weapons should have been immediate. Of course, with 17 platoon being beyond wireless range of "D" Company, this would have required intimate co-operation from our tanks. Shooting the tank lieutenant who refused to pass my message to Major Garceau might well have ensured better co-operation in the future. I'm serious: we lost good men on the Hitler Line, all of them better than that snotty tank lieutenant. Getting to the Hitler Line 36 hours earlier would have surprised the enemy, and that's at least half the battle.

But even if the tank lieutenant had got word to Garceau giving the whereabouts of his long-lost 17 platoon, I would have been ordered back. My subsequent experiences convince me that there would not have been an immediate order to the tanks and to me to push on as fast as we could with the object of closing with and attacking the next enemy position.

We simply took one bite at a time. Having achieved our (always limited) objectives, we dug in for the night while the tanks went back a mile or two to harbour. And the enemy had all the time in the world to be ready for us when we tried our next little bite.

The next day, 18 May 1944, Garceau marched with me at the head of my platoon, leading the company in single file until we came to a crossroad. From there, he pointed out to me some farm houses about 150 yards away and to the right of the road that led towards the enemy. He said: "Send a patrol to ensure that there are no enemy there. Then take up position around the farm for the night." I found it perfectly natural that he should walk with me at the head of my platoon. I now ask myself whether my company commander was not simply trying to ensure that 17 platoon took its objective, its *sole* objective, without getting lost in the mists until supper-time.

As soon as Garceau had left to return to his command post, I went off with Corporal Colas and two of his soldiers to see what was in that farm, leaving Sergeant Careau and the rest of the platoon along a ditch hidden by a hedge parallel to the front to cover us, if necessary. We had crossed the road that led to the enemy and were within five paces of one of the houses when, fifty yards from us, I saw coming down the road from the direction of the enemy a German soldier followed by others. I dropped to one knee and made a sign to Colas and his two soldiers not to move, for the enemy patrol was heading towards where 17 platoon was awaiting it, and I saw that we four could complete the patrol's encirclement. But when the number of Germans had reached eight, I began to wonder who would be encircling whom. Happily, the number did not go any higher, and not one of the Germans glanced to the left where we four were waiting, completely in the open.

Careau told me later that he was at the crossroads telling the platoon war stories from Sicily, when the leader of the patrol opened fire on him with a Schmeisser submachine gun. It was to be the last shot fired by the enemy. Careau's reply was a grenade. At the same moment, I ran on to the road behind the German patrol and, on one knee, fired into their backs. . . and missed. I saw the German corporal turn his head an instant after I saw my bullet raise the dust next to his head. Had my first shot counted, more of the German patrol might have survived. With the German corporal's submachine-gun out of action, I might have decided to advance on the remaining seven at once and demanded their surrender. But that did not happen.

The whole patrol was now in line in the ditch, alongside the road that it had been coming down. Since the German corporal was armed with a submachine-gun and I with a Lee-Enfield rifle that was not even semi-automatic, I jumped into the grain field next to the road to reload. That done, I jumped back on to the road to fire another shot. I repeated the manoeuvre two or three times until those of the Germans still alive started to crawl through the hedge that bordered the road. At this, I crossed the road, followed by Colas and the two soldiers. I continued firing, standing, and now at point blank range. Careau had also been firing from his side.

It was now obvious that the Germans were beaten. Therefore, each from its own side, our two groups advanced on the enemy. Five were dead; one, wounded in the stomach, was lying on his back screaming "Doktor"; another, wounded in the knee, was on his knees with his hands in the air; the last one, unscathed, was standing with his hands in the air.

One of the soldiers who had been with Sergeant Careau was armed with a .45 Tommy-gun. Saying, "This is the only doctor you'll get," he fired on the German who was screaming doctor, killing him instantly. I felt my rifle swing a couple of degrees in the direction of the murderer; alone, I might well have put him to death on the spot. The main reason I hesitated was that I doubted that the summary execution of one of their comrades would have been good for my platoon's morale. After all, each of my soldiers felt closer to the one with the Tommy-gun than to the dying German soldier. I cursed the holder of the Tommy-gun, telling him that we did not shoot the wounded.

But why did he do it? Maybe the screams of the wounded German unnerved him. Maybe he was ashamed at not having fired during the skirmish (only Careau and I had fired). Maybe he wished to show me that he was tough and just as much a bandit as he imagined I was. Or maybe he was simply a bandit.

When I asked Colas why he had not opened fire with his Tommy-gun, he told me that it had jammed. Since the same thing happened to me several times a few months later, I can well imagine how he must have felt. However, during this little battle, only the three leaders used their weapons. And even here, the German corporal stopped using his at precisely the wrong moment. Instead of all eight of them crowding into a ditch a foot deep and presenting perfect targets to Careau and me, the German patrol should have turned about at my first shot and charged me in line, each of the men firing from the hip. It's what I had expected them to do. Had they done so, they would have lived and I would still be in Italy. The lessons: (1) when fired on, shoot back at once, without thinking, automatically; (2) when encircled, attack immediately what appears to be the weakest point.

A third lesson I learned the next day: be merciful only when victory is assured, as I was on 17 and 18 May, but not when the enemy is still able to fight back. That's what von Clausewitz taught. As we see below, I should have read him before 19 May 1944.

Shortly after we had destroyed the enemy patrol, the CO of the West Novies arrived in his Jeep, coming up the road down which the enemy patrol had been coming. I remember thinking there might have been some promotions in the West Novies had their colonel arrived a little earlier. The West Novies' CO, noting our success, said that he would bring his battalion forward at once. He didn't, but his idea was good. The fact that the enemy patrol had been coming down the road as though it owned the place, indicated that the enemy was not expecting our immediate advance to the Hitler Line. And this is why we, the R22eR or the West Novies, preferably both, should have advanced at once, with tanks and our anti-tank guns. We could not possibly have done worse in the afternoon of 18 May than we ended up doing on 19 May, when the enemy was fully prepared for us.

In so far as 17 platoon is concerned, this is what happened on 19 May 1944. At dawn, we advanced towards the Hitler Line. We attained our objective without incident. With the other platoons of "D" Company, our task was to act as a firm base for Major Potvin's "B" Company, which was to be part of the main attack on the Hitler Line.

As soon as we were in position, the leader of my right-hand section – I believe it was Corporal Colas, told me that he saw Germans about 150 yards in front. I at once went to Colas' flank and through the sights of his section's Bren Light Machine Gun (LMG) I saw about ten Germans who obviously had not the slightest suspicion that we had arrived. I should have said: "17 Platoon, at the instant I open fire with the Bren, all, rapid fire on the enemy in front." And I certainly believe I would have given this order had I carefully studied my map the previous evening. The German soldiers in front were not simply an isolated outpost but an integral part of the Hitler Line. In any case, I sent a messenger to find Garceau to ask permission to attack. Shortly, the messenger returned: "The Major gives you permission to attack; but it's not an order; it's not an order." At the moment, I found amusing his insistence that I was attacking at my own discretion. Later, I came to realize that he was not so stupid.

Having given an order to the 2-inch mortar detachment to cover us if necessary, I advanced with Colas and five or six men of his section to where we had seen the ten or so German soldiers, who had now taken cover. About thirty yards from their bunker, we came on a knee-high barbed-wire obstacle hidden from us until then by the grain. We had just crossed the obstacle without difficulty when a mortar bomb landed between Private Gaston Simard and me, gravely wounding Simard in the stomach.

I turned to see what had happened. On seeing Simard, I told Colas to help him. Then, at last, I looked around me, and realized that we were in the middle of the Hitler Line, surrounded by enemy bunkers, and we were without any support. I then ordered Colas's section to rejoin 17 platoon in the rear, while I dropped to one knee in front of Colas and Simard. Once Simard was bandaged, my intention was to help Colas carry him back to our position. But after a few moments, Colas was wounded by a bullet that broke his thigh bone.

At the same moment, "B" Company must have appeared on the battlefield, for during the next two hours bullets and shells whistled over our heads and even lower. A bullet hit my helmet, stoving it in so much that the steel of the helmet struck my forehead. Blood ran into my eye and for an instant I thought that I was dead; but I got off with only a concussion and a headache.

Finally, I concluded that "B" Company was not going to reach the Hitler Line and thus help me evacuate my two wounded. Because of the German wire, I could not carry them back one after the other in my arms: standing up, one would not have lived five seconds. So, I took off my equipment, keeping only my pistol, and, having promised Colas and Simard that I would come back for them, I slid on my back under the barbed wire and then crawled back to "B" Company, which had not been able to go beyond the line where I had left my platoon before my stroll in and out of the Hitler Line.

The failure of the regiment on 19 May depends uniquely on the error made at division or corps headquarters. The error consisted in thinking that the enemy had abandoned the Hitler Line and that a simple reconnaissance in strength was all that was necessary to smash through it. (Obviously, the error was similar to mine; but at least I was risking my own skin along with those I commanded). Once the enemy had woken up and the early-morning mist had dissipated, with only one artillery battery in support and our tanks God knows where, "B" Company could not advance without cover against the machine guns of the Hitler Line.

Back in our lines, I eventually reached "D" Company's command post in a house, since I was hoping for a second attack, this one crowned with success, in which I could take part to go to the rescue of my two wounded soldiers. For some time we were joined by

Colonel Allard, for he had come forward to see whether we were still able to turn the day around. In our room, which did not seem very strong to me, there was a fine big table, solid as Gibraltar, and when the enemy started to shell the road a few yards from us I had an almost overwhelming desire to duck under it. Alone, I wouldn't have thought twice about it. But in front of the colonel, there was nothing to do but hope that the enemy would continue to shoot straight.

The tanks supposed to support "B" and "C" Companies were almost all burning: they had come on to the battlefield in single file, thus presenting ideal targets to the German 88 mm guns without themselves being able to fire back.

Although I saw only three knocked-out tanks when I got back to the "D" company lines, I'm told that in the British tank squadron supporting us eleven or twelve of its fourteen tanks were flamers and its OC was killed.

It became evident to me that there would be no second attack that day. I then asked my company commander, Major Garceau, for some stretcher bearers to accompany me into the Hitler Line. It was my second error of the day. What I should have done, with Garceau's approbation, was to go alone, unarmed and with my lieutenant's stars removed, but with a white flag, to the middle of no-man's-land, there to parley with the enemy to ask permission to enter its position with one stretcher bearer to pick up my wounded one at a time. I had already led two of my men into a mess that day. I should have thought hard before exposing others.

In any event, out of consideration for me, Garceau gave me five stretcher bearers. Since we had only one stretcher, one soldier besides me would have been enough. Having put aside our weapons and having put on Red Cross armbands, we left the cover of the trees at about the same spot as that whence my aborted attack had started. On seeing us, and probably thinking that we were a fighting patrol, the enemy fired a couple of bursts from a machine-gun or submachine-gun at us, raising the dust at our feet. We continued to advance, waving the Red Cross flag at the end of a stick.

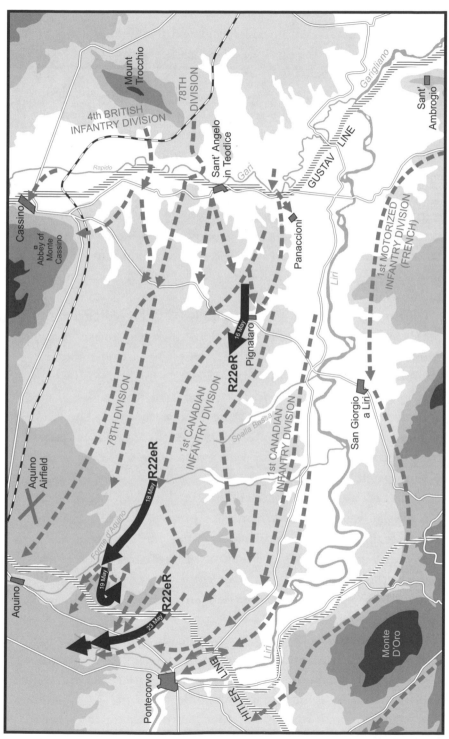

The Royal 22nd Régiment and the Gustav and Hitler Lines

Back in the German lines, I recognized the German corporal whom I had had in the sights of a Bren early that morning. I told him that we were there to take the wounded back behind the lines. He said that he was glad to hear this, while expressing the desire that we go behind his lines. I replied that this did not suit me at all. The corporal then pointed out to me that he was the one who was holding the Schmeisser; he was aiming it precisely at my middle. I accepted the force of this argument.

The enemy had already bandaged Colas' thigh and had placed him in their bunker. The German corporal told me that Simard had died of his wound. I asked to see the body. This was allowed me. So far as I could judge, Simard had died of the wound caused by the mortar bomb: the enemy had not shot him while he was lying on the ground.

Despite the bandage, Colas's wound was still bleeding and the flies were bothering him, so I covered his thigh with my tunic and teamed up with one of the stretcher bearers to carry the corporal on our stretcher until we arrived at a German medical post, where we were received benevolently. I was able to leave Colas there confident that he was in good hands. Colas survived. The New Year following the war, I was most happy to get a card from Montreal from the corporal. He signed it: "*Votre reconnaissant Cpl. Aimé Colas.*" ("Your grateful...")

Our task as stretcher bearers completed, we got into a truck. On the way, we passed a German army propaganda unit, proud to be able to film six Canadian prisoners, all in a pile. Having no desire to make Dr. Goebbels happy, I told my brother stretcher bearers to lean their arm with the Red Cross armband over the side of the truck, all the while pointing at the Red Cross with their other hand. Everyone did this.

This displeased our guards, who already seemed somewhat unhappy that Canadians appeared able to make war with lieutenants (*oberleutnants*) twenty-one years old. So, a Hitler-*Jügend* type, who also had his Schmeisser pointing at my middle, asked me if I thought that killing German soldiers was good. Using tact for the second time that day, I gave him a philosophical-type answer, to the effect that "war is stupid and all that." What I found really stupid was that it was he who was holding the submachine-gun and not I…but I didn't tell him that.

Possibly it was my having to be tactful twice during the afternoon of 19 May 1944 that completely used up all my *savoir vivre*. At any rate, back in our own army two months later, I never again thought before speaking as I did during the first of my eleven days in the hands of the German army.

Arriving at a German command post, I went in for my interrogation before a captain who wore the Iron Cross at his throat, the Knight's Cross. We argued for a long time: I told him that they had no right to take us prisoner, still less to keep us prisoner, for we had entered their lines voluntarily with the sole aim of picking up wounded; we were unarmed and wearing Red Cross armbands. He replied that as a combatant officer I had no right to wear this armband. "Maybe," I replied, "but your corporal did not know that when he took us prisoner."

Finally, recognizing that it wasn't working, I told him: "I am of a military family, and I cannot accept the dishonour of being made a prisoner." The German captain, in a paternal tone, replied: "I assure you, Lieutenant, the Court of Honour will acquit you of any guilt in this matter." Then I told him: "So long as I have reason to believe we will all be repatriated, I will not try to escape; but as soon as I come to realize that we won't be, then it will be my duty to escape."

At once, the captain grabbed a phone to plead my case. At least that's what I thought…at first. After that, at each stop, I demanded to be paraded before the CO to require again our immediate return to our own lines. But no one higher than a lance-corporal interpreter would speak to me. Finally, it dawned on me that my sympathetic German captain with the Iron Cross must have said on the phone: "I have a completely mad Canadian lieutenant in front of me: don't pay him any attention." In one shot and in the space of a few minutes I had made myself "*impossible à vivre*" ("utterly impossible") to the hierarchy of the German army.

During the interrogation, the German captain asked me why we had not sent tanks forward to pick up the wounded. Obviously, if our tanks had been able to reach the Hitler Line to pick up wounded, they would have been able to smash through this damned line…instead of burning stupidly at the entrance to the battlefield. Instead of explaining all this, I looked stupid: "Tanks, what tanks?" Apparently my fellow stretcher bearers acted similarly.

I cannot end this account without expressing all the admiration that I felt for my first company commander in action, Major Ovila Garceau, and my first platoon sergeant, Sergeant Maurice Careau. No young lieutenant could have faced the enemy for the first time better backed up. I knew the two men only for five or six weeks, because I first joined the Regiment on the Ortona front on 16 April 1944 and Colonel Allard sent me to "D" Company the next day. By the time I rejoined the regiment on 25 July 1944, Garceau and Careau had both been killed.

Getting one of my men killed, another badly wounded and taken prisoner, and myself and five other stretcher bearers taken prisoner also was a defeat, pure and simple. The best that I can say about it is that at least it wasn't dishonourable.

Chapter Two

Prisoner of War and Partisan

After our interrogation by the pleasant German captain, we six stretcher bearers passed the night of 19-20 May 1944 in a stable. I think I recall that at dawn the headache caused by the bullet that had stove in my helmet the previous day had practically gone. And, to my everlasting regret, the bloody ecchymosis on my left temple left no scar at all! At any rate, after eating some black bread to get us going, we were on the road on foot with our guards. There we met a German general with his fine car stuck in a hole. His aide-de camp ordered us to help get the car out. Knowing that, according to the Geneva Convention, officer-prisoners were exempt from all work, I knew that I had the right to tell the enemy general to go to hell. However, I had led the five stretcher bearers into the mess in which we now found ourselves; and I did not know whether the general was conversant with the Geneva Convention: near the front and unarmed in the hands of the enemy, it's not a bad idea to be polite. We got the general out of his hole in nothing flat.

Still, I sometimes wonder if he was not the general in the car immediately behind the one that was completely destroyed by the ten pounds of plastic high explosive (HE) that I placed on a road southeast of Florence seven weeks later. Certainly, I hope he was!

I soon became separated from my five stretcher bearers. I hope they did not find the next twelve months too boring. The one I have seen, Paul-Emile Lamouche, described our being taken prisoner and his subsequent year as a POW in a short article in *Maclean's* of 3 April 1995. We have exchanged letters since, and finally met in 1999.

We were a couple of days in a transit camp (a third-class hotel, six or seven prisoners in a room, no furniture at all, very little to eat). Two of the prisoners were Indian army Sikhs, I believe. They spent most of their waking hours chanting. The German sergeant who came in to tell us it was time to go kicked the two Sikhs. On leaving, I found myself in an open truck in the rain with ten or so other prisoners, when our solitary guard put his rifle in the hands of one of the prisoners so that he, the guard, could very kindly pull over us a tarpaulin. Obviously, I should have profited from the occasion to take French leave. If I did not do so, it was certainly at least in part because we were in the middle of a town filled with German soldiers. But possibly it was mostly because I did not have a cup of *ersatz* coffee in my body.

It was around 22 May that I arrived in my first true POW camp. It was not far from Rome and on our arrival a German lance-corporal interpreter, in saluting me very correctly, as though I were an *oberleutnant*, offered his excuses that I would have to pass the night in the other ranks' quarters, because I could not enter the quarters reserved for officers before being deloused and defleed. He also expressed his regrets at the need to take my steel helmet, of which I was very proud, for no one alive had one more stove in than mine. He added that prisoners were not allowed to keep their helmets because there was a danger that they would use them to dig holes, exit holes, of course.

Arriving the next day in the officers' corner (separated from the other ranks by another row of barbed wire), I quickly realized that the German lance-corporal was right to distrust steel helmets. Next to the stove used to heat the cabin in winter, there was a wood-box that hid a hole six or seven feet deep. At the bottom was a tunnel maybe thirty feet long and just wide enough that one man at a time could dig, with the steel helmet lying there. We would go into the tunnel naked since we came out of it stained with clay, and, while our uniforms could hide the stains on our bodies, we had nothing to get the stains off our uniforms. Besides, our tunnel was a very tight squeeze: there simply was no room for clothing.

There were six other officers, all American if I remember correctly, when I joined the group in the cabin. Most of the time these imbeciles talked of the meals they would eat after the war. Since we got two meals a day – very thin soup and a piece of bread – I would have preferred that they had talked of something else.

So, I spent quite a bit of the time in the tunnel, even though we realized that we would be moved before we could reach our goal: the hole made by a bomb dropped from a plane outside the second row of barbed wire that kept us in place. Besides, we were beginning to be short of space for the spoil from the tunnel. All this earth went into the attic on top of the ceiling of the cabin's only room, but the ceiling was only heavy cardboard. We hoped every time the German sergeant came to check that we were all present, that he would not slam the door: it would not have taken more than that for several tons of earth to come down on his head. It would have been embarrassing.

One day I got permission to go to the kitchen to get some hot water, because there were some scabies-causing bugs in the straw on which I had slept on 18 May (in the farm Major Garceau had pointed out to me as my objective), and a good bath seemed to me to be useful. The corporal cook, a Briton, in giving me some hot water, also gave me a loaf of bread, saying it was to give us more strength to work on our tunnel. I placed the loaf under my tunic, against my skin eruptions, but my fellow prisoners did not complain. On the contrary, it took us a good half-hour to figure out how to cut this loaf into seven perfectly equal pieces.

In returning to the officers' enclosure, I was stopped by a soldier who asked me to kindly cut the barbed wire that separated him from us on the night our tunnel was completed, so that the whole camp could slip out by the same tunnel! I absolutely believed that the whole camp knew about our tunnel, including the Germans. Maybe they figured that so long as we were working on it (which required at least fifty more feet of digging), we would not think of something even more stupid, from the German point of view, at any rate.

One day, a British soldier came up to the barbed-wire fence separating us. He asked to speak to me about a medical problem: my Red Cross armband, which I wore during the whole time I was a POW, had led him to believe that I was a physician, an MO. With regret, I had to explain that I was merely a provisional stretcher bearer, utterly unqualified in my assumed specialty.

Around 26 May, I left by truck with a couple of hundred other prisoners in the direction of Laterina, the last of my camps, not far from Arezzo. Because of British Spitfires, the trip took 44 hours; during this time we had nothing to eat: whenever a Spitfire flew within ten miles of us, it was always *our* soup that got blown up.

At Laterina, many of the prisoners were among those who had been liberated at the time of the armistice with Italy in September 1943 and were subsequently recaptured by the Germans, who had taken practically all of them in North Africa in the first place before handing them over to the Italian army to guard.

On 30 May, around 1800 hours, the Germans gave us some *ersatz* coffee (roasted acorns) before having 90 other ranks and 30 officers climb into four open trucks. Or rather, 26 officers, for I was the 26th, and I protested that it was contrary to the Geneva Convention to crowd more than 26 men in a truck of that size. This far from the front, I figured that I could get away with playing barrack-room lawyer. The German staff-sergeant in charge, who took life very seriously, then had our truck go forward, followed by an abrupt halt, and 26 officers slid on their arses towards the front of the truck. The four remaining officers joined us. But I at once resumed my place at the back of the truck.

Before taking his place beside the driver, the German staff-sergeant warned us not to salute the Italians as we passed through their villages with two fingers making a "V," the "V for Victory" sign, for that would cost us a bullet through the offending hand while the Italians that replied would get a bullet in the head.

With the delay, the officers' truck was at the end of the convoy instead of in the middle, supposedly because officers were more apt to escape, something that I certainly did not note during my time in the German POW camps.

We traveled about 50 miles non-stop. Three guards sat on the tailgate facing us; two were armed with rifles, the third with a Schmeisser sub-machine-gun. My idea was that the three of us seated at their feet should rise as one man, grab the muzzle of the weapon that was in his face, and then roll its German soldier over the back of the truck. Obviously, it was essential to act as one man!

Those at the back of the truck with me were much more ready to discuss the matter than to act. Finally, I asked them to quit talking about it: the English word "escape" is very similar to the Italian "*scappare*," and our guards had ears. At the same time that I asked them to shut up, I said to them: "Then it's agreed, any action tonight will be individual effort."

After 50 miles, the convoy stopped to give us a chance to stretch. Our three guards got down from the truck to chat with their comrades from the other trucks, while slinging their weapons from the shoulder. The convoy had stopped in a sunken road eight feet below the level of the surrounding fields. We were all in our stocking feet: our boots were in a pile with the staff-sergeant to deter escape.

I noted that we were about eight or nine feet from the field, an impossible standing leap with boots on, but maybe possible in stocking feet. I asked the American standing next to me: "Do you think you can jump from here to there?" On his "No," I was off. To be impulsive is advantageous when one has to jump over the heads of guards busily peeing. I landed on top of the bank at the edge of the field. I was at quite a distance before the guards could climb back into the truck to send their first burst of automatic fire my way. I was flat on the ground, rather wondering if, after all, I really should have left the truck. But in the half-light of 2200 hours and the half-moon, the bursts missed. After one or two minutes I continued southward (I was even pointed in the right direction in jumping out of the truck) and the other 29 officers, three or four Canadian and British, the rest Americans, continued their trip towards imprisonment in Germany.

Once on my feet, I removed the Red Cross armband that I had worn until then. My duty towards my two wounded men completed, well or badly, I became a combatant again. I wrapped my feet in my ankle puttees (my boots having remained behind in the truck) and marched southward (I could easily distinguish the North Star behind me), waking up, as I passed between farms a good dozen dogs. I discovered the Gothic Line along my way, when I found myself at the bottom of a trench six feet deep. Happily, I was its only occupant and I got out almost as fast as I had gone in.

Arriving in a bean field, at 0300 hours, I ate to my stomach's content for the first time since 19 May, eleven days earlier. Since the place seemed isolated, I decided to spend the rest of the night there. On awakening three hours later, I saw passing by on the main road a *carabiniere* (policeman) peacefully pedaling away on his bicycle. That convinced me to move. I crossed the road and found myself at the approaches of the Prato Magno, a chain of small mountains (highest point, the Uomo di Sasso 5,043 feet) stretching for 20 miles northwest of Arezzo. Going up a narrow path, I suddenly found myself face-to-face with three peasant women. In my best Italian, I said to them: "*Sono tenente canadese; scappare di Tedesce; o fame.*" "I am a Canadian lieutenant; I have escaped from the Germans; I am hungry." The three Italian women kindly pointed out to me their farm in a neighbouring valley, where I went to get a meal very much better than raw beans: bread, cheese, and red wine, all produced there.

A little after noon the same day, 31 May, always moving southward, I saw a château before me. Taking it for granted that only a fascist could live there, I did not present myself at the front door. Rather, I went around it, sticking to the woods. For some time I sat there looking at the tennis court.

I went down into the little village of Campiglioni (in the commune of San Miniato in Alpe), which was at the foot of the château. There, since my story seemed to be successful, I repeated it: "*Sono tenente canadese; scappare di Tedesce; o fame.*" I was served the best minestrone soup that I have had in my life.

Before sitting down, I had carefully asked that the fascists of the château not be told of my presence. But suddenly there in front of me was Signora Georgio Garabelli, a relative of Vittorio Emanuele Orlando, prime minister of Italy during the First World War. My luck continued: here I was in the bosom of the premier democratic family of Italy!

Signora Garabelli invited me to Villa Story where I met her husband. Here I took a much-needed bath, and the Garabellis gave me an excellent supper, counting the raw beans, my fourth meal of the day, civilian clothes, 400 lire, and a place to sleep for the night. This was an out-building: had the Germans turned up and found me in the château, probably I would have survived; no one else would have.

The next day, 1 June, I set off at dawn into the Prato Magno, passing between Montemignaio to the east and Vallombrosa to the west. I saw a truck going by on a road that circled upwards around the mountain. I climbed to the top of the mountain, called Risala, to see who owned the truck. On separating the branches of the last tree, I saw *three yards* in front of me five German soldiers searching for signs of partisan activity with their binoculars. Very quietly, I placed the branches back where they belonged. The Garabellis had given me tennis shoes, open in front to make room for my toes, very useful for leaving the observation post silently.

Towards midday, I noticed a small cabin in a valley, an unlikely spot for an enemy detachment. Since it was time for lunch, I entered and found eight partisans: seven amiable young bandits, most even younger than I, who were there because they did not wish to make war for Mussolini; and Ignatz, a Pole about thirty, who was willing to fight only for Poland. "*Sono tenente canadese; scappare di Tedesce; o fame.*" It took no more than that for me to become the ninth bandit. Instead of continuing southward, I decided to stay with them to see what could be done to screw up the Germans of the Prato Magno.

I had asked the Garabellis to burn my uniform: it would have cost them their lives had the Germans found it on the premises. But in case they had kept it for me, and since I prefer to make war as a soldier, after five days, at dawn, I again presented myself at the Villa Story, accompanied by one of my partisan comrades. Hearing us knocking, one of the female servants opened a shutter and cried: "È *Guglielmo*!" ("It's William!") Why William? Because my parents named me after my great-grand-father, William Henry Pope, and on arriving at the Garabellis five days earlier, when I was asked my given name, I replied "Guglielmo."

The Garabellis offered us breakfast: my comrade ate in the kitchen, I in the dining-room. Not only had my uniform not been burnt, but because it was stained with Corporal Aimé Colas' blood, it had been washed! Better yet, since I had not attacked on 17 May with my best shirt on my back, the shirt's collar had been turned so that I would not look quite so shabby.

A day or so later, I went to Mount Uomo di Sasso to meet the leader of a band of 150 partisans; he went by the war name of Potente. I asked him why they did not go down at night to attack the German trucks, which travelled at night hidden from the Spitfires. Potente replied that they did not have enough weapons. I believed that he was giving the true reason, and I tried to make him understand that with 150 men he should be able to ambush one truck at a time and thus build up their stock of weapons bit by bit from the Germans whom they killed.

Later, Potente's men told me that their task was to occupy Florence, presumably when it was free of Germans. Potente was a Communist: he was thinking not of making war against the Germans but of winning the peace. This I understood later, after the war, when I saw what had happened in Yugoslavia with Tito's victory, but Tito at least fought the Germans as well as the non-communist Yugoslavs.

For the next three weeks I lived with my band of eight in the mountains in charcoal burners' sod huts, full of fleas and lice. But at least my fleas and lice did not get fat since I turned my underwear inside out every day, forcing the little buggers to work to get back on the inside track. I had no intention of letting them have a completely free lunch.

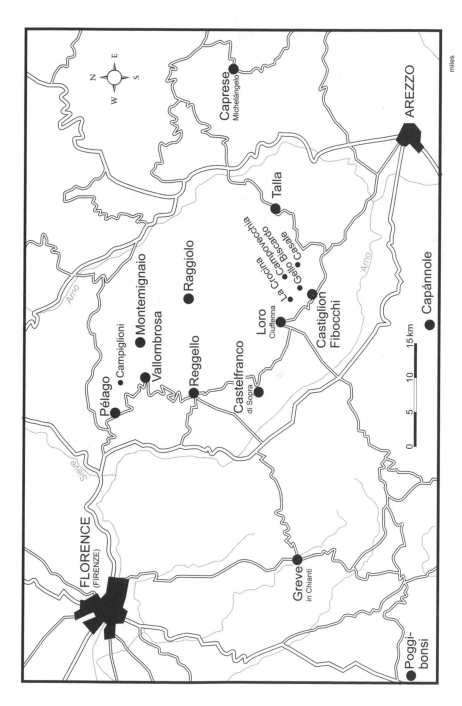

Area of Harry Pope's Partisan Activities

Usually every three or four days we'd go down to Montemignaio to find food. And normally the people would give us food freely. But when people would not receive us kindly, we would enter their houses anyway to search in their drawers until we found a fascist flag (ALL the Italian flags at that time bore the fascist symbol!) or, even better, a portrait of Mussolini. We would then accuse them of being dirty fascists and take twice as much as we would have otherwise.

One day, around mid-June, one of our group announced that he knew where a rich fascist lived in Castelfranco di Sopra and that we should go and rob him. All being in agreement, we set off southwest, even though we were leaving Prato Magno to venture into the plain towards a large village through which passed German trucks.

Arriving in the village, we crossed over a brick wall about nine feet high that separated the property from the main road. We were busily kicking the front door of the house when a German convoy of some 30 trucks entered the village. The door of the house remaining closed and the house itself being part of row housing, we headed back towards the wall. We got back to the foot of the wall a few seconds before the German convoy stopped on the other side. Ten feet from us, silhouetted against the stars, a German soldier was standing in the back of one of the trucks. Ignatz whispered in my ear: "*Guglielmo, non sparare!*" ("William, don't shoot!")

I have had many crazy ideas in my life, but to open fire with a duck-shooting shot-gun on maybe 60 German soldiers, many undoubtedly armed with Schmeissers, and all blocking our only line of retreat? No, that's an idea that I never had!

After a few minutes, the Germans continued north, and we returned to the door. Finally, it was opened by a female servant, the owner being in Florence. Once inside, we divided into three groups: one for money, one for wine and liquor, and the third, the serious pair, Ignatz and I, for food: potatoes, beans, bread, and ham.

We then found a garage with a spacious attic wherein to spend the night and start serious work on our haul of wine. Had anyone revealed us to the Germans, we would all have been shot out of hand, if we were lucky. Unlucky, we would have had a session with the Gestapo first. The next day, Ignatz and I and another one or two helped the others to stay on the narrow track as they staggered up our mountains to get back to our sod huts.

About a week later, on 20 June 1944, Ignatz and I and two or three others went again to Montemignaio. On arriving, we met about 30 of Potente's band, all very proud of themselves because they had met a six-man German patrol in the village that morning and had killed three. Potente's men seemed perfectly happy either to go back into the mountains or to celebrate their victory on the south bank of the river that divided the village, far from the two approach roads from the north that the Germans would have to take. I asked them if they thought that their attack would lead the Germans to take revenge against the population. Why not then divide at once into two groups to prepare ambushes along the two approach roads? But Potente's men, those remaining in the southern part of the village, had had enough war and wished now only to drink wine.

Early that afternoon, the German army came back in strength in the northern part of Montemignaio. Behind a wall in the southern part of the village with Ignatz and the two or three others of my little band, maybe 300 yards from the enemy, I decided that, although we were very late, we should try to cross the bridge that led to the northern part and then try to take the enemy in its right flank. I turned to explain the plan to Potente's partisans: not one remained, so the four or five of us started off for the bridge and heard an enemy machine-gun firing on our left flank; the enemy was outflanking us before we could outflank it.

Then Ignatz, for whom this was not the first battle behind the lines, told me that we would soon be encircled, that we four or five, armed as we were, could not face machine-guns. Finally, if Potente's partisans did not have the guts to defend their own people, there was nothing that a Pole and a Canadian could do. So, we headed for the mountains in our turn.

We came back a few hours later. The women of the village – there were no men left – no longer treated us as liberators, as they had done in the morning. Through their tears, they spat on us. Some 20 houses had been burned. We entered the church. At the foot of the altar, shot, lay one 15-year-old boy and ten men, the older with their long white beards floating in their blood. The German army had entered the village with three tanks and had put to death all the males that were there. I was not proud of my day.

Would it have been better for Montemignaio if the partisans had taken my advice and ambushed the German troops? Almost certainly not. The killing of the three German soldiers that morning had been inadvertent. The partisans had not been looking for a fight. Suddenly meeting a German patrol, they had to kill or be killed. But from that moment, German revenge became inevitable. Killing more Germans, as they came to kill these civilians would certainly have led to the Germans killing more than eleven. Indeed, they might well have burned the entire village and massacred everyone in it. Once the three German soldiers had been killed, the only way for the people to be spared any reprisal would have been for the partisans to defend Montemignaio until Allied forces fought their way there two months later. But only the most highly motivated and best-trained troops, which the partisans certainly were not, would have had a fighting chance of holding off the German army for two months.

Before the German army came back on the afternoon of 20 June 1944, I would have better employed my time going about Montemignaio urging the population to head for the hills. But that would have required more foresight than I possessed.

Several days later, Potente formed the 22nd Garibaldi Assault Brigade (Lanciotto), a thousand men of his own band, as well as others from north of Florence. Hoping for a little more action now, I offered him my services a second time. He placed me in 8th Company to co-operate with its commander.

For a week, nothing happened, apart from talk of the eventual occupation of Florence. Finally, on 2 July, 8th Company was ordered to go to the village of Talla, about ten miles to the southeast, to destroy a band of about 50 other partisans or convince them to join us. Apparently, these men were not much better than the fascists who lived at the expense of others and took no action against the enemy. It seemed to me that the description fit us perfectly, as well!

We were about 60 in number to go down to Talla. I marched at the head of the company with its commander and the political commissar, called Roméo, with whom I got on well, which may have saved my life. As we got close to the village, the company became more and more spread out; when the commander, the commissar, and I arrived at the hall where the whole Talla band was sitting down having lunch, I doubt that anyone else in the company had yet set foot in the village.

The three of us entered together, I shouted, "hands up!" presumably in Italian, aiming my *carabiniere* rifle, while my two comrades gathered in both their arms the weapons of the guests, stacked in a pile at the entrance. If so much as one of the Talla band had had on him a pistol that day, things would have ended badly. Not a sound was heard, except for the noise made by my two colleagues as they dragged the 50 weapons out the door. At last, one of the guests got over his shock. The one who had the muzzle of my rifle most directly in his face said, in perfect English: "You can't take those weapons; they belong to us."

I was in the act of threatening a captain of the 8th Army, thus my superior officer, since the R22eR was also part of this army, even if I was personally detached from it at that moment. So I quit the hands-up business and turned around to start pulling back the weapons of Talla. Finally, I got my two colleagues to understand my problem.

At once, everyone moved outside and the Talla band decided to join Potente. I learned that the captain's name was Gordon Rowbottom, that he was there with two of his corporals, that all three were members of the LRDG (Long Range Desert Group), that an American plane was supposed to drop them by parachute south of Arezzo to report on the traffic on the main road, and that the plane had dropped them north of Arezzo. Now, having nothing else to do, they placed mines on roads to blow up German trucks.

I immediately offered him my services, and he accepted. Like a good staff officer, the second-in-command of the brigade made sure that there would be no shooting and had now arrived in the village. When I told him of my decision, he told me that I had to ask Potente's permission. Not having the slightest desire to trek back into the mountains, especially when it seemed Rowbottom would be up to something before I got back (always assuming that Potente agreed to releasing me), I told the brigade's second-in-command that I had joined Potente voluntarily, that I had made no engagement to serve under him indefinitely, and that I was now going where the chances of action against the Germans seemed very much better. With the second-in-command not convinced, I finally told him to go to hell and turned my back on him. At that, according to one of the British corporals, the partisan pulled out his pistol to shoot me in the back. But the political commissar grabbed his arm. The British corporal added that if the second-in-command had shot me, he, the corporal would have shot him. I thanked him for the thought.

I think that Potente would have preferred to have me along for his group's occupation of Florence. An officer of the 8th Army might have been useful to give some sort of cachet of legality to the murders there of non-communists that Potente was doubtless planning. Of course, at some stage Potente might have decided that I had seen things I should not have, and that I should go to the wall also.

I was now part of a band of 12 or 13 that included six Brits, a paratroop captain (Rowbottom), two paratroop corporals, a tank lieutenant, and two soldiers (one a corporal), a South African soldier, two French Foreign Legion soldiers from Marseilles, one Russian Cossack (a non-permanent member) and two Italian guides.

Some were prisoners in Italy when the armistice with Italy opened the doors of the clink. Some had subsequently been recaptured by the Germans, but had escaped again, somewhat as I.

Rowbottom's band had all that was needed to make war, including explosives, all of it dropped by parachute. I was at last properly armed: a Sten-submachine gun and three grenades.

On 3 July (the day after my enrolment in the band) we tried to blow up a Roman stone bridge near La Crocina to please the peasants, who found it annoying to have an enemy tank wandering around their neighbourhood. Our 25 pounds of plastic HE did no more than make a small hole. The next day the enemy returned by another route with two tanks and infantry to burn all the houses along the road and shell Gello Biscardo and Campovecchio. In our view, it did so not in reprisal but as part of a scorched earth policy: leave nothing either for the partisans or for the Allies.

The evening of the same day, 4 July, Rowbottom, his two paratroop corporals, the British tank lieutenant, the Cossack, and I went down into the plain. Having crossed the main road between Castelfranco di Sopra and Castiglion Fibocchi (where there was a German divisional HQ), we placed explosives around a telephone pole as well as on the wires themselves, all joined to little tubes that looked like pencils but contained an acid that took an hour and a half to dissolve a metallic barrier and so set off the detonator.

Having rearranged the enemy's communications, we returned to the main road, where the Cossack placed in the centre of the road the ten pounds of plastic HE that he had been carrying. We placed a steel wire about three feet above the level of the road and attached it to a tree on one side of the road and to a small rock on the other. Under the rock we placed a mechanism that opened like a book as soon as the weight of the rock was removed.

While I was a battle drill instructor in England in January 1944, we played a lot with these instruments. The last explosion I engineered occurred when one of my fellow Voltigeurs lieutenants – Jean-Marie Tremblay – opened his shaving kit in the early morning, leaving him with a blackened, smoky ruin in his hands. This was considered a bit much. Which was why it was the last explosion.

The opening of the mechanism activated the detonator, which activated the explosive fuse leading to the plastic HE, which lay in the middle of the road awaiting the first truck, the unfortunate one that would jar our steel wire suspended over the road.

While the captain and one of his corporals were placing our snare in place, the rest of us formed a guard around them. I had suggested to the captain that before leaving the road we leave our visiting card – a poster with something like this written on it: "With the compliments of the 8th Army." I was thinking of the young boy and the ten men shot in the little church at Montemignaio. But Rowbottom did not agree. When hiding in the middle of an enemy division, it is not a good idea to incite a game of hide-and-seek.

With my first suggestion rejected, I had another one for the captain: to remain around our snare to massacre those who would come to the aid of the men that had discovered our ten pounds of plastic HE under them. Patiently, Rowbottom explained to me that two minutes after the explosion, enemy reinforcements would be on the scene in numbers far greater than our own. Our attack weapons, he said, were our explosives; our submachine-guns were there only for defence if by ill luck we came face-to-face with the enemy: something that he had no intention of provoking.

I sometimes wonder whether it was not this conversation that gained me my first mention-in-despatches, which I got on Rowbottom's recommendation. Maybe he said to himself that I would certainly get it posthumously, so why not recommend me? It would please my father, even if it could not console my mother.

We were only half a mile from our snare, climbing the path leading to our woods, when suddenly the night behind us vanished in the light of an explosion that we heard two seconds later. Still another instant, and a German voice crying "*Helfe, helfe!*" ("Help, help!"). After that, silence for about two minutes, followed, as the captain had foreseen, by the sound of enemy machine-guns firing in all directions.

Next morning, the road was still blocked by a petrol-transporting truck, which was still burning. (We had sprinkled our bomb with thermite so that it would burn well: with a petrol truck this was a demonstration of excessive zeal.) The peasants who were our neighbours told us that four German soldiers had been killed in the explosion and that in revenge the four Italian men living closest to the explosion had been put to death by the enemy. Even I judged that it would have been tactless to tell the peasants that we were the instigators of the tragedy. At any moment, the peasants could have revealed us to the enemy.

Why did I not refuse to be part of the bomb-laying sortie from our mountains? The answer is simple: I was a soldier wishing above all else to take action against the enemy. Having joined Rowbottom's band, I could not refuse to go with him to the road west of Castiglion Fibocchi.

But having at least attempted to defend the civilians of Montemignaio against reprisals, even though I had had nothing to do with the killings there, I should have done what I could to defend the civilians of Castiglion Fibocchi. What I should have done, once Rowbottom refused my suggestion to await the German counterattack, was to slip away and remain behind alone. Lying in ambush with my Sten submachine-gun, I could at least have killed some of the enemy and tried to let the others know that Italian partisans had had nothing to do with our bomb.

Of course, I would have been on my own. I cannot see Rowbottom's forgiving my disobeying his orders in the face of the enemy and thus endangering the rest of his band. Had he not shot me, I think that the two French Foreign Legionnaires from Marseilles would have; they never forgave me for putting into one pot to soak all the different types of dried beans that we had stolen. I was told never again to meddle in their soup making.

The monument commemorating those massacred in reprisal there has 31 names. The horrible possibility exists that the Germans came back a day or so later with 27 others, whom they executed at this spot.

After the explosion of our bomb, we judged that it would be a good idea to move to Casale, an hour and a half to the east. With the assistance of two mules we transported all our explosives. But if there is an experience that I prefer not to repeat, it is to pass in the woods from one flank to the other within the area of an enemy division with two mules that will not stop braying.

On 10 July, we repeated our deadly joke on the same main road, but this time east of Castiglion Fibocchi. Since the Cossack had disappeared - maybe being the bomb-carrier did not suit him - I now held the bomb in my two hands as though I were entering the dining-room with a birthday cake. We were on a little path that led to the main road about three hundred yards away, when, through the tall hedges that bordered both sides of the road, we heard

German voices. We were in the middle of a field kitchen. So, we five or six took off our boots to hang them around our necks, and then continued on tip-toes.

Arriving on the main road, I placed the bomb in the middle. The captain then inserted two detonators, each joined by an explosive fuse to a mechanism that would cause an explosion should a wheel pass over it. The mechanisms, naturally, were placed in the tracks made by truck tires. We did not use steel wire because we did not wish to waste all our beautiful work on a motorcyclist.

We had gone only about a hundred yards when the explosion took place. We took off at a gallop, our boots still hanging from our necks, laughing like eighth-grade students who had just played a mean trick on the school-mistress.

Again it was a truck loaded with petrol that we had blown up, and again the main road remained blocked all night. But this time only one German soldier was killed. The general commanding the division was in a vehicle immediately behind the blown-up truck and did not find this at all funny. Result: FOURTEEN Italians were put to death and it was announced that henceforth it would be a hundred for one. In addition, the Germans conscripted two hundred men from Castiglion Fibocchi to patrol the main road and placed sound detectors alongside it. One must believe that the German army did not know that it was confronting individuals who from time to time worked in their stockings.

The monument there lists the names of the 14 killed. The oldest was 71 and the youngest, 12. To the Germans seeking revenge, any male would do. It should also be noted that the date of this massacre – 12 July 1944 – was also two days after the bomb exploded. No doubt the deliberate delay added to the horror.

The enemy reprisals had the desired effect: during the remaining ten days that we were behind enemy lines, we detonated no more bombs. Even if some, but not I, could say so much the worse for the Italians if the Germans killed them because of us, we could not hope that the peasants would not report us to the enemy to save one hundred of their own people.

From this, two lessons. First, atrocities can be useful for an unscrupulous enemy: they had the desired effect. Second: it is not permissible to wage war using methods an unscrupulous enemy considers unjust (example: bombs placed on roads by night), if one does not have the means of protecting the population against the enemy. One must control the territory and be ready to defend it to the end.

What we did at Castiglion Fibocchi was immoral, a sin. *Not* because we killed German soldiers. That was our duty, which we carried out most efficiently. Our acts were immoral, sinful, because we ignored the results of our acts on the civilians among whom we lived. A soldier's duties include the protection of civilians. The fact that the Italians were co-belligerents rather than allies is utterly irrelevant. Even enemy civilians, the Germans, had the moral right to our protection.

Probably our two bombs helped the Allied cause. After all, we did blow up two petrol trucks and blocked a divisional road for two nights. But even if our two bombs were literally vital to victory, this still would not have justified what we did. No cause, no victory, is worth a single innocent life, and our actions claimed 45. Besides, we could have made it clear to the Germans that the two bombs were the work of British paratroopers with which Italian partisans had absolutely nothing to do. Of course, this would have greatly increased the risk to us. But, in fact, our risk would still not have been any greater than that faced by an infantryman in any attack on a defended locality.

The fury of the Germans against the partisans was not without reason. Many partisans were so only until the Germans launched their counter-attack. Then they hid their weapons and said "*Sono contadino*" ("I'm a farmer"). Short of partisans, the Germans then killed all the males whom they found in the area. I do not in any way excuse the German army: the ten men and the young boy sprawled at the foot of the altar in the church in Montemignaio and the 45 killed in July 1944 west and east of Castiglion Fibocchi had nothing to do with the partisans, and those who put them to death knew it perfectly well.

During the next ten days, in the middle of an enemy division as we were, with the field guns in place less than a mile behind us and the observation posts maybe 500 yards in front, we could not remain too long in the same spot.

But even now, although we knew that the enemy was all around us, we could act foolishly. For no good reason that I can remember, one night we slept on the dirt ground floor of an Italian farm house. Since the chickens also slept there, we were surely better off where we were the next night, a couple of hundred yards away in the woods! Much better off indeed. For at about 0300 hours, the man on watch woke us all very quietly to tell us that the Germans were in the house in which we had been 24 hours earlier. Had we still been sleeping in the farm house, it would have been the Germans that woke us. And it would have been our last reveille.

Finally, on 19 July, six of us former prisoners, long since dressed in civilian clothes, succeeded in crossing over to the Allied lines, the enemy believing that they were peasants going home now that the front had been quiet for several days.

At 0100 hours on 20 July, our two Italian guides came back to tell us that our army would appreciate seeing us on its side of the lines with all the information that we had about the enemy. We therefore went down into the plain, stepping very carefully over German communication wires as we did so: the peasants had also told us that the enemy had said that it would kill one hundred Italians if anyone interfered with their communications, as we had done two weeks earlier.

At last, to our credit, we gave some thought as to what would happen to Italian civilians if we took further action against the enemy.

Down in the plain, the three paratroopers and I took off our uniforms and put on civilian clothes given us by a sympathetic peasant who may well have been damned glad to see the last of us! Also, we put down our arms, something about which I was not at all pleased, since I remembered that this whole affair had started two months earlier when I went without arms to meet the enemy. But when I suggested to Captain Rowbottom that we should cross over as a fighting patrol, he did not agree.

Of course, we should have crossed as a fighting patrol. Here was our chance to inflict casualties on the enemy *without* leaving Italian civilians open to enemy reprisals. Our actions against the enemy having led to the deaths of so many Italians in reprisal, we should at least have tried to avenge them by killing as many German soldiers as we could as we made our way back to our own lines. Probably this would have been riskier than sneaking across in civvies. But it would have been honourable, at last. And we would have started our little encounter battle with the great advantage of shooting the Germans in the back.

So there we were, all six of us (the three paratroopers, the tank lieutenant, the British infantry corporal, and I) at 0600 hours, with a group of peasants, surrounded by cows, the infantry corporal holding a live hen by her neck, arriving at a German post, side-by-side with the enemy, trying to convince the guards to let us pass to return to our little farms near Arezzo. But those controlling the checkpoint were in poor humour. They told us, "You're going there to help the English." Which was perfectly true – much truer than the guards could possibly imagine. In any case, the guards told us to go back whence we came.

On the way, having always the bad habit of talking too much, to make small talk with the upstanding family head next to me, I told him who we were. He damned near had a heart attack. His cries of distress quickly convinced us to leave his company.

All six of us then tried another post, without a cow this time (but the corporal still with his unhappy hen by the neck, the unhappy bird died, strangled before she and he could cross the lines together). But the Germans again refused to let us through, rather impolitely, so that we thought that it would not be a good idea to try it the same way a third time.

During the morning, our two Italian guides, the tank lieutenant, and the corporal (still with his deceased hen) all managed to cross through the lines, leaving only the three paratroopers and me. We then set off across country with a new Italian guide, who demanded that we stay five minutes behind him. But the tank lieutenant, already back with the British, had indicated to our artillery where to shoot, that is to say, at the Germans, which, of course, was precisely where we were. After a particularly impressive explosion very close to us, we never saw our guide again.

Thus, there we were at 1400 hours on 20 July, without a guide and without a map. Because I spoke the best Italian of the group, it was decided that I should lead. Face to face with a German, I was to say: "*È questa la buena strada por passare la fronte?*" ("Is this the right route to cross the lines?"). If the German addressed us in Italian (an Italian evidently better than mine) then the captain was to speak in German, giving the impression that he was an Italian who spoke German.

We started off again across country, very slowly, as though we were four simpletons who had all the time in the world. When it seemed to us that the Germans were watching us a little too severely from their positions, we sat down; far from any thought of ours to worry the German army that day! We passed through small woods and little paths, avoiding, as much as we could, the forward slopes.

After a couple of hours, for the distance between the lines was enormous, we arrived at a tributary of the Arno river. It was almost dry, but where there was some water we came across a man taking a bath. We surrounded him. I asked him: "*Dove sono i Tedesce?*" ("Where are the Germans?"). Unhappy man if he had answered me in German, for each of us had noted where there was a rock big enough to crush a man's head. But the man replied to me in Italian, indicating by a wave of his arm that the enemy was somewhere to the north: we had crossed through the lines without realizing it!

We then left the river to find a road leading south. All together, we deliberately marched in the centre of the road, as we did not wish to sneak up on a nervous lad with his finger on his Bren's trigger, until an English voice gave us the order that we were expecting: "Halt! Advance one and be recognized!" No doubt it was Captain Rowbottom who advanced first. Little matter, the Grenadier Guards platoon that was receiving us served each of us our first cup of tea in a long time: an overflowing mess-tin, in fact. And I have not varied my recipe since: much sugar drowned in mechanized milk (condensed milk).

Chapter Three

Aide-de-Camp and Platoon Commander

After crossing the lines on 20 July 1944, we all told our stories, one after the other, to a British Intelligence Corps captain. He told me that he regretted we had not judged it appropriate to attack the enemy artillery battery that, from our home under the stars, we could see very well the previous evening at a distance of about 1,000 yards. So I said to him: "Give me a platoon of thirty men and I will lead it on patrol across the enemy lines to destroy that battery this night." Evidently, having just crossed the enemy lines so easily towards the south, I took it for granted that I could do it towards the north just as easily. Back with the regiment, in December I had to make patrols (and my last attack) which I found not at all as much fun as the one that I suggested to the British captain. In any case, he had never heard of a patrol going five miles deep into enemy territory, and he spoke no more to me of this enemy battery that bothered him so much.

My first night back on our side of the lines I spent at a British corps HQ. But before I could be admitted to half-decent society, I was met by a corporal with a long-handled pitchfork. "Please take off *all* your clothes, sir, and place them there where my pitchfork can just reach them. Very good, sir. I will now throw them into the fire we've got going here. Now, sir, would you go into the showers right there and scrub hard, especially your head and hair." I do not recall what sort of soap I was provided, but it did the trick: finished the lice, fleas, and scabies. The corporal, too, had confidence in his debugging routine: when I came out of the showers he did *not* use his long-handled pitchfork to hand me first a towel and then a *clean* uniform. It seems to me that I was the only one to receive the full clean-up treatment. But then the others had not lived a month in thoroughly infested charcoal burners' sod huts.

Next day, I headed south in the back of a three-ton truck as guard for several German POWs. For the occasion, I had a rifle, which I was not convinced would do the trick, for one of the prisoners was a paratrooper who insisted on remaining on one knee. Precisely the position I would adopt if I were about to take a flying leap out of the truck and thought that I was dealing with a guard too stunned to recognize the significance of the crouch. Not only did I find this insulting, but, having myself escaped by jumping out of a German truck seven weeks earlier, I was damned if I was going to let one of my prisoners now pull that trick on me by jumping out of a British truck. Luckily, the truck's driver was a German Jew. I said to him: "Tell the paratrooper that he is to sit squarely on his arse for the rest of the trip. If he so much as moves from that position, I will take him and one other prisoner out of the truck, march them into the nearest woods, and execute them both." The driver did as I had told him to. Having spent seven weeks noting the extreme brutality used by the German army against Italian civilians, I was sure that the German paratrooper would take my promise of summary execution as normal and therefore as deadly serious. I was right. All the POWs were as good as gold for the rest of the trip, and I handed over as many POWs as I had started with.

It took me five days to find the regiment. In passing from one British formation to another, I reached Rome where I met together on the street two or three of my former students at the Findon Manor Battle Drill School. Since they had heard that I had been killed in action between 19 and 23 May, they were horrified on seeing me, believing me to be a ghost. They quickly enough got over their shock and then, I believe, were dismayed that I was not indeed a ghost. Anyway, when the British told me that all soldiers who had spent two months behind enemy lines were automatically sent home, I told them that I was taken prisoner on 21 May (and not 19 May, the correct date). As proficient in lower mathematics as I, they then said that I was short one day to complete my two months, but the British could send me back to my country anyway. I told the British that all I needed from them was a piece of paper marked RTU (Return to Unit). The British replied that they should rather send me to the Canadian reinforcement depot. "We don't have any," I answered. Either the British believed me or they wished to be rid of me; in any case, I left the British with my piece of paper marked "RTU."

Because I had not gone through the regular channels to rejoin the regiment, I was still on the X-6 List, that of the missing. It would have screwed up the guardians of military bumph had something new happened to me while I was still officially missing. So, when the regiment headed back towards the front, I tagged along with "A" echelon, or maybe it was even the "B."

While this was going on, unfortunately the GOC 1st Canadian Corps, Lieutenant-General Tommy Burns, learnt that I was back and got off this telegram to the Chief of the General Staff through CMHQ in London:

Personal. Murchie from Burns.

Please transmit the following to Maj Gen Pope.

' From Harry. Escaped after 11 days. Spent 7 weeks behind enemy lines. Now back with the regiment in best spirits and health.' Have seen Harry and he is very well and has done remarkable job. Am very happy about this.

I was ordered to lunch in the "A" Mess of General Burns' HQ with him, five brigadiers, two lieutenant-colonels, and two captains. After lunch, the general asked me if I wished to be his aide-de-camp (ADC). I replied "No." Five days later, the order arrived at the Regiment to send me to Corps HQ to become ADC. But General Burns could just as easily have sent me back to Canada. He wished above all to relieve my mother's anxiety! It was my mother's beautiful eyes that protected my skin during the battles that the regiment had to wage against the Gothic Line!

I found it humiliating to be taken from my regiment on the eve of battle. However, as an ADC for 50 days I learned things I could not have learned remaining in command of 17 platoon.

Several times during the 50 days, I went forward to visit my regiment. My Jeep with its big black "17" on a white background (the unit sign for Corps HQ) was not a popular sight forward of Brigade HQ. One fine August afternoon I was tooling along on a gravel road more or less on the skyline in the lines of the 4th Recce (the Princess Louise Dragoon Guards, or PLDG) when a voice that I recognized shouted to me from one of the slit trenches on my left: "Why don't you go and get a tank, you'll raise more dust!" I left my Jeep to look after itself in the event of the expected enemy shelling and jumped into the slit trench of my old drinking partner, Larry Parlow. I do not remember whether the enemy did shell us. Certainly no one got hit. *That* I would remember: it's all right to draw fire on yourself, or on the corps commander's borrowed-without-his-knowledge-or-permission Jeep, but drawing it on the Plugs who were minding their own business and had not invited you and, in any case, did not expect anyone to come in on a bright sunny day on a dusty road in full view of the enemy.

Larry was no longer a lieutenant; he was a trooper. I never found out what had happened. An officer getting into trouble in England was usually sent home, and once back in Canada got promoted because of overseas experience! That Larry had not accepted that option was entirely to his credit. It must have been difficult for him in the Plugs with about ten of his RMC classmates there also and all still lieutenants.

Every day, the general, the driver-operator, and I would head off in the GOC's Jeep to each divisional HQ in the line. The general would drive, I would read my map, the driver-operator would listen to the Light program (for the forces) on the BBC. When the General would ask me where we were, I would tell him without hesitation, and then the General would ask me where that church steeple over there was on my map, indicating that I had not quite got it right. This went on for a couple of weeks until a kind soul asked me whether I knew how Burns got the Order of the British Empire

(OBE) *between* the wars. I didn't know. "Well he got it for inventing the modified British grid system: the maps we are using." From then on, when the general said where we were and I did not agree, I shut up.

One day, I accompanied the general to an airstrip. There being no ops tent close by, I minded my own business, relaxing quietly, while the general went up in an air OP. Soon enough a British lieutenant-colonel came running up with the news that Sir James Grigg, the secretary for war, would be arriving by plane very shortly, and would I mind telling him what was happening on our front? Of course I wouldn't mind: hell, this civilian won't know that my map is not up to the hour (or maybe even up to the day).

Everything went swimmingly with the minister. "Splendid," he said, "now, General Sir Harold Alexander [the GOC-in-C] is arriving in his plane in a couple of minutes. Would you mind giving him all the information you have just given me?" Of course I minded, very much, in fact. But I was stuck. During my presentation, General Alexander fixed me with unwavering cold blue eyes. At the time, I thought the general realized that I was skating and, without saying a word, he was indicating to me that subalterns had better get up earlier in the morning before trying to tell their GOC-in-C what was happening on *his* front. But maybe General Alexander's coldness on this occasion was caused by the entirely proper contempt he must have felt for a young and obviously fit infantry lieutenant that had got himself a soft and safe job at corps while four out of twelve of his brother lieutenants were getting killed on the Gothic Line. It is sad that his decency and tact, which I was to learn to appreciate within two years, prevented him from asking me what I was doing out of the fighting. Had he asked, I would have told him, and I might have been back with my regiment in time to be useful.

In early September 1944, Major-General Dudley Ward's 4th British Infantry Division, which was in 1st Canadian Corps under General Burns's command, was ordered to close up to the Marecchia River so that the Mighty Maroon Machine, 5th Canadian Armoured Division, could break through into the valley of the Po. I usually went to the ops tent before breakfast to see what had happened overnight. The morning after the order to 4th British Infantry Division, I found a whole gaggle of general staff officers exclaiming over the message from this division posted on the board: "Patrols set out for the Marecchia River but because of inclement weather returned." This "inclement weather" was to continue, and the Mighty Maroon Machine never did make its breakout.

Always, until then, when the general arrived at a divisional HQ, I would hop out of the Jeep, go to the divisional commander's caravan, knock, and say, "Corps Commander to see you, Sir." Then I would shove off to the ops tent to update my map with the latest-known positions of our side and the enemy. Everything was done as usual for the visit to General Ward, except that I did not shove off at once to the ops tent.

I had already been up in front of several colonels, a brigadier and a major-general; so I knew how a subaltern got spoken to. I was interested in hearing how a lieutenant-general dealt with a major-general. Hanging around outside, practically under the caravan's steps, I heard Burns say: "Dudley, do you think you could push on a little faster?" He might just as well have added: "Why, that's very kind of you, I think I will have a spot of tea."

Burns should have been in touch with 8th Army as soon as the "inclement weather" message arrived from 4th British Infantry Division and demanded Ward's immediate replacement. Instead, of course, Burns was gone in a couple of months. He was a decent, hard-working man, an excellent staff officer, a "brain" as proven by his contributions to the *Canadian Defence Quarterly* in the 1930s, but not a commander. Of course he could give orders, but he could not *inspire* and, in war, that's what counts.

When 1st Canadian Infantry Division landed in Sicily on 10 July 1943, its Canadian commander should have been slated, in Ottawa's mind, to become GOC 1st Canadian Corps in Italy should it subsequently be decided to send another division to Italy, as was in fact done. And the general staff officers of 1st Canadian Corps should have come from 1st Canadian Division and, to a lesser extent because of its lack of battle experience, from the newly arrived 5th Canadian Armoured Division.

Burns did command 5th Armoured Division before assuming command of 1st Canadian Corps, but he did not command 5th Armoured in any important battle on a divisional scale. In other words, he had not proven himself as a commander in battle as had the commanders of 1st Infantry Division and 5th Armoured Division before 1st Canadian Corps fought its first battle as a corps on the Gustav and Hitler Lines.

Moreover, Burns simply did not fit into the happy-warrior mould of Major-General Chris Vokes of 1st Infanty Division or of Major-General Bert Hoffmeister of 5th Armoured Division. It was like having a clerk, a brilliant clerk, but still a clerk, trying to lead commandos who have cheerfully killed with knives and are contemptuous of anyone who hasn't.

One day, I went with Burns to call on the 8th Army's Commander, Lieutenant-General Sir Oliver Leese. We found him sitting in his canvas bathtub in the middle of his compound with a couple of General Staff officers nearby, presumably ready to write down whatever of significance might occur to their general while he was soaking wet and unable to wield pen and notebook. On seeing us as we hove in sight, he gave us a cheery wave with the hand that held an enormous sponge, "Hallo Tommy, hallo Harry," finishing with a mighty splash, as he brought the sponge down vigorously on his head. I do not recall the subsequent events. I suppose Leese found a towel and then his trousers and then conferred privately with General Burns. At least, I was not needed, which meant that I shoved off to the ops tents to get up to date.

It would have been impossible for Burns to come anywhere close to matching the informality of our greeting. I do not mean that the path to success in the 8th Army was to greet your subordinates naked, sitting in your bathtub. I do mean that if in contrast to *that* you smile so rarely that you're nicknamed "Smiler," then we do not have a very good fit.

Another day, Burns decided to make an unannounced inspection of 5th Armoured Division's Rear HQ. Perfectly legal. But if even I could see that it was a tactless thing to do without *first* asking General Hoffmeister if he would like to come along, then I am sure that

Bert Hoffmeister must have been mad as hell when he found out. Of course, *I* rather enjoyed the afternoon. It started off with Burns asking a couple of staff-sergeants standing in a truck with their backs to us where the camp commandant was. One of them, looking casually over his shoulder at this officer wearing an armoured corps black beret, gave a not very helpful answer. I then quietly climbed up behind the two and, in my mildest tones, said, "Staff, when the Corps Commander asks you a question, I think the least you should do is come to attention." The poor bastards were still standing at attention when we disappeared from sight.

We found the camp commandant, a major. After Burns had finished telling him what a shit-house of a camp site he was running, the general strode towards his Jeep. However, I found that I had time to point out a few more faults to the unhappy major. He punctuated every one of my phrases with, "Yes Sir, yes Sir," all the while trying to bring his arms more stiffly to attention at his sides. A couple more nits from me and he would have forced his arms out of their sockets at the shoulders.

I was happy to have been party to anything that made life miserable, however temporarily, for these rear-echelon types. But, still, it was not sensible of Burns to have done it. If he had been looking for reasons to fire Hoffmeister, fine. But he was not out to get Hoffmeister. But what he did do was add to Hoffmeister's desire to get rid of *him*. Probably 5th Armoured Division's Rear HQ was a little neater for a few days, but it would have been much neater much longer had Burns casually mentioned to Hoffmeister that he would like to take a stroll through a rear divisional HQ some day soon.

General Burns mentioned in a letter the "adventurous undertakings" that I proposed to him. It was the last such that earned me my return to the regiment. One evening in "A" Mess, the brigadier responsible for the artillery, the Corps Commander Royal Artillery, was telling us that now that we were in the valley of the Po, we were short of hills from which to observe the enemy. Therefore he was thinking of sending an officer by boat behind the enemy lines to find targets for the artillery. (We were bordered by the Adriatic.)

Since I had been a bombardier (corporal) in the militia artillery in 1940 before going to RMC in Kingston; and since at RMC we had done much artillery study; and since I had just completed 50 days as a partisan behind enemy lines; and since to win a Military Cross sitting under a haystack with a radio for a week behind enemy lines seemed to me much more intelligent than to do so among shells and bullets, I proposed to the brigadier that I do the job.

He replied that I was no doubt the ideal candidate – but it was up to me to get the general's permission. I set out to do this at once, knocking on his caravan's door around 2100 hours. His reply was brief and brooked no reply: "God damn it to hell, man, no! You'll be going back to your regiment as soon as the current action is over."

Evidently it was impossible for the general to say yes: if I had not come back, how could he have explained that to my mother? But I risked my skin much more with the regiment on the Savio, the Ronco, the Lamone, and the Senio in October, December, and January to come out of it with two more wounds and my second mention in despatches than I would have sitting quietly under a haystack for a week. The artillery captain who got that agreeable week instead of me was awarded the Military Cross!

When I was back with the regiment at the end of September, after 50 days as ADC, identical to the number of days I had been a partisan, Colonel Allard at last sent me back to "D" Company, which I had left as an unofficial stretcher bearer under German escort four months earlier. Since Lieutenant Léo Jobin, an old Voltigeur like me, was commanding my old 17 platoon, Captain Tony Poulin gave me the last platoon of the regiment, number 18.

Thus it was that as the sun was setting on 18 October, I was at the head of 18 platoon, leading it to the front and thinking that at that moment my replacement as ADC was having a cocktail in "A" Mess. And when the enemy started to shell on the other side of the road, the shells were landing a hundred yards from us, I asked myself if sometimes I didn't show excessive zeal. The feeling was cowardly, and obviously nothing came of it. But it is necessary to see only one soldier of one's regiment, uniformed as oneself, shredded by a shell, and I had seen enough on the Hitler Line on 19 May. After that, it is hard not to take enemy shelling very seriously.

It was 19 October 1944, the day after we re-entered the line, and we were advancing towards the Savio river along a railway line, with Cesena on our left. On 20 October, we reached the river, 18 platoon was on the left of the regiment in position on the crest of a hill facing the river, with a railway bridge immediately to our left. The bridge, naturally, had been destroyed.

Between us and the river there was about 200 yards of flat ground and I decided to go alone in daylight to the river to see what there was to be seen. In the regimental war diary for 20 October at 1300 hours there is a report eleven lines long concerning a patrol to the Savio. The intelligence officer (IO), the senior lieutenant of the battalion at the time, was Lieutenant Marcel Richard, who had been one of my seniors at RMC in 1940-41. I see his initials ("JMR") at the foot of the report but there is no indication who made the patrol; a strange omission for Muck. It is possible then that it is my report made directly to the IO with the author's name suppressed out of tactfulness, unauthorized patrols being, after all, unauthorized.

What makes me think that it is my patrol is the detailed description of the railway bridge in my sector. In referring to mines, however, the report states (in English): "Along the near side of the river is a wire which carries signs bearing the word '*Minen*'. These signs face both ways. There is a pathway which was used by the patrol on this side of the river. This might indicate that the Germans report our side of the river to be mined." This wire with its signs was not simply there as a warning: the wire was an integral part of the minefield! At about every five yards the wire was attached to exploding mines encased in concrete on little posts about six inches high. All that was needed was to push a little too hard on the wire – with one's foot or leg in walking, for example – to find the war very unpleasant.

Therefore, if this patrol report is really mine, I should certainly have made absolutely clear the situation regarding the mines. If the report is not mine, then I am even more in the wrong, for this

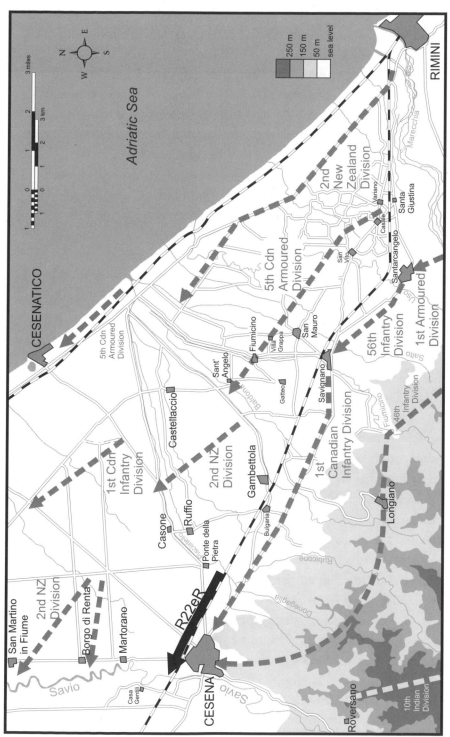

Advance to the Savio River

means that I kept for myself information essential for the success of all the battalion's patrols.

That same evening of the 20th, after dark, I commanded another patrol to the river, this one official, that included a tank lieutenant, an engineer lieutenant, two of our pioneers, and, according to the war diary, of an officer from the Carleton and York Regiment (CYR) and an NCO.

Our task was to discover if the infantry, supported by tanks, could make an assault crossing of the river without a bridge. And if a bridge was necessary, the engineer officer was in the group to decide on what type.

I had been aware of the presence of mines since my stroll to the Savio 12 hours earlier. Therefore I took the lead as always, but now with my bare arms trailing along the ground. If there be those pleased to say that I must have looked like a monkey, let them think of a better way to find a tripwire in the dark! As soon as I felt the wire, I had the pioneers come up. They then cut the wire to make a path for us big enough to allow us to pass through at our leisure (or in a hell of a hurry!).

After having gone a short distance southwards along the bank, which was about ten feet high, I found a spot that dropped more gently to the river. The enemy, that was not stupid, but had reason to believe that we could be at times, was equally aware of this spot. Therefore when my whole gang had followed me into the trap, at the instant when I was about to put a foot into the water, the enemy opened fire on us with a machine-gun from a distance of 50 yards.

I turned like a top; indeed, I had completed my 360 degrees before realizing that all the others had been content with 180 and were already back up on top of the bank. Since we were a recce patrol, not a fighting patrol, there was nothing wrong with that. Therefore I followed the example of my colleagues, and we dove through the minefield gap that our pioneers had made, all of us breaking into loud laughter – because we'd had a close one. I have not the slightest idea how all the bullets could have missed the tight little group that we were in the trap into which I had led the patrol.

According to the war diary, practically the same thing happened to "C" Company's patrol: a machine gun had fired on them point blank. But that patrol got a lieutenant and two soldiers wounded. The diary does not state the nature of the wounds. In fact, in reading the Diary, one gets the impression that they were machine gun wounds. But I have the impression that at the time I was told that the "C" Company patrol coming back in a hurry like mine hit the tripwire, causing one or more mines to explode – something that would certainly have happened to my patrol also had I not gone alone on patrol that morning.

Here, as always, the two patrols were in no way supported by their company or by battalion HQ. As soon as either patrol came under fire, mortar bombs, 2-inch from their company, 3-inch from the battalion, should have come down on the enemy side of the Savio. Since neither patrol had crossed the river, these bombs could have been fired without danger to the patrols. There was no excuse for this neglect. Nothing else was happening on the battalion front. But the weapons under the direct control of the CO (3-inch mortars, MMGs) were ordered to fire only when the battalion was attacking or being attacked. The anti-tank guns, as far as I could determine, were given tasks only during consolidation and in defence. At the company level, no one had any tasks at all except the attacking platoons or the patrols. I never heard of a 2-inch mortar being fired, and certainly the Brens of the reserve platoon might as well have been LOB (left out of battle).

I, of course, was no better. Before setting off on this patrol, I should have had my platoon sergeant standing by with my 2-inch mortar detachment ready to fire across the Savio as soon as I fired a Very pistol flare. Naturally, because 2-inch mortars could *not* be sighted with any degree of accuracy (unlike the 60 mm mortars that we had in Korea), I would have had a bomb or two fired across the Savio beforehand, and then told my sergeant to be damned sure that the mortar was fired at the same angle when my flare went up. When a patrol is fired on by the enemy, it does not also need one of its own mortar bombs landing on it.

The next evening, 21 October, according to a note in the war diary, the regiment was supposed to make the enemy believe we were attacking on our front to draw the enemy's attention while the 2nd Brigade attacked for real on our right. The note ended thus: "'D' Company will have two parties [at the river] making noises, throwing stones into the river and firing TSMGs [Thompson submachine guns, Tommy guns] and Schmeissers. Lieut W.H. Pope is to be in charge of these parties."

I have no recollection at all of having played the fool that night. I remember fooling around only when I do it on my own account. Or maybe the orders were countermanded when the enemy sent a patrol into our lines that night and nobody on our side had then the time to play games.

The next day, 22 October, and thus two days after I had walked alone in the morning along the Savio, Lieutenant P. Leblanc of my company went on an official patrol with a section to cross the river. When he was in the water up to his knees, "a burst of enemy machine gun fire caught them," as says *l'Histoire du Royal 22e Régiment* (page 325). Leblanc was shot in the thigh, no bones broken, and once a stretcher bearer had got him out of there, we thought he would get himself an agreeable holiday with a not-too-serious wound. When I saw him in hospital several months later, his leg had been amputated above the knee.

On the same page of *l'Histoire*, I read: "On the morning of the 23rd, Lieutenant Pope led a patrol to the far bank of the Savio and discovered that the enemy had withdrawn." And on page 153 of the *Mémoires du Général Jean V. Allard*, I read: "The next morning Lieutenant Harry Pope swims across the river and confirms the fact" (that the enemy had abandoned the far bank).

I find none of this in the war diary, because I'm certain I never swam across that damned river! It seems to me that if one takes a bath in a river towards the end of October, one is not likely to forget it, especially if one has reason to believe the enemy will interrupt the swim.

Instead of wasting three days on patrols, we should have made an assault crossing of the river on 20 October. If the tanks could have crossed with us, fine; if not, they could have supported us by firing on the enemy machine guns from our bank.

But I should have thought of making these recommendations to Brigadier Bernatchez, commander of our brigade, when I reported to him the night of my unsuccessful attempt to cross the Savio. Not much point in thinking of this half a century late. But maybe Bernatchez should have thought of all this without any prompting from a young infantry subaltern. I do not know if he also had the tanker and the sapper report to him. Surely he should have. After all, they saw as much of the river as I had before the machine gun opened up on us. It was not necessary to wade or swim across this small river to see that a Bailey bridge could quickly have been slung from one bank to the other. If not a Bailey, then the tanker and sapper could have been able to tell the brigadier what sort of a bridge would have been needed to get tanks across. It was not a major obstacle. It was not the Rhine! It was not even comparable to the Ronco; and it did not have the 20- or 30-foot dikes of the Senio. The Savio had no elevated dikes at all; the water merely flowed about ten feet below the top of its banks.

But this was no longer the case by 23 October. By then, the 2nd Brigade had crossed the river on 21-22 October, heavy rains had turned the Savio into a raging torrent, and the sappers could not bridge it until the night of the 23rd. And this bridge, a folding boat bridge, was soon swept away. 2nd Brigade almost paid very dearly for the failure of 3rd Brigade to make an assault crossing on 20 October. Finally, the enemy having withdrawn from in front of us at least two days previously, we crossed the Savio on 25 October and advanced six miles behind those who had preceded us. Arriving in our new positions behind the CYR around midnight on 25 October, I was again on patrol (official), with one of my corporals, to a river separating the CYR from the enemy. My task: determine whether the river was crossable. Now that I think about it, it seems to me that a simple phone call to the CYR would have settled the question more easily, from my point of view anyway.

So there we were, the corporal and I, at 0300 hours looking at that damned river, the Ronco. With the continuing rain, the river was in full flood: even in a boat it could not be crossed. Therefore, at 0500 hours (after the corporal and I had spent the whole night marching), the war diary states: "Lieut Pope reports back from the Carlt and York Regt. Reports they attempted to cross the river but could not owing to mud and quicksand." Evidently, they really wanted me to take a bath! If I had tried to cross the river, I would have headed for the Adriatic at 20 miles an hour, and I saw no quicksand. As for mud, it was not necessary to go on a recce to find out there was mud along a river. There was mud everywhere else.

We quit the front on 29 October. I had been at the front for eleven days without seeing the enemy, but in December that would change.

After spending all of November in reserve, the regiment entered the line on 1 December. That day and the next, "D" Company remained in battalion reserve, though not without casualties: as 18 platoon waited in line in a ditch alongside a road, an enemy shell landed a few yards behind me, wounding two of my men. At last, around 0100 hours, 3 December, "D" Company set off in the fog to catch up to the enemy, which had just retreated along our axis of advance. In other words, our task was to advance to contact, not my favourite operation of war because it seemed to me that the "contact" too often was a machine gun burst in the face at point-blank range.

About 0200 hours, the company commander, Captain André Langlais, a couple of his signallers, and I were next to a barbed-wire fence that separated us from the main building of a farm a few feet away from us. The company was in single file behind us. We heard something move close to the house. "The Germans!" exclaimed one of the signallers. I barely had time to say, "No, it's a horse," when an enemy machine gun next to the house opened fire. Even if the bullets were not coming directly in our direction, we decided to move before the German soldier improved his aim.

So, while Langlais placed the company in a defensive position south of the farm, I left with two sections of 18 platoon, nine of us, towards the north. The farm was stuck alongside a railway embankment, maybe six feet high. Having crossed over the embankment, we took up position in line along the embankment, thus behind and about ten yards from the enemy's position and the house.

The soldier responsible for the PIAT being among us, I told him to fire a bomb into the house. At the moment the bomb exploded I was going to lead the assault into the rear of the enemy position, which, obviously, was encircled. But while the soldier was placing the detonator in the bomb's nose, there was an explosion on the other side of our embankment and sparks fell on us like rain. Nothing dangerous in that but I said to myself that if the others in the company were amusing themselves by firing PIAT bombs into the enemy position, they must be just about to attack and it would not be a popular move on my part were I to fire my PIAT bomb into the crowd. So I countermanded my order to fire a PIAT bomb, and I decided to remain in place, behind the enemy, to await events.

And I waited. I do not know whether I thought my signaler, with his wireless, would have been useful if I had thought to bring him. Certainly I would have liked to ask Captain Langlais what was happening on his and the enemy's side of the embankment, for after a little while I started to fall asleep. I thought this idiotic and to keep myself awake I tried to scare myself with such thoughts as: "Imbecile! Here you are on the wrong side of the enemy lines again. It's no time to sleep: if we're behind an enemy post, that means all the rest of the German army is behind you!"

Fortunately, we eventually heard movement on the other side of our embankment. I had one of my soldiers throw a grenade, gravely wounding a German soldier. Seeing a stretcher bearer appear to help the unfortunate fellow, I told the stretcher bearer, in a mixture of three or four languages, that they were encircled but that their lives would be spared if they surrendered immediately. At once, the stretcher bearer gave a shout, and his twelve comrades climbed out of their trenches as a single man, all with their hands high above their heads.

We then, at last, crossed back over the embankment to accept the surrender. It was at that moment that I noticed that our company had disappeared. At sunrise, Langlais could not leave the company completely in the open, not a hundred yards from a solidly entrenched enemy position. It wasn't kind of me, but when I realized that the nine of us had taken fourteen prisoners, I laughed in their faces. And I laughed the more when the stretcher bearer demanded to be set free, emphasizing the enormous Red Cross that covered his front from his neck to his belt. Since I had been taken prisoner on 19 May when I went unarmed, voluntarily, into the enemy lines to pick up my wounded, I was certainly not going to let go a stretcher bearer taken by force of arms in an encircled position (or which believed itself encircled!).

One of my men expressed his dismay at the company's leaving us to fend for ourselves. He did not share my satisfaction at our pulling it off by ourselves and, moreover, with no losses on our side.

At this moment, we realized that the house was full of Italian women and children. I was horrified at what I had almost done in ordering that a PIAT bomb be fired into this whole group of non-combatants. What saved their lives, and left my conscience at peace, was *not* a PIAT bomb fired by another platoon of "D" Company, but rather a rocket fired from a *panzerfaust* by one of the German soldiers! This rocket saved many lives – those of the women and children and of German soldiers shot in the back in their trenches, and maybe one or two members of 18 platoon had the Germans turned quickly enough to receive us.

But nothing could be done for the German soldier wounded by our grenade. I had him carried in a poncho by two of his comrades when we all retraced our steps for maybe half a mile, looking for our company. On the way, the wounded soldier died, and I left him alongside the road: I had already lost much time, and I did not wish to lose more simply for the pleasure of presenting 14 rather than 13 prisoners to my company commander.

Concerning all this, the regiment's war diary contains this note at 1030 hours on 3 December:

> Twelve prisoners of war arrive at Tac HQ [Tactical Headquarters]. They are identified as coming from No. 1 Company, I/870 Grenadier

Regiment, Infantry Division 356. They were taken at 0200 hours by Lieut. W. H. Pope and two sections of "D" Company at approximately 414330.

Certainly I should have taken these 14 (not 12) at 0200 hours; but it was closer to 0600 hours before we completed our task. Also, it all happened 800 metres farther north, that is at 414338.

ROYAL 22ND ACTION HACKS INTO NAZIS

Platoon Accounts for Many

Killed and Prisoners;

Supplies Captured

By William Boss

With the Canadian Corps on the Adriatic, January 16 [1945] - CP - A neat platoon action led by Lt. Harry Pope of Ottawa, son of Maj.-Gen. Maurice Pope, military staff officer to Prime Minister Mackenzie King, brought in 14 prisoners, killed three Nazis, wounded another, and accounted for eight mortars, four machine guns and a bazooka...

Langlais rearranged his platoon dispositions, ordered Pope to take on the enemy. With two sections the Ottawa officer went around to tackle the Nazis from behind. The little scrap revealed two machine-guns instead of one. At the sound of fire more enemy rushed out of a nearby house, of these, three were killed and one wounded...

I do not quote two paragraphs of Bill Boss that are identical to mine. I quote above only the two others, full of suds as they are. These that Bill Boss found, God only knows where, six weeks after the fact, I frankly prefer enormously to mine. I quote Boss simply as an excellent example of the tendency to exaggerate feats of arms. May God keep me from doing so! Possibly, Boss got his "facts" from an unsuccessful citation for the Military Cross for me. If this is so, it's well the citation got nowhere: I could hardly have framed BS like that!

It goes without saying that we were lucky. If the enemy post had had a wireless, it could easily have sent word back and we would have been encircled.

In any case, after I had delivered my 13 surviving prisoners to Langlais, we all returned to the farm next to the railway embankment, where the company took up a defensive position for the day, with

18 platoon in reserve around company HQ, which was in the house that I had *not* bombed.

After nightfall, Langlais left me in command of the company while he went to a Battalion "O" Group. I was junior to the other two platoon commanders, one had been a captain in England, but I had joined the company before them, having done so originally in April. Shortly after Langlais had left, the other two platoon commanders told me that there were snipers everywhere and that they were pulling their platoons back to safer territory. CSM Irené Roy, MM, asked me what company HQ and 18 platoon would do. "We stay," I replied. "That's what I thought you'd say," he said. Hell, I had taken the position with eight men when it was defended by fourteen Germans. Was I now going to abandon the position because the other two platoon commanders saw snipers everywhere?!

The next morning, 4 December, at about 0600 hours, 18 platoon advanced alone to the Lamone River, about 1,000 yards north-northwest of our famous farm, where the rest of the company remained. We found no snipers along the way: it never occurred to me that we would. Having arrived, I was on the second floor busy house-clearing with my platoon sergeant, when we saw the door connecting us to the next room opening very slowly. At the same time a voice made itself heard: "Austria, Austria, Austria." Or maybe he was saying "*Osterreich.*" To be truly polite, dealing with the 22nd, he should have announced himself with "*Autriche!*" In any case, it was evidently a deserter from the German army who thought that he would be received better as an Austrian than as a German.

With his hands high in the air, our new prisoner clearly had a wristwatch, and my sergeant saw it. At once, the sergeant grabbed his arm to take his watch. "Stop," I told him. "When I was a prisoner, the Germans examined my watch to make sure it wasn't a German one. When they recognized that I wasn't wearing one stolen from them, they gave me back my watch. Every prisoner for whom I'm responsible will receive the same honourable treatment. Give him back his watch." Much dismayed, the sergeant obeyed.

My platoon was now in position around the house, a few yards from the Lamone. There seemed to be no more Germans on our bank of the Lamone and all seemed quiet. So, leaving my sergeant in command, I decided to take the prisoner myself to the company CP, which was still in the house next to the railway embankment. Arriving there, I phoned the battle adjutant, Captain Cme Simard, MC. "Cme," I said to him, "I'm sending you something rare: a prisoner who still has his watch. He has gone through 18 platoon without losing it and he has gone through 'D' Company without losing it. I want you to promise me he won't lose it at Battalion." I forget what Captain Simard replied. All that I know is that the entry in the war diary for 1145 hours of 4 December is: "'D' Company has taken a prisoner. He is identified as coming from Infantry Division 356." No mention of his watch.

Coming out of the line a couple of days later, Captain Langlais asked me what our heavy shelling had been like along the banks of the Lamone the night of 4-5 December, when 18 platoon was there all alone. "What shelling?" I asked.

"I ordered you to withdraw your platoon three hundred yards the night before last so that you wouldn't be caught by any shells landing short," said Captain Langlais. "So that's why my signaller was trying to wake me! Well, he wasn't able to. Nothing hit our house and we all slept through it all, except the signaller and, I hope, those on guard." We were lucky. *Not* because our artillery did not drop a load on us but because the enemy didn't check us out that night. Fast asleep: a hell of a stupid way to be taken prisoner – or shot! But I had not slept at all the night of 2-3 December, when I was behind the German outpost, and hardly, if at all, the night of 3-4 December when the other two platoon commanders were worrying about snipers and taking their platoons back. So, on the night of 4-5 December, with my platoon 800 yards forward of the rest of the company, thank the Lord, alone at last, I went to sleep.

On 5 December, the company CP and the other two platoons joined us along the Lamone. During the night of 5-6 December, the RCR and the Hasty Pees failed in their attempt to establish a bridgehead on the other side of the Lamone: two companies had succeeded in crossing, but a German counter-attack had thrown them back to our side. Thus, instead of us attacking through the RCR on 6 December, that regiment took our place along the Lamone while we fell back a mile with the object of doing, during the night of 6-7 December, what 1st Brigade had failed to do the preceding night.

During the evening of the 6th, we were told that the attack of our brigade, the 3rd, was put off for 24 hours. Even later in the evening of the 7th, we learned that the attack was again postponed. On the 8th, there was no talk of an attack.

At noon on the 9th, we were told that there would be no attack that evening. Finally, during the night of 10-11 December, we got serious.

The Carleton and York Regiment of our brigade having established the bridgehead, "D" Company passed through the CYR at 0630 hours 11 December. 18 platoon was in reserve and soon 16 and 17 were in contact with the enemy who were spread among some farm buildings maybe 150 yards in front. Knowing that my platoon would have to make the attack if the other two could not take the farm, I went to the company CP where Captain Langlais was in the front line with the artillery forward observation officer. The decision was made to fire a few rounds at the farm.

I then went to see what was happening on the right of the company. In this way, I again met L/Cpl Trudel. He who had loudly proclaimed to 17 platoon, which I then commanded, during our attack against the Gustav Line on 17 May: "Our lieutenant is a bandit: he likes to kill." Well, early in the morning of 11 December, Trudel was still with 17, in charge of a Bren in the front line on the extreme right of the company. He asked me: "Lieutenant, what should I do with my Bren?"

Giving evidence of a tactfulness that was highly abnormal for me, I replied that I was no longer his platoon commander and that he should ask the lieutenant who was. But Trudel found this response, when the enemy was within a hundred yards, perfectly idiotic. So he repeated the question, adding: "He knows nothing." Then I told Trudel: "The artillery is going to fire on the farm. The rounds will fall on this side of it. Place your Bren as far on the right as you can and fire in enfilade as much behind those casas as you can. That will give the enemy the impression of being surrounded: shells in front and bullets in the back."

Trudel followed my advice, and it worked as though on wheels (*comme sur des roulettes*). Very soon, a German stretcher bearer (again one!) climbed out of a trench 100 yards in front of us. I shouted at him to come over to us, which he did at the double. I took him by the collar and with my Luger in his back I turned him around to face the position that he had just abandoned. "Tell the others to surrender," I ordered him.

He obeyed me, and about ten Germans, led by an officer, came out of their holes and ran towards us. I therefore took a few paces forward and accepted the Luger that the officer handed me. In the war diary, the entry for 1308 hours 11 December reads: "Eight prisoners, including an officer, are taken by 'D' Company."

Again, as on 3 December, the stretcher bearer protested that we had no right to keep him prisoner. I told him that he was not acting as a stretcher bearer when he ran towards us with his hands over his head.

On 17 and 18 May, 17 platoon, which I was then commanding, had captured several German pistols. At that time, I had chosen a Mauser for myself, but when I went back into the German lines on 19 May to pick up my two wounded soldiers, the Mauser, and all my weapons – had stayed behind. When I came back to the regiment on 25 July, I learned that the quarter-master had not counted on my returning and had dispersed all my equipment. The soldiers of my old 17 platoon paid me the highest compliment possible between comrades-in-arms: they told me that they had expected me to come back and they therefore had put a Luger aside for me. They then gave it to me. So the Luger that I had just captured on this 11 December, I saved for my company commander, Captain André Langlais, for I already had mine (and of course I still do).

To give the Luger to Langlais greatly upset the new commander of 17 platoon, who insisted that since the German prisoners had come through his platoon the booty should be his. I told him that this would have been the case had he been in the front line when the unsurrendered enemy was a hundred yards away.

* * * * *

But back to Trudel. The first time that he had impressed me was on the Ortona front in April 1944, soon after I had joined the regiment. The company was in reserve, and I had the time to go from trench to trench to invite the men to buy Victory Bonds. When I reached the trench that Private Trudel occupied with another, Trudel said to me: "I heard you explaining all that to the others, Lieutenant, and it makes a lot of sense. But I had already decided that I wasn't going to buy any and since I'm a stubborn bastard ('*j'ai une tête de cochon*'), I'm not going to buy any, regardless of what you say now." I had no difficulty at all understanding, indeed approving of, this point of view.

The last time that I saw Lance-Corporal Trudel was at Avellino in March 1945. I had just got out of hospital, compound fracture of the left ulna: a German tracer bullet through the arm on the Senio, New Year's Day, and was spending two weeks at the reinforcement centre before rejoining the regiment (which I succeeded in doing, going through Marseilles on 18 March). To give me something else to do besides drinking beer (naturally there were gallons of it far from the front), I had been named junior officer on a succession of courts-martial. One day, going along the corridor leading to the court-room, I saw Trudel lined up with the other accused. "*Pourquoi?*" ("Why?") I whispered in his ear. He replied: "I insulted an English RSM." I told him: "Don't let on you know me. Accept me as one of your judges."

Apparently, at the regiment it had been decided in February that Trudel's leadership qualities were such that he deserved to qualify as corporal at the Junior NCOs' School, in English, naturally. However, Trudel did not speak English, and did not wish to go on the course.

Thus, on arriving at the school, Trudel went on an extremely solid drunk and, unfortunately, decided to sit down for a little while in the tent of the school's RSM.

In his years of military service Trudel had learned most of the four-letter words used by the English when all is not right in their world. Also, he probably knew all the curses employed in *la belle province.* Thus it is perfectly understandable that the British RSM felt injured when Trudel explained to him why he, Trudel, was not going to leave the RSM's comfortable chair and, in consequence, what the RSM could do about it.

What the RSM did about it was to throw Trudel in the clink.

Thus, after 30 days in close arrest, here was Trudel before a court-martial. We were three officers as judges: a major, a captain, and I. Also, there was a second major, the judge-advocate, who, as a lawyer, was there to guide us as to the law, if necessary.

The evidence given, I, as the junior, had to give my opinion first. "It's obvious," I started by saying, "that he's guilty of conduct to the prejudice of good order and military discipline. On the other hand, he seems to be a good fighting soldier. After all, his company must have had confidence in him to send him on this course. Coming out of the line, and feeling out of his element among people he could not understand, he took one drink too many. [One!] No doubt, he did not know he was in the RSM's tent. Finally, he has already lost thirty days' pay because he has been thirty days under close arrest. Therefore, I recommend: guilty, admonished."

Happily my colleagues did not know military law as well as I did, for with the minimum punishment, "admonished," pay is not lost for the time spent in close arrest. No doubt the judge-advocate knew this as well. Maybe he let me lead my colleagues into error because he was sleeping, but more likely he did so because he was not a bad fellow and judged that, if for once I was recommending the minimum, I must have good reason. After all, I had already given proof of my devotion to law and order by recommending the penitentiary for each deserter who passed before us.

I never saw Trudel again.

* * * * *

With the surrender of the German troops around the farm on the morning of 11 December, it was again necessary to make an advance to contact.

Why we waited until nightfall, I do not know. It would have been far more intelligent to advance in attack formation at once, with the battalion's anti-tank guns following close behind the leading company, in the hope of catching the enemy off balance. Why give a dozen hours to set up its machine-guns to receive us as we stumbled along in the dark? The least we should have done was to send a recce patrol forward to determine the next enemy position, and *then* have the company advance in daylight to close with the enemy. And then advise Trudel, still i/c Bren, what to do to convince the enemy to surrender! We were not dealing now with paratroopers or Hitler *Jügend* who would fight to the death. We were facing rather demoralized infantry men, perfectly happy to catch us in the open with machine-gun fire but eager to surrender when we had given them serious reason to believe we were well positioned to kill them.

Anyway, around 0200 hours on 12 December, 18 platoon was leading the company in single file about 300 yards from the canal Fosso Vecchio. We were advancing in a northwest direction along the via Boncellino. It seemed to us that the enemy would not be far away. So we stopped to think about what we were doing. I think that I went to discuss it with the company commander, André Langlais. At any rate, when I got back to the head of my platoon, one of my soldiers told me that he had heard German voices in front of us.

I listened, but I heard nothing. Still, as a precaution, and having again talked to Langlais, I crossed the road with my platoon and continued the advance in line, that is, in attack formation. I was in the centre, flanked by three or four soldiers on each side of me, with the reserve section and my sergeant about 50 yards in back. The rest of the company followed on the other side of the road, in single file in the ditch.

After having advanced like that for about 100 yards, we were approaching a little road, the via Martini, which was on my side of the via Boncellino and at right angles to it. Behind the via Martini, the enemy was awaiting us. When we were about 15 yards away, four enemy machine-guns opened fire on us simultaneously, killing one of my soldiers on my right and a soldier behind Langlais in the ditch on the other side of the road.

Probably because I was slightly ahead of those at my sides, in the flashes made by the continuous bursts of machine-gun fire I saw a ditch on our side of the via Martini, the enemy being on the other side of the road. So I went forward and jumped into the ditch, thus allowing the enemy bullets to pass several feet over my head without any hindrance from me or my head.

Since those with me had not seen that there was cover, the ditch, a few paces in front, they sought cover about 100 yards back around a farm. It was a normal reaction, and even desirable: impossible to advance completely in the open without any support against four solidly entrenched machine-guns. In the circumstances, it was reasonable to regroup under cover to determine a more intelligent way of taking the enemy position.

I was alone in my ditch with four machine-guns that would not stop firing above my head. Normally, taken by surprise by an enemy shooting at me, I had learned to reply without a moment's hesitation with my submachine gun. Maybe I had not yet learnt this good habit, early on the morning of 12 December 1944, or maybe I judged that a single submachine gun wasn't going to shut up four machine-guns. Also, I presume that I judged that my first duty was to go find my platoon.

Obviously, what I should have done was to raise my head just a little bit – when the machine-guns weren't firing right along the ground – and fire a good burst or two of my submachine gun at one of the machine guns ten yards from me. Maybe I would have done this, had at least one member of my platoon been in the ditch with me, for then I would have felt obliged to get as many of the enemy as possible to shut up the better to get us out of the trap. Alone, all I had to do was crawl a few yards to the rear to find my platoon in short order.

It was then that I realized that I was carrying, for the first time, a couple of grenades on my belt, two grenades with which I could very easily have blown up two of the enemy machine-guns. Having done that, I might have thought of looking after the remaining two with my submachine gun. Talk of missing out on a Victoria Cross!

Having forgotten my two grenades precisely at the wrong moment, I have often thought of them since. The lesson: the first time that a platoon commander goes into action, he must arm himself to the teeth: submachine gun, pistol, grenades, knife at least. Like that, always armed in the same way, he will find that four enemy machine guns firing in his face point blank at 20 yards distance at two o'clock in the morning will not leave his mind a blank so that he forgets what he has on his body.

Platoon commanders were taught to carry only a pistol, in its holster, to leave their hands free for their map and for their wireless. This nonsense was almost certainly a carryover from the Great War, where, in the beginning, officers went into battle carrying their swagger sticks! Fighting was for the men, not for officers, whose sole job was to lead their men into battle. Well, officers must *lead by example, starting with killing*. And for this task the platoon commander needs more than a pistol. The wireless set, during the assault, must be back with the platoon sergeant. During the actual assault, the platoon commander has absolutely no time to hear anything at all from his company commander. His sole thought must be to close with and destroy the enemy.

Apart from forgetting that I had a couple of grenades on my belt, I also started the action badly: I should have found a position for my 2-inch mortar behind one of the farm buildings on the start line of our advance in attack formation, about 150 yards from the four enemy machine guns. I should also have placed the reserve section and the PIAT in a defensive position on the ground in front of the farm buildings. Had I done all this – and instructed my sergeant to have the 2-inch mortar, PIAT, and reserve section open fire on the enemy should we (the two attacking sections and I) come under fire, then the night might not have been a dead loss for us. I suppose, too, that I did not do all this because I wasn't convinced the enemy was close at hand. A poor excuse indeed! At least when I got back to my platoon around the farm buildings, I should have, belatedly, organized my platoon to fire back on the four enemy machine guns with the 2-inch mortar, PIAT, and at least my three Bren machine guns. Firing on fixed lines as they were, we could have fired on them with very little risk of a prompt and accurate reply, and their gun flashes would have been perfect targets for us. Since I already knew the troops where we were fighting were prone to surrender when heavily engaged, I cannot explain why I did not do what had to be done to add to the 14 prisoners that my two sections and I took on 3 December, the ten whom Trudel and I took on 11 December (and the 15 additional prisoners 18 platoon was to take on 14 December).

Naturally, if our enemy on this occasion turned out to be paratroopers or Hitler *Jügend*, we would have had a real fight on our hands. But that was what we were being paid for, anyway.

Here again, of course, battalion HQ was at fault in not having at least two of our six 3-inch mortars ready to fire instantaneously on the enemy side of the Fosso Vecchio. "D"Company had been ordered to advance to this obstacle. It was entirely reasonable to assume that the enemy would defend it. As it happened, the enemy had installed four machine-guns on *our* side of the obstacle. Fine: if our 3-inch mortars had been ready to open fire on the Fosso Vecchio and had done so as soon as the enemy opened fire on 18 platoon, this would have at least been disconcerting to those manning the four machine-guns and might well have caught those in a backup position. Also, as soon as it was realized that the enemy was forward of the Fosso Vecchio, it would have been easy to have the 3-inch mortars *immediately* drop their range by a couple of hundred yards to land the bombs on the four machine-guns. *Provided our 3-inch mortars had already ranged in on the Fosso Vecchio.* But, as always, since this was not a full-scale set-piece attack with artillery and all, troops were ordered forward to advance into no-man's-land naked: completely unsupported by the weapons available to battalion HQ.

A few hours later, at dawn, I went on patrol with a section of five men to the scene of our setback. Noting that the enemy rearguard had abandoned its position, having accomplished its task of slowing our advance, I decided to continue to the canal, the

Fosso Vecchio. When we were about 20 yards away, a German soldier, I believe he was a sergeant, came out of a house on the other side of the Fosso Vecchio to walk towards the canal, that is, directly towards us.

I at once dropped to one knee to let him get closer. The rest of my patrol, in Indian file behind me, presumably followed my example. In any case, the German soldier was perhaps 40 yards away when he saw that his enemy was watching him. He then started to run forward in the hope of taking cover behind a tree; but before he could do so, I fired on him with my Tommy-gun until I was enveloped in smoke and could see nothing. He collapsed against the tree, presumably dead, since my corporal later told me he could see the dust coming out of the enemy's greatcoat where my bullets were hitting.

It was now a good idea to get out of there: if the enemy thought that it was at liberty to wander, as one man had been doing moments earlier, then that must mean we were almost in their territory. So we returned whence we came without loss of time. Back with my platoon, I asked my corporal why he had not followed my example when I opened fire. He replied that because the patrol was in Indian file, I was in the way. Although I regarded it as considerate of him to have thought of that, I explained to him all he had had to do was to take a pace to the right or left.

But it was my fault. I thought it so natural to fire on the enemy, with no emotion at all except the desire to shoot straight, that I took it for granted that all would act as I did. With the apparent exception of myself, it is not normal for a man to kill another man, and it takes a most rigorous training and a precise direct order to give the average infantryman the desire to fire at a man whose only fault is to wear a uniform of the wrong colour.

In the time I commanded a platoon, I never learned to give preparatory fire orders. In going out on patrol on 12 December, I should have told the section not only to do as I did if I opened fire, but, also that if we were close to the Fosso Vecchio when we met the enemy, all those not firing to the front should fire on the house just on the other side of the via Boncellino, 200 yards on our right and close up against the Fosso Vecchio. It had seemed to me that this was an ideal place for an enemy post. Later that day, I learned that I was right. It would have been well to make the lives of the occupants of that post less agreeable at dawn, before they tried to cut mine short in the afternoon.

In the afternoon it was decided that another platoon of "D" Company should launch an attack against this presumed enemy post – and without any artillery support: occasionally the ration of shells was restricted. They had to be kept for the real war in north-west Europe! The commander of the other platoon having convinced the company commander that the sending of a recce patrol would be less costly, the honour fell on 18 platoon, mine.

Therefore, after lunch, I went off with one of my corporals to see if I was right in believing that there was an enemy post around the house stuck up against the Fosso Vecchio. Having thought a bit about it (for once!), I decided that to go directly towards the house along the main road of the area, the via Boncellino, would not be very smart. Therefore the corporal and I went along a little path towards the north for 200 or 300 yards before breaking out of the cover of some trees and heading directly across a field towards the houses, about 150 yards away.

Happily, the enemy machine gunner who saw us first was nervous. We had gone only about ten paces in to the field when he opened fire on us. I immediately fired back with my SMG and even though the damned thing, which had worked perfectly at dawn, jammed after only one round in the right direction, that was enough to shut the machine-gunner up. Obviously, with our task accomplished, we did not stay around to dispute the field of battle with the entrenched machine-gunner. In nothing flat, we were back on our little path, whose surface was perhaps ten inches below that of the field. It was from there, flat on our stomachs, that we noted with interest that our enemy could shoot extremely accurately when he put his mind to it: his repeated bursts were cutting the grass two or three inches above our heads.

We were lucky that he had not done as I had a few hours earlier: if he had waited until we were in minefield, as he should have done, my corporal and I would still be in Italy.

Since I was sure that there was an enemy post around the house, I should not have tried to approach the house across an open field. Granted, this was better than trying it along the main road, but I still should have increased the odds in my favour. Assuming that we could get no support from the battalion's 3-inch mortars or the 13 Bren-gun carriers of the Carrier platoon, I still had my own 2-inch mortar and three Bren guns, quite apart from the 15 or so rifles of my riflemen. And I had my PIAT. What I should have done was line up my whole platoon under cover along the road from which my corporal and I had broken cover in our ten-pace jaunt into no-man's-land. Then I should have started hostilities with three PIAT bombs fired at the house simultaneously with the landing of half a dozen 2-inch mortar HE bombs on the presumed enemy post. This should have been immediately followed by several 2-inch mortar smoke bombs on the enemy. *Then* I should have broken cover at a fast trot towards the enemy position, covered by my three Brens and the 15 riflemen – to whom, for once, I would have given a fire order: "As soon as the enemy opens fire, all rapid fire on the enemy." Of course, as soon as the enemy did open fire, my job would have been done, since it was simply to determine whether there was an enemy position around the house.

The point is that in any action against the enemy, one should use all the weapons that one has, with a view always to inflict the maximum number of casualties on the enemy while taking the fewest losses oneself. Certainly, this is what I did in Korea but there I was never allowed to make patrols: "Stay in your command post on your hill!" (The patrols that I did make were all unauthorized.) I suppose that in Italy, since I *never* sent anyone on patrol (doing them all myself), it never occurred to me to organize support for myself. However, it most certainly should have occurred to my company commander to organize support with all the weapons under his command for every patrol that he ordered. What else did he have to do?

Incidentally, the fact that "D" Company could not get any artillery support for the contemplated attack on the enemy position, should *not* have precluded our attacking it. The company had four 2-inch mortars, four PIATs, and at least ten Brens. Surely this should have been enough firepower for a neat little company attack on a small enemy post. Moreover, could we not have prevailed on the CO for 3-inch mortar support, plus a few direct-sight rounds from a couple of our anti-tank guns (whether or not the enemy had a tank hiding there)? With all that landing on the enemy, I think it would have been a case of graciously accepting a surrender rather than having to make an assault. But even if an assault proved necessary, one that arrived on the enemy position within 30 seconds of the last bomb landing would probably not have cost *us* a single casualty.

But even in the absence of any decision by my company commander to attack the enemy post, there was nothing to prevent me going back to my platoon and placing my 2-inch mortar where it could drop a few HE bombs on the enemy position, while my three Bren machine gunners lay ready to fire on any German soldiers foolish enough to show themselves by changing position to avoid our bombs. This might have been enough to induce the enemy to surrender, as on 11 December.

I would not have ordered an attack by my platoon on my own authority. I hated losing men, and it would not have been fair to my platoon to get them to take risks that had been refused by another platoon commander. Of course, since a platoon attack, *well prepared,* was a perfectly reasonable proposition, I certainly would not have protested an order to attack.

Apart from several patrols to maintain contact with the adjoining units and sub-units, "D" Company did not do much else on 12 or 13 December. But on 14 December, it became interesting again. The regiment's advance having been held up for more than a day, Colonel Allard decided to throw "D" Company against an enemy position solidly entrenched around a brick factory, a half-mile to the north of the places I have just described and also a half-mile southeast of Bagnacavallo, which was still in enemy hands.

Eighteen platoon formed up for the attack in a barnyard close behind the start line. For some reason I can certainly no longer remember, I decided to brush my teeth before the attack. I was crossing the barnyard, toothbrush in hand, with my men standing around, when I realized, with some dismay, that what I thought was straw covering solid barnyard was straw masking the top of liquid manure four or five feet deep. Moreover, the pit was about eight feet square. After the first unfortunate step, I had to swim for it. I did, and I got out, minus my toothbrush, for which I did *not* search. There was a hand pump in the barnyard. I got as much of me under it as I could and had my batman work the pump to get most of the more solid pieces of manure off me. Here, my wearing of puttees and britches instead of battledress trousers proved helpful: manure slides off puttees more easily than it would off trousers. Although none of my men laughed, not that I would have noticed while I was swimming for it, I do believe they enjoyed all this, and that their morale was thereby boosted.

Unfortunately, no mobile laundry and bath unit (MLBU) came close to us for the next few weeks, so that during this time I could have given Li'l Abner's friend Big Barnsmell a run for his money.

Although two days earlier there had not been even a single shell to be fired in our support, on 14 December "D" Company had in support the field artillery of the 1st Division, the medium artillery of the 1st Corps, the medium machine-guns and the 4.2-inch mortars of the 1st Division, three tanks, and two fighter planes! In addition, naturally, there were the regiment's 3-inch mortars.

With all that, it will surprise no one that it is my impression that the enemy in the brick factory surrendered without firing a single shot. In any case, the *Histoire du Royal 22e Régiment* is in error on pages 338-9 in saying "The platoon of Lieutenant Pope,…advances directly towards the brick factory under a murderous fire." I do not forget "murderous fires" and I was not subjected to any during this attack. Also, I didn't advance directly towards the brick factory because 18 platoon was in reserve during the first phase.

The factory having been captured by the other two platoons of the company, 18 platoon swung left to take a group of houses from some 300 or 400 yards away. We had hardly left the main body of the company when one of my Bren machine gunners, Private Taschereau, a cousin through my Taschereau grandmother, began firing his Bren from the hip towards the left, in the direction of the rest of the Regiment. Taschereau, quicker than I, had noticed that "D" Company's attack had got behind an enemy post, which was now between us and the regiment. Looking where he was firing, I noticed that this enemy post was well supplied with white handkerchiefs. So I told Taschereau to cease firing and we accepted the surrender of some 15 Germans. Probably it is of them that the war diary speaks at 1715 hours, 14 December: "'D' Company takes another fifteen prisoners. Two are wounded and are evacuated. They all belong to 5 Company, 290 GR."

Arriving on our objective, I decided to do house-clearing with a new corporal who had arrived in 18 platoon that very day after having been seriously wounded on the Gothic Line in September. Having kicked in the front door, I told him to throw a grenade into the room, which he did. After four seconds, the grenade having exploded, I jumped into the room, to jump out again just as quickly. Despite the smoke, I noted that there was a brand new grenade at my feet.

The second grenade having gone off as it should, I explained to the corporal that it was not correct to introduce grenades into rooms I was occupying: it's a case of throwing grenades in before and not after I enter. Since I expressed myself with much more energy than one might gather from these few lines, it seemed to me the corporal had fully understood the correct procedure for house-clearing.

So I jumped into the room a second time, to come out again just as quickly. Yes, it was truly so: the third brand new grenade was there at my feet. After this last explosion, I told the corporal that I was fed up and that he was going to enter the room first. So I took him by the back of his collar and pushed him into the room. And no, I did not put in a grenade. All that was, in fact, for nothing since there were no enemy in the house.

I don't believe the corporal was trying to get rid of me. After all, he had only that very day arrived in the platoon and didn't know me well enough for that. I believe that he was simply horribly nervous, almost shell-shocked.

The position having been taken, 15 prisoners in the bag, and no losses on our side, I felt for a few instants the ecstasy of the conqueror: I had power of life or death over all before me. I did not know it at the time, but I was never again to have this feeling of glory.

And even this time, the enemy did not allow me to rejoice in my conquest for more than a few moments, for, at last, its artillery reacted and its defensive fire (DF) came down on us. So I jumped into a hole like the others, and all sensation of victory went up in the smoke of the exploding enemy shells.

A short time later, a platoon of "C" Company came up to replace us on the position that we had taken. Thus, 18 platoon set off to rejoin "D" Company around the brick factory. And then, while on the way, we met the "murderous fire" noted in the *Histoire du Royal 22e Régiment*. We were half way back, completely in the open, when the enemy decided that it was a good time to launch a second defensive fire, this one maybe 50 yards from us, maybe less. It goes without saying that I did not try to calculate the exact distance. Like all the others flat on the ground, I had not the slightest desire to raise my head so much as an inch. I lived with a single desire: that the enemy artillery continue its perfectly accurate fire – the shells were landing in an open field – and not fire 50 yards further, where we were.

The enemy did not disappoint me, and after a few minutes we were able to rejoin the company without loss, but all with the firm resolution either to find or to dig a really good slit trench.

But my day was not finished. I still had two patrols to make. The first, a contact patrol to "C" Company, almost became a disaster for some of the regiment's scouts because I could not mind my own business. The second, a recce patrol that I made at night with a corporal and a private, was quite simply a disaster, even though we accomplished our task: to determine whether the enemy occupied a certain position. The enemy occupied the position and shot straight - as we will see.

A short time after 18 platoon had rejoined "D" Company around the brick factory on 14 December, I returned alone on a contact patrol to "C" Company, which was now occupying the position that my platoon had taken earlier that afternoon.

On arrival, I saw some soldiers in camouflaged uniforms some 150 yards in front along a railway embankment. Since they looked like German paratroopers, I immediately opened fire on them with my submachine gun. At the same time, I invited the Bren gunner on the spot to open fire also.

Fortunately, the latter preferred that fire orders be delivered to him along more regular channels than those of a lieutenant of another company who was wandering where, possibly, he had no business (since I forget whether Captain Langlais had ordered me to go to see whether "C" Company was well established in my former position).

Fortunately, I said, because after two or three bursts, it seemed to me that the soldiers at whom I was shooting were not acting at all in a normal way. That is, they had not immediately thrown themselves on the ground and then fired on me. So I ceased firing, which allowed the five or six members of the regiment's scout platoon to re-enter our lines!

And the crowning touch was that the platoon sergeant congratulated me on my shooting! "You shoot damn close, Lieutenant," he told me, "we heard your rounds hitting the bank behind us." And he said this without irony. I greatly doubt that I would have been as polite had someone from our side fired on me. On the contrary, I believe that I would have acted exactly as though it was the enemy firing on me. In any case, after that I returned quietly to my platoon.

During the night of 14-15 December, another contact patrol was made, this one by a German soldier coming from one of their posts some 300 yards in front; he was not aware that his army was no longer the proprietor of the brick factory. Despite this, a short time later Langlais told me that he had just received an order to send a patrol of three men to determine whether the enemy was at the location from which our new prisoner had just come. If the enemy was not there, then an infantry section, backed by a tank, would go and occupy the position, a little woods of a few trees or big bushes.

Since Langlais was telling me the orders that he had received because he was passing them to 18 platoon, I told him that since we knew that the enemy was at the place in question, it was useless first to send a recce patrol. "Therefore," I continued, "I will go with a fighting patrol of one section as soon as the tank that's to support us is ready." With the orders that had landed on us, I knew then I would be fired on at point-blank range before the night was through, but I preferred it happen during an attack that we could win rather than during a perfectly useless recce patrol.

But the orders were: recce patrol first and, afterwards, occupation of the position only if the enemy was not there. There was no question of an attack. I greatly doubt that we could have found a tanker naive enough to venture with only half a dozen infantrymen to an isolated little woods 300 yards in front of our lines. Talk about a perfect target for a *Panzerfaust* at dawn!

Thus, mad as hell, I left with one of my corporals and a soldier from his section to go ask the Germans of the little woods whether it was really true that they were there.

The corporal whom I took with me was the one who had "helped" me in house-clearing that afternoon by throwing grenades into the room that I already occupied. I took him with me not as a punishment but simply because it was his turn, my other two corporals having gone on patrol in turn with me two days earlier.

Before we could even quit the company lines, the enemy decided to send us a few shells to harass us. And with success, for following in single file behind me and the corporal, the soldier was hit by a shell fragment that broke his leg.

After having taken 38 prisoners in 12 days with the loss of only one of my men (the soldier killed next to me near the Fosso Vecchio on 12 December), I was losing another man for absolutely no reason at all. Mad with anger, I returned to my company commander to get the stretcher bearers and ask him to let me do the patrol alone. But Langlais was bound by the orders that he had received: a patrol of three men. However, like the good lawyer he has since become, he added that since I started with three, the corporal and I may now continue, just the two of us.

Convinced that I would not return from this idiocy, I emptied my pockets of all that might identify me, something I should have normally done anyway, not as a grandiose gesture.

I had no identity disc to take off, because since my sojourn with the Germans I did not wear one. If civilized armies no longer shoot their prisoners, it's because there is a convention that an escaped prisoner does not take up arms again against the enemy that spared him. Moreover, if I were taken prisoner again, I had no desire to be asked awkward questions concerning my activities during the 51 days I was at liberty with partisans and paratroopers behind enemy lines. Therefore, in enemy hands a second time, I was either going to give my mother's family name (du Monceau) or that of my paternal grandmother (Taschereau). Of course, I had no intention of being taken a second time, but with a bullet in the gut three feet from an enemy position, say, the best intentions in the world change nothing: you're either dead or in the bag.

In emptying my pockets, I came across my second Luger (the one captured two days earlier) rolled up in my gas cape on the back of my belt. I now gave it to Langlais, an indication that my anger was not directed at him. In fact, we got on well.

At last, the corporal and I left again on patrol. To get the damn thing over with, I headed straight for the little woods. When we were about 60 yards away, we got down on all fours, the corporal on my right and slightly behind. We continued like that until we were about three or four feet away from the little woods.

"A noise, if it is loud and close enough, almost escapes the hearing…" Thus the English author Graham Greene described in *The Comedians* the sensation, or rather the lack of sensation, caused by gunshot at a distance of three feet. All that I remember is that suddenly there was a jet of flame that passed between my arms and under my body.

It took me an instant to realize that I had been shot at from a trench into which I was on the point of falling. My Tommy-gun was hanging by its strap from my shoulder. Therefore, on my knees, I immediately shot back. But the damned thing that had worked altogether too well that afternoon when I fired on our own scouts – and missed! – now jammed after one round.

In any event, our task was accomplished. We now had the proof desired by higher authority: the position was occupied by the enemy. The proof was to become weightier in a few seconds. With our task done and with my jammed Tommy-gun in my hands, I decided that three feet from an enemy position was not the place to do my IA (immediate action). After all, if my SMG continued to fire only one round at a time, I would begin to look stupid there on my knees. Therefore, I yelled to the corporal something like "Débarquons!" ("Let's get the hell out!").

In any case, he understood that it was time to retreat and we ran side by side as fast as we could in the direction of our lines. Since this was not the first time that I had got a whole bunch of very-well-armed people very angry with me, I ran zigzag; the corporal straight ahead.

Now that I think about it, it was probably not clever of me to go zigzag. Often at night, machine-guns are on fixed lines. If, on that particular night, the machine-gun that opened fire on us after six or seven seconds had been on a fixed line, then in missing me on a zig it would have got me on a zag. But on that night, the machine-gun was not on a fixed line. And running straight ahead, the corporal presented the better target. Thus he was the one that got the burst in his back.

For the second time that night, I went to the company CP to get the stretcher bearers. Having helped them bring in the corporal (I do not know if he lived), I went at last to the company CP for the last time that night to make my report. And then Langlais made a mistake. As I entered the CP, he said to me: "Harry, I have just got the order: the patrol is cancelled!"

I'm quite certain that I did not reply, "André, it is honest of you to tell me this," and I'm absolutely certain that in offering my comments on the events of the night of 14-15 December 1944, I needed all my English and all my French, the better to swear.

And since then, I have discovered that the regimental war diary makes absolutely no mention of this patrol. It was as though cancelling the patrol also cancelled the loss of my two men! But it didn't. I lost two men for absolutely nothing. If the information obtained by a patrol is not worth putting in the War Diary, then getting this information is not worth risking the life of a single soldier.

But I am certainly not without fault in this affair.

In the first place, I should have laid down precisely what action to take when the enemy fired on us. Certainly I should have done this, because I took it for granted we would be fired on. Obviously, the action to take was to fire back at once, as I did. But if I had thought of telling the corporal and the private that, I might have asked myself if I was bringing the right corporal with me. After my experience in house-clearing with him that afternoon, I should have asked myself whether I wished to be close to him when he started to fire his SMG! If he had fired his SMG (in the right direction, of course) and even if his had jammed after only one round, like mine, that would still have doubled our chances of getting back whole to our own lines.

Second, before setting off, I should have made sure that my Tommy-gun was working perfectly. After having used it (incorrectly!) that afternoon, I should have cleaned and oiled it.

Third, I should have hooked at least two grenades to my belt. It is plain stupid to go on patrol, especially at night, without grenades. In addition, I knew that I was going to go to an enemy position, and even if I could have determined the enemy was there without being fired on, I knew I would get close enough to throw some grenades. It's silly to be in a position to make life shorter or at least more disagreeable for the enemy without taking advantage of the occasion. Also, with my SMG jammed, if I had immediately thrown a couple of grenades, it is highly likely that the enemy machine gun never would have opened fire on us.

Fourth, the order to take the corporal on patrol with me did not require me to have him follow me right to the enemy position. If I had thought a little before setting off, I would have told him to take up a position about 75 yards from the enemy position to give me covering fire or to return with a report of the events in case I did not return. And my chances of getting close to the enemy position undetected were infinitely greater alone than when there were two of us. Alone, one can stop to listen or to change direction. With two that can't be done since it is hardly possible to talk a few feet from an enemy position. Even signals are forbidden, the enemy also having eyes.

Finally, I should have thought a bit before going on patrol. If I had done that, I would no doubt have decided that to head straight for the woods was not very bright. I should have headed at least 50 yards to the right or left and then have tried to approach the little woods from one flank or the other or maybe even from the rear. It was plain stupid of me to go to within three feet of a place where, with reason, I was convinced that the enemy would be. What I should have done was to take a small pack full of grenades with me. Then ten yards or so from the suspected place, I could have amused myself throwing grenades. I would certainly have found that more amusing than being fired on from three feet. And without any doubt, this method would have given me the proof that higher authorities required that the enemy was there: the enemy would not have suffered in silence if a whole pack of grenades had come down on its heads. There is nothing like a grenade with a four-second fuze landing in his trench to make a lad move.

But, in summary, the principal lesson of this patrol was probably that while being impulsive had already got me out of a hole, this same characteristic could get me into one too. But that I already knew.

At the time, having received an order tantamount to a death warrant, I suppose I would have thought it cowardly to do otherwise than what I did: head straight for the enemy position.

I think, however, that this patrol may be the reason why I never lost a man on outpost or on patrol in Korea. Being specifically forbidden to command my patrols in the valley (no-man's-land), I never presumed to give the commanders on the ground, lieutenant or lance-corporal, more than general instructions or advice, never orders. I surrounded them, as I did my forward sections, with close-in registered targets of all the weapons that I commanded or could call on, especially my private artillery, my four 60 mm mortars, ready to have their bombs landing within 30 seconds within 30 yards of my men.

One of my lieutenants, many years later, told me that those I commanded in Korea knew that I would not get them killed stupidly. No remark could have pleased me more. Even more than the remark to my wife by Brigadier-General Marcel Richard, R22eR: "Harry had no desire to die for his country; he simply wanted to make sure that the maximum number of Germans died for theirs!"

Once again, we have an example of the overly cautious "one small bite at a time" approach. If, during the night, it was thought desirable to occupy the small woods, surely this could have been thought of during the afternoon so that immediately after 18 platoon returned from its left hook, we should have been sent off to take the small woods, backed by the three tanks and all the supporting fire, on call, that had terrified the defenders of the brick factory into surrendering. We had made a breach in the enemy's line: why on earth wait until it patched up something in rear before we remember that there's still a war on? We honestly seemed to be scared stiff of making a breakthrough. And yet getting *behind* an enemy position is always the way to take more than one's own weight in prisoners. First, a set-piece frontal attack, if necessary, then, *always*, exploit the success *immediately* by getting everyone except the cooks through the gap – without ever forgetting the anti-tank guns.

Even though it seems that it was too much to ask that, simultaneously with the taking of the brick factory, the idea of taking the little woods occured to the battalion, the battalion should have supported the three-man patrol that it was ordering to the little woods. A few 3-inch mortar bombs landing on the enemy there as our patrol was setting out would have been helpful. And with this target thus registered beforehand, it would have been possible to have a half-dozen or so bombs come down on the enemy as soon as it opened fire on us, the time of flight of the bombs giving my corporal and me all the time in the world to get away before the bombs landed. Of course, for this to work would have required the company commander to be in a forward trench with his wireless or telephone to give the fire order to the 3-inch mortars and not sitting in his command post doing nothing except waiting for me (with luck) to return and report the disastrous results of so utterly unprepared and unsupported a patrol.

The only time I remember seeing any of our battalion anti-tank guns in action in Italy was in this brick factory position. But the solitary gun next to our company CP was not used on the enemy. One bright day, a Jeep, not belonging to "D" Company, came roaring up from the rear. The driver waved cheerfully back at those of us trying to flag him down and continued on his merry way until he was flagged down by chaps in field-grey uniforms who were not smiling. As soon as the driver was safely out of the Jeep, our anti-tank gun at last got a shot in – as a matter of fact, *six*, according to the war diary. The Germans had got themselves a Van Doo but they did not get much of a Van Doo Jeep.

Chapter Four

The Senio River

Shortly after my disastrous patrol, that is, at 0220 hours on 15 December 1944, Major Joseph-Fernand (Joe) Trudeau retook command of "D" Company from Captain Langlais, who was second in command, despite having commanded the company in action since the beginning of the month.

On 15 and 16 December, "D" Company stayed quietly in place around the brick factory captured on 14 December. But on the night of 16-17 December, the regiment was ordered to change position while remaining in the front line. Thus, at 0030 hours on 17 December, "D" Company was on a night march on small paths, a distance of two miles in a direct line to the north. Probably it was a march of a good three hours, because obviously we could not go in a direct line.

As soon as we had arrived, Trudeau told me he had just received an order to send a patrol with a PIAT to destroy an enemy tank somewhere on our front. Therefore he said to me: "Pope, send your two soldiers on the PIAT to destroy that tank."

During the whole time I commanded a platoon in action, I had never sent anyone from my platoon on patrol; all the patrols I did alone if they were my idea; accompanied normally only by a corporal when the order required a two-man patrol.

Now, here I was being ordered to send two of my soldiers to do something utterly impossible: to go, loaded down with a PIAT and bombs, into the enemy lines to search for, find, and fire on a tank no doubt surrounded by infantrymen! And all this without the slightest previous reconnaissance; without even having seen the enemy positions by daylight. To find that tank before dawn, it would have been necessary to ask every enemy soldier met en route: "*Wo ist der Panzer?*" ("Where's the tank?")

Therefore I replied: "Major, you may order me to go and destroy that tank, and I will go, alone, but I will not pass your order to anyone in my platoon."

And it continued like that the whole night through! We were comfortably seated at a table with a couple of heavy stone walls between us and the German self-propelled gun (SP) that was ineffectively firing 88 mm shells at us from time to time. (Maybe, instead of an SP, it was "my" tank!) And between us there was a bottle of a good country wine, because the house containing the company CP was full of enormous barrels, each holding at least ten thousand litres of the stuff. At each half-hour, approximately, Trudeau said to me: "Pope, send two men." And I replied: "No, Major, you may order me to go and I will go; but I am not passing that order to anyone else."

Phone calls from the battalion kept asking if the patrol had set out yet. To this, obviously, we had to reply "No." But, happily, after some time, the question from the battalion became: "Has the patrol returned yet?" To this, naturally, "No." Finally the battalion lost interest and we no longer received any awkward questions about the phantom patrol, and the war diary does not mention it.

Of course, what we did was all wrong. What the company commander should have done was phone the battalion and say: "Every order to 18 platoon to carry out a patrol, Pope has done himself, accompanied in their turn by one of his three corporals. You are now ordering that the two men on the PIAT go into the enemy lines that they have never seen by day – we're not even sure where the enemy lines are, but we assume they are in the general direction in which our trenches face, nor do we know the distance to the enemy lines. Assuming the two men with the PIAT can penetrate the enemy lines, once they've found them, and can do so without getting shot, you then want them to wander around in the enemy lines looking for the enemy tank, destroy it and then return to our lines. Pope refuses to order his two men on the PIAT to do any of this. However, since the order must be obeyed one way or another, Pope will carry it out himself, alone. He is now strapping the PIAT (which weighs 40 pounds) to his back as well as three bombs in which he will have inserted their fuses. He will leave our lines in five minutes. Since this time when he enters the enemy lines he will be armed, with both his Luger and a Tommy gun, he will not be taken prisoner again. Therefore you will not see him again." This little speech might have awakened the battalion to the sheer idiocy of the order. If not, my last act as a platoon commander would have been honourable: carrying out an idiotic order myself, rather than ordering any man under my command to his death.

But, of course, my men were not idiots. They would have seen that what they were being ordered to do was utterly impossible. Had I disgraced myself by passing on the order to my two men on the PIAT, they would have gone a few yards forward of our lines, laid down for a couple of hours, and then returned to report that they had not been able to penetrate the enemy lines. Indeed, if I had been a coward and passed on the order, I hope that I would at least have had the decency to tell them to do precisely that. But, at the same time, I would certainly have dropped in their esteem for not having done what I did do: refuse to obey the order. Had I obeyed the order, they would have had the right from then on to wonder about any other order that I gave my platoon.

Which brings us to the moral of the whole affair: *Patrols must never be ordered casually.* Every patrol forward of our lines puts men's lives at risk. Before ordering a patrol, the commander must ask himself: "Is the task that I am setting possible, and, if it is, is what I wish to accomplish with this patrol worth the lives of every man on it?" And the next question is: "How can I best support the patrol?" In other words: "What artillery, mortar, machine-gun support can I give it?"

Either on Christmas Day or the next, Colonel Allard told me he was sending me as an instructor to the Junior NCOs' School for a month. I replied that if he did that he would be condemning me to a month-long drunk. Maybe recalling my infamous drunk of 10 May in Naples, he then left me in peace with 18 platoon.

Although the colonel could not have known about the trouble I had getting out of England to join the regiment, he certainly knew that I had escaped from the Germans to rejoin it and had become ADC to Burns only under protest. Thus he could understand why I could not accept the honourable out that he was offering me of leaving my platoon and taking a rest after almost four weeks of fighting. By now I was sufficiently well established in his esteem that I could talk about going on an extended drunk. Allard would certainly not have taken my remark as a threat. After seeing the sorry state that I was in when I arrived late for his officers' conference on 12 May 1944 after my bender in Naples, he would have known as well as I that anyone threatened by my going on a two-day drunk, let alone a month, would be me! On 28 December 1944, the regiment went back into the line southwest of Bagnacavallo.

The war diary has this entry for 0125 hours on 29 December 1944: "'D' Company reports the ordinary oil they are using on rifles and grenades freezes when exposed. Can the winter oil be obtained?" With my Tommy-gun having already, at embarrassing moments, jammed twice on me after one shot, I can well believe I was the initiator of this request. Since my Tommy-gun was to embarrass me again two nights later, I can also believe that the quartermaster did not get the (thinner) winter oil to us very quickly.

At 0210 hours on 29 December 1944, all the companies were ordered to advance to the banks of the Senio River. Glancing quickly at my map, I saw that 18 platoon's objective was a casa situated about 100 yards from the Senio. On arriving, I wondered whether I'd reached the right objective, because there were two or three houses there.

Deciding then to do what I should have done before starting, I entered one of the houses to study my map carefully. But that was another error, because the house was in ruins. Since we had advanced unsupported, it was neither our guns nor our mortars that had given the casa its smashed look. And since we were the first of the 8th

Army on the scene and no one had fired on us during our advance, I knew that the casa had not been smashed by enemy defensive fire. Therefore, I should have realized that the enemy had blown up the casa to render life more unpleasant for us, and then I should have asked myself what I would have done in addition to make life still more unpleasant for my enemy.

Anyway, I entered the casa with four soldiers, two of whom were linesmen.

In England, all officers were issued pocket-lamps because they were very useful for finding an objective, such as a pub, in the blackout. But when an officer left for the front, his pocket-lamp was taken away from him, the convenience of officers making war on their arse in England being infinitely more important than the needs of those making war in the face of the enemy.

So, once in the house, I took out my bit of a candle and my matches. Once the candle was lit, I started to study my map, when it suddenly occurred to me that with the enemy a 100 or 150 yards away along the top of the embankment of the Senio, it would be smarter to hide my light. So I told one of my soldiers to shut the door of the room in which we were while I continued to study my map on my knees.

The resulting explosion certainly fixed the problem of the light, for there I was on my arse, cuts on my hands and a thigh and my eyes full of dust. However, I saw well enough to get on my feet and go charging out of the house, swinging my submachine-gun from one of my soldiers to the next, and shouting: "Who's the ********
of an imbecile who threw a grenade in there?"

After a couple of moments, everything calmed down when I realized that it was a joker from the other side that had placed on the door what the regiment's war diary rightly calls a booby-trap. One of my soldiers then told me that I was truly impressive coming out of the house with my submachine-gun swinging in all directions.

In any case, my luck continued, for while my four companions in the room had to be evacuated, I got off with two or three hours at the regimental aid post (RAP) to get washed, have my cuts bandaged, and especially to get the dust out of my eyes. As far as I was personally concerned, it amused me to win my second wound stripe with a second "wounded remained on duty."

The Senio, maybe 30 feet wide, flowed between elevated banks at least 20 feet high. Their slope was at least 60 degrees, and the enemy had prepared defences on both banks. Anyone wishing to take up a position on our side of our bank would have to deal with the enemy entrenched on the top and 20 feet away on the enemy side of our bank, and also with the enemy entrenched 50 feet away on the other bank.

During the night of 29-30 December, another platoon of "D" Company had tried to install itself on our side of our bank, but withdrew, apparently without casualties.

During the night of 30 to 31 December, it was 18 platoon's turn. After midnight, I received the order to attack at 0410 hours with the 13 men which I had left. But it seemed to me perfectly idiotic to try to dig trenches ten or 20 feet away from a solidly entrenched enemy who was supported by other soldiers also solidly entrenched on the other side of the Senio, 30 feet away. So, on the phone, I asked my new company commander (the third since 1 December), Captain Yvan Dubé: "Yvan, do you see any sense in this attack?" He replied: "Harry, it's an order from Corps HQ and you will do it."

Orders had arrived from the C-in-C that the 8th and 5th Armies were to spend the winter where they were, no more advances. So the geniuses at 1st Canadian Corps, five miles from the front, without the slightest military experience properly speaking, on looking at their maps had decided that the Senio would be a splendid boundary between us and the German army, left bank to the Germans, right bank for us. Very fine, but the imbeciles at Corps HQ did not realize that for that to work it was necessary that Field Marshal Kesselring agree. *Failing that, it would be necessary to make an assault across the river and take both banks.*

Since no one saw fit to visit 18 platoon, positioned as it was 100 yards from an enemy-held embankment that towered over it, I do not know whether my company commander, or the CO, or anyone higher in the chain of command ever had a look at the 20- or 30-

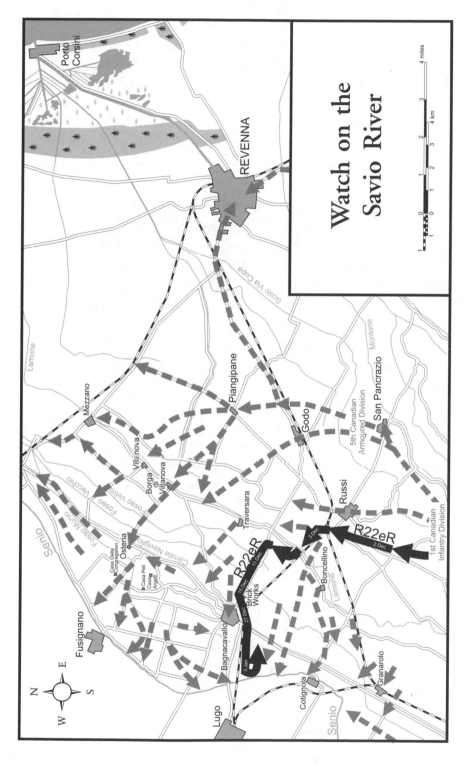

Watch on the
Savio River

foot-high banks of the Senio. Certainly, they should have. I cannot imagine anyone from my company commander on up looking at the bank facing us, realizing that the enemy was dug in on top of it, on the other side of it, and on the opposite bank 50 feet away and then *not* concluding that trying to dig in on our side of it was insane. Having reached this only possible conclusion, each commander in turn should have told the next one up that the order to attack was insane but that since the order had to be obeyed, he would lead the attack personally. In other words, my superiors should have done, in essence, what I did a couple of weeks earlier. And it is possible that their acting in this way would have made corps HQ realize the attack had to be cancelled. But if corps HQ continued in its stupidity, then the commander leading the hopeless attack would have been acting honourably in taking the same risks that he had been obliged to force on his subordinates.

What is not permissible is to pass on an order that the officer who must carry it out tells you is insane, do absolutely nothing about it except to repeat it, not go forward to see why the order is insane, and then remain in your CP waiting for the call to come in for the RAP carrier.

It was noted that at 0420 hours 30 December 1944, "Major F. Trudeau is ordered to get the platoon [not mine] back on the bank." Twenty-four hours later he was no longer commanding "D" Company. It is certainly possible that it was his inability "to get the platoon back on the bank" that led to his being replaced by Captain Dubé. If such was the reason, it was grossly unfair. No platoon could have stayed six feet from the top of the east side of that bank, even if it had not been mined. In the time it would have taken the platoon to dig in, every last man would have been machine-gunned. The platoon would have got back on the bank all right and this time to stay – dead.

If I'm right that Major Ferdinand Trudeau was replaced because he could not get a live platoon on to the bank, the curtness of Yvan Dubé's order to me is understandable: he was damned if he was going to tolerate a platoon commander not carrying out orders now that *he* was in command.

As a matter of fact, Yvan's order to me was even more insulting. He didn't say: "It's an order from Corps HQ and that's the end of it." What he did say was: "It's an order from Corps HQ and you will do it."

No one else ever dared question my courage in battle. The insult angered me at the time, but that was the end of it. I only record it now because a friend, both of mine and of Dubé's, whom we both greatly admired and whose death in Korea through someone else's careless handling of a firearm we both greatly deplored, found it difficult to believe that Yvan would have spoken that way.

I do regret, most deeply, however, that Yvan did not come forward to look at the bank and hear what I had to say about the enemy positioned on it and on the west bank. Had he done so, I think that he would have wished to convince Allard and so on up to corps, that corp's notion of our occupying the east bank without making a full-scale attack on *both* banks was sheer bloody nonsense.

A few minutes before our attack, two or three flamethrowers of the Regiment, Wasps in Bren carriers, arrived to shoot napalm onto our bank. Since the path wasn't close enough to the embankment, and since the carrier drivers did not wish to venture off the path, not a drop of oil fell on the enemy; all the oil landed on our side of our bank.

Anyone seeing the carriers close to the embankment, as I did, would have seen that it was simply not conceivable that the Wasp-carriers could climb the 60-degree slope to the top of the embankment: it was highly unlikely that enough traction could be gained and, moreover, the slightest bump on the way up and it was highly likely the carriers would flip over upside-down. Had anyone higher in rank than I come forward at 0400 hours on 31 December 1944 to see the Wasps close to the foot of the embankments, it might have prevented "A" and "C" Companies being sent in to their hopeless attack on the embankment on 3 January 1945.

Obviously, the napalm did not help us in the slightest: on the contrary, the flames thawed the ground to make what was awaiting us at the top of the embankment work better —*Schuhmeine* (shoe mines: they took your boot off, with your foot still in it). But having already said all that I had to say about the idiocy of the orders received, I judged that there was no point in trying again to get my platoon out of this attack, where the chances of success were zero and therefore where the risks were completely unjustifiable.

So, at 0410 hours, with the eight men that made up two sections, I covered the 100 yards that separated us from the embankment. There, I must admit, the napalm was useful, but in a strange way: the enemy soldiers, judging that we would not be so stupid as to attack without placing the flames in the right place, that is, in full on them, stayed at the bottom of their trenches without moving. So, without being bothered, I went up the embankment to six feet from the top with Tremblay and his three soldiers, while a corporal did the same thing 50 yards away with his three soldiers. And all nine of us started digging our slit trenches six feet below the crest. It would not have been intelligent to dig any higher up the embankment; and that is in sight of the Germans on top ten feet away, or of those 20 feet away on the other side of the embankment, or even of those on the other side of the Senio 50 feet away.

Shortly, there occurred one or two explosions in the section of the detached corporal. When he arrived with his section at the bottom of the embankment where I was, I went down to see what the trouble was. The corporal was shell-shocked: in digging, his spade, and perhaps the spade of another member of his section, had hit a *Schuhmeine* and his spade had flown up and hit him squarely in the face. I was busy shaking him and slapping him to get him to get his wits back as quickly as possible, all the while trying to make him understand that to have his platoon commander furious with him was worse than *Schuhmeine*, when there was an explosion above us and the other section arrived at my feet, rolling down the embankment.

Tremblay, whose foot was the cause of the explosion, in rolling – he could no longer walk – with great presence of mind, had taken off his belt. Arriving at my side, while giving me his belt, he said, "Lieutenant, my foot!" It had been blown off. So, using his belt as a tourniquet, I tightened it around what was left of his leg. And we all returned where we had been at the start of this stupid affair. (In

January 1945, when I saw Tremblay in hospital, they had taken his leg off above the knee. Apparently the explosion had forced his shin up into his knee, destroying it.)

As I wrote above, the war diary reports that "Men of the pioneer platoon are sent forward to neutralize these mines." So, a little later, but still in darkness, the pioneer sergeant and I went towards this damned embankment. During the delay, the enemy had regained courage, and I could now see heads at the top of our embankment. The sergeant saw them also. "Germans!" he said. "No, they're tree trunks," I replied, knowing perfectly well that there never had been trees on the top of these embankments. One had to get this night over with; and with the orders that I had been given, it seemed to me that it would have been pretty useless to try to explain to my superiors the difficulty of lifting mines in full view of and ten feet away from enemy machine-guns.

The battalion simply had not the foggiest idea of where the mines were in relation to the enemy. Possibly my company commander had no idea either. Certainly, he does not seem to have explained the situation to the battalion HQ.

So, we continued to the base of the embankment, to the spot where I had applied a tourniquet an hour earlier. On our arrival, an enemy machine-gunner stopped dreaming of Lorelei long enough to fire a burst at us from maybe 20 yards. Once again, I immediately replied with my submachine-gun. And once again only one round came out, but it was enough to get us back unwounded the 100 yards to my platoon. The war diary makes no mention of our attempt at lifting the *Schuhmeine*.

This was an unfortunate omission, unfortunate for the *thirteen* who became casualties because of *Schuhmeine* on 3 January 1945. Proper acknowledgment by battalion of the deadly profusion of these mines might have led to a plan that did *not* send two rifle companies smack into them.

Now here, back with my platoon, I failed in my duty. I knew where the enemy was: on top of and on the reverse slope of "our" embankment. I should have immediately got my 2-inch mortar, nicely hidden behind a haystack, dropping bombs on the enemy.

Once again, in other words, I neglected an opportunity to mortar the enemy where I knew it to be. I know then I did *not* go along with the "live and let live" philosophy: if we don't shoot at them, maybe they won't shoot at us. Hell, in *this* case they owed me: they had already tried to machine-gun me and had taken the foot off one of my section commanders. Certainly, I used my Tommy-gun with gay abandon, as our scouts could attest from my trying (unsuccessfully!) to kill half a dozen of them a couple of weeks earlier. But I seemed to have a blind spot concerning my 2-inch mortar. I was to pay for this within thirty-six hours.

My batman, Private Bill Long, had made it plain to me that he much preferred being batman to my friend, Lieutenant Fritz LaFlèche, MC, who, on the Gothic Line and elsewhere had told Bill that his job was to collect interesting loot: Schmeissers and suchlike. With Fritz wounded and evacuated, Bill Long inherited me. With my platoon at one-third strength, I decided that I could afford no luxuries; besides, I already had the only "loot" I cared for: the Luger given me by the men of my old 17 platoon when I came back from the wrong side of the lines. Thus I detailed Bill number two on the mortar, loaded down with mortar bombs. The least that I should have done for Bill's sake, if for no other reason, was to have his load of bombs fired off every time we halted. By 15 December 1946, when he dropped me a line, Bill was out of the army, married, and living in Waterloo, Quebec, "still at the same job," presumably his pre-war one. He did not mention mortar bombs. So I suppose that he had forgiven me for that.

For the remainder of 31 December, we stayed quietly in place under or alongside the haystacks that were in 18 platoon's position. After the experience of the mine attached to the door, we did not again try to find shelter in the surrounding houses.

After being up all night 31 December - 1 January, I was still sleeping in my CP that was under the biggest haystack in the area, when around midday "C" Company phoned me to say that it could see enemy heads along the top of the embankment facing my platoon. Perhaps it was Major Trudeau, DSO, who was offering me this unintended insult. After always firing without hesitation on all that was in front of me – unless the enemy indicated they wished to surrender – I was deeply humiliated that another company should think itself obliged to ask me to do my duty.

By not mortaring the heads that I could see on the top of the dike in the dark after 18 platoon's unsuccessful attack on 31 December, I let the enemy dominate us. Thus the enemy felt perfectly free to fire its machine-guns at us at will. I paid for this very shortly.

Belatedly, then, in an attempt to get enemy heads down or, preferably, off, I got out from under my haystack as fast as I could, and having told my platoon sergeant to get the 2-inch mortar ready, I stood alongside the haystack to indicate the direction of fire by pointing with my right arm. The enemy had already started firing tracer bullets at us before I woke up and I found one of our smaller haystacks on fire. This made me yet more furious: after having blown up all the casas of the area and then placing booby-traps in them, now the bastards wanted to burn down our miserable haystacks over our heads!

Insulted, humiliated, and furious, I did not realize that if I could see the heads of my enemies, they could see me from the top of my helmet to the soles of my boots. I think that my mortar had already fired a bomb or two without getting so much as one of the enemy heads 150 yards from us, when among the maybe half-dozen tracer bullets coming at me that I could see in the air simultaneously, one suddenly caught all my attention. "*******, I'm going to get it in the gut!" I had just time to think, when the bullet went through my left arm, fracturing it. The principal bone, the ulna, of this arm was bent at belt level, causing the bullet to veer away from my stomach.

I must assume that on this day, the Germans were firing only tracer bullets. Had they been firing one tracer bullet for every three normal bullets, as our machine-gunners did, that would have meant 24 bullets coming at me simultaneously. I cannot believe that I could have survived that many. My guardian angel no doubt had the competence to deflect an infinite number of bullets. But, after nine months of looking after me, he might well have got fed up and said, "If this idiot wants to stand there when there are 24 bullets coming at him, he can go to hell.....Literally."

In any event, it was the end of the battle. Two paces, and I was behind my haystack. As soon as a dressing had been applied, I left the field on foot, accompanied by a stretcher bearer, who carried the Red Cross flag at the end of a stick. All had become calm; there were no shots from one side or the other.

I am not proud to have to admit that I felt a sense of relief. I had found it profoundly demoralizing to have been unable to protect my platoon from the insane order to "attack" the bank of the Senio River and dig in ten feet from enemy machine-gunners, with the resulting loss of a foot by one of my section commanders. Also, before going back into the line after Christmas, I had realized that I had a moderate case of flu (about one degree of fever) and I was tired: I was the only one of my platoon that had been there when we started our series of attacks and advances a month earlier. Now, I could quit the battlefield honourably.

Later, reading of what some others had done when wounded, I realize I should have stayed with my men until dark. It would have been good for their morale. They were not fools: they, too, could see that our attack on the embankment of the Senio was senseless. My staying with them a little longer when obviously I didn't have to, would have encouraged them a little. My wound was not in any way life-threatening and there was nothing to prevent my continuing to direct the 2-inch mortar fire, but more intelligently, while lying flat on the ground and peering around my haystack. Starting with a smoke bomb would probably have been a good idea. Of course, having the phosphorus smoke bombs of the 60 mm mortars that we had in Korea would have been ideal: bits of burning phosphorus dropping into the enemy trenches on top of the embankment would probably have caused enough quick jumping about by the enemy to give my Bren gunners something worthwhile to shoot at. And that would have been excellent for *our* morale.

Later, when I was in hospital, I heard that my friend Lieutenant "Muck" Richard, the IO, had indicated that he considered that I had shown excessive zeal in drawing on myself enemy fire to get it off my men. But as we have just seen, it was not that at all. I was thinking only of blowing off every enemy head in front of me. I did not succeed, and certainly there were smarter ways of going about it. Still, I am satisfied that at the moment an enemy bullet ended my career as a platoon commander in the 22nd, I was facing the enemy giving a fire order to my platoon.

In the regimental war diary for 2 January 1945 one reads:

> 1445 (hours) Brigadier J.P.E. Bernatchez DSO, OBE, Comd 3 Cdn Inf Bde, arrives at our Tac HQ. Plans for an attack on the east bank of the Senio are now being made.

It seems that neither the brigade commander nor the CO recognized the impossibility of taking the east bank while the enemy was dug in on the west side of the east bank as well as on the west bank. General Allard's *Mémoires* are decidedly not helpful here. At page 163, after noting that the regiment quit the front on 22 December 1944 to spend Christmas at Piangipane, the general writes, "Without knowing it, I had commanded my last battle at the head of the *Royal 22e Régiment*."

Allard remained in command until 1000 hours on 13 January 1945, when he went on leave. The last, disastrous battle of the regiment in Italy took place on 3 January 1945, with Allard in command. True, the general starts his next chapter, at page 165: "In January 1945, the Regiment takes part in the first skirmishes (*escarmouches*) on the banks of the Senio."

The battle of 3 January 1945 was *not* a skirmish. It was a battalion attack with two companies forward, "A" and "C." The CO's operation order, given at 2235 hours on 2 January 1945, stated, "Enemy: West bank is held in force all along. Far side of east bank is mined and wired."

Apparently, the CO did not know that 18 platoon had discovered two nights earlier that the *near* side of the east bank was thickly mined with *Schuhmeine*. The war diary notes that at 0435 hours on 31 December 1944, "The RAP carrier is sent to 'D' Company" and at 0500 hours "'D' Company reports that there are mines on the bank of the river." Since there is no mention in the war diary of the pioneer sergeant's going forward with me to attempt to lift these mines, one gets the impression that the battalion simply took it for granted that the *Schuhmeine* were on the far side of the east bank. Maybe, no one else in the battalion HQ, was aware that there were mines on our side of the bank. It was a puzzling mistake to think that the enemy would put mines *behind* its position on the crest of the embankment. Perhaps at the battalion no one even knew that the enemy occupied the top of the east bank.

I have no recollection of my company commander contacting me again after ordering me to attack. This was a tragic mistake for "A" and "C" companies. The lesson is not complicated: *after a defeat (mine), it is necessary to determine what went wrong.* The battalion should have treated my defeat as a reconnaissance and asked me all that I had learned. If it had done that, Tremblay would not have lost his leg for nothing, and the disaster awaiting "A" and "C" companies would never have occurred.

Continuing with the Operation Order:

> Own Troops. – Normal support arms, plus 1 Regt of Med Arty and four M-10 SP guns. "INTENTION R22eR will attack and capture east bank of river in front of present positions in view of dominating the river.

The operation order fills more than two pages of the war diary and the battle itself four. In addition to the weapons specifically listed as being in support were 26 2-inch mortars, ten Wasps (flame-throwers), MMGs, 3-inch mortars, Cab rank (Spitfire planes).

The flame-throwers were supposed to climb the east bank and, once on top, spray the west bank. As I wrote above, I doubt very much that these tracked flame-throwers, or any other vehicle, could have climbed the 60 degree slope of the bank. Moreover, as they reached the top, with their bellies exposed, they would have been destroyed by rockets from the west bank before getting off a single squirt. In the event, there is no mention in the War Diary of any flame-thrower getting on top of the east bank, nor of any flame-thrower being destroyed. I do not understand how even the most elementary recce could have failed to demonstrate the impossibility of the task assigned the flame-throwers.

The battle ended after about two hours with no platoon of R22eR able to remain on its objective, the east bank. The battle cost R22eR six killed in action and at least one who died of wounds: Private Alexandre Conrad Leduc, "who stepped on a German anti-personnel mine" during "A" Company's attack and died of wounds after much suffering on 23 March 1945 (as recounted by his nephew Harold Leduc, "A Story of Service and Suffering" in *Legion Magazine*, January/February 1999). In addition, the two who died on 7 January 1945 may well have received their mortal wounds on 3 January. And over and above these senseless losses of, presumably, at least nine killed, we must add several times that number of wounded, including 13 wounded by *Schuhmeine*.

It seems that neither Allard nor Bernatchez realized the impossibility of taking and occupying the east bank as long as the enemy was in well-prepared positions on the west bank a mere 50 feet away. They knew all about successful assault crossings, the taking of *both* banks, and *seem* to have assumed that taking just one bank would be only half as difficult!

There is nothing in the war diary about consulting with the new commander of 1st Canadian Infantry Division, Major-General Harry Foster, or with the new corps Commander, Lieutenant-General Charles Foulkes, about winning the east bank by simultaneously crossing the river and destroying the enemy on the west bank before returning to the east bank, which could henceforth assert its dominance over the west bank as the enemy crept back. Foster and Foulkes might well have answered, with an implied sneer, that any good regiment would be able to take and occupy the east bank *only* without fussing. And, in any event, the extra ammunition did not exist for an assault crossing of the Senio.

Had they wished to go to division and corps to protest the original plan (to attack only the east bank, the plan actually carried out), I think that they would have had a better chance of success had Major-General Chris Vokes still been GOC 1st Canadian Infantry Division and Lieutenant-General Tommy Burns still been GOC 1st Canadian Corps. Both knew and respected Bernatchez, Allard, and the R22eR. Moreover, having been ADC both to Burns and to Foulkes (in early 1946), I think that I can say Burns was more open to an argument based on sound tactics than was Foulkes, who I believe, would have been disinclined to amend his orders, however ill-conceived. Moreover, though he was a sapper, Burns *did* see action as a subaltern in the Great War, where he won the Military Cross. And, I think, this experience would have guided him to the sensible conclusion that both banks had to be attacked simultaneously.

It is tragic that the fact, as clearly recorded in the war diary, of the east bank's being sown with *Schuhmeine*, which even the most modest military experience would alert a commander to the fact that this meant *our* side of the east bank, was ignored in the plan of attack. Had proper cognizance been taken of these mines, the frontage of attack of each company would have been restricted to the frontage that could be cleared of these mines, under cover of smoke and very heavy interdiction of the surrounding enemy, before the forward platoon of each of the two assaulting companies passed through the gap. The second and third platoons should then have followed hard on the heels of the lead platoon, with the second swinging in one direction along the top of the bank and the third swinging in the other. The idea, simple enough, is not to have all your men in line charging through a minefield. And surely, after eight men and I of 18 platoon set off three *Schuhmeine* in five minutes or less, it should have been obvious that we had a problem here, if not always deadly, at least horribly maiming.

The two-company attack on the east bank of the Senio was Allard's biggest mistake. When word got back to him of what was happening, he came up and ordered that the troops be withdrawn. The attack was a disaster.

The two-company attack on the east bank of the Senio on 3 January 1945 was a mistake, just as it was a mistake when I was ordered to lead 18 platoon in our attack on the east bank on 31 December 1944. And my lack of success on 31 December *should* have led to my being questioned as to the reasons. Instead, was it simply assumed by my company commander and at battalion HQ that I just didn't have it in me? I don't know. Equally possible – and one I prefer if only because it's not grossly insulting to me – it may simply have been assumed that if an unsupported platoon at one-third strength couldn't hack it, then surely a two-company attack, massively supported, could.

The fundamental problem on the Senio was that *all* the commanders all the way back to corps, (except the poor bloody platoon commanders and their men who had to carry out the orders!) were relying on their experience of a series of successful river crossings to think that occupying the east bank of the Senio would simply be more of the same. And, indeed, simpler: no river crossing needed. And, therefore, no need for any recces.

But, for example, the banks of the Savio were not elevated as were the banks of the Senio. And, in any event, we had not dug in along our bank of the Savio. We stayed a couple of hundred yards back along a ridge from which we could fire on any enemy soldiers who decided to come back to the east side of the river to see how we were getting along. And we stayed there until a river crossing had been made, regrettably not by our brigade.

Also, on the Lamone, which had high banks like the Senio, we went up to the east bank where 18 platoon found several solid houses and where we encamped, happily detached from the rest of "D" Company, which remained 800 yards back for 24 hours. But note that we went up *to* the east bank. We certainly did not go *up* the east bank. Although we had no indication that the enemy was dug in on top of "our" bank, I took it for granted that it would be dug in on its bank 50 or so feet away, and ready to put a bullet through the head of any idiot taking a peek over the bare top of our bank. Again, as with the Savio, both banks were taken when a successful assault crossing was made.

When on patrol and approaching the Fosso Vecchio, which had no high banks, I was able to kill with my Tommy-gun a German soldier carelessly strolling on the opposite side. But I did not then continue to our bank of the Fosso Vecchio and there lie down with my patrol to give the surrounding dug-in enemy posts a lovely opportunity to exact immediate revenge. Instead, of course, I brought the patrol back to our platoon. By the next day the regiment had crossed the Fosso Vecchio in strength.

The point is that each of these water obstacles had to be treated differently. And in each case, recces were made before orders were given for their assault crossing. In war, in a sense, the enemy is the directing staff, the group responsible for overseeing the competence of officers under instruction, as at staff college, for example. Success in one operation does *not* mean that following the same method will work the next time out. Indeed, against a competent enemy, using the same method twice in a row could prove fatal. At least, it should. And even if a method has proven successful several times in a row, this does not turn it into an immutable principle of war. *Every* operation must be regarded as a unique event: before a plan of attack or defence is decided on, *all* the factors that make it different from anything previous must be considered. And if it is concluded that the factors are identical, then the plan still must be different. It must always be taken for granted that the enemy will have figured out why it lost the last time out and will be readier this time should we try the same plan again. I come back to this below in describing our operations in Korea. There, God help us, we kept on doing things in exactly the same way for almost two solid years, and got clobbered whenever the enemy decided to give us lads a bit of on-the-job training.

We arrived at the foot of the east bank of the Senio before dawn on 29 December 1944, and orders were given at 1900 hours that same day: "'C' Company's forward platoon and one platoon from 'D' Company [not mine] were to take up positions right on top of the east bank of the river." If recces were made before these orders were given, either they were inadequate or the fundamental difference between making assault crossings and occupying a defended bank supported by another one 30 feet away was simply not thought through. Even during the whole of 30 December, no one visited 18 platoon and thus the order to attack at 0410 hours the next day that I received also could not have been thought through.

In hindsight, I wish that I had thought a bit about how to get my new company commander to come forward to have a look at the bank of the Senio towering over us. I might have been able to convince him that the only way to assault the east bank successfully was to assault the west bank as well. In other words, make an assault crossing. My phoning him and asking: "*Yvan, vois-tu du bon sens dans cette attaque?*" ("Yvan, do you see any sense in this attack?") was, I suppose, tactless. In the middle of the night, ordered to do something that I knew to be mad, I was not at my most tactful.

When next we go to war *everyone* will be inexperienced. Generals, colonels, and company commanders will be giving orders without having the foggiest idea of what it will be like for the platoons that have to carry out the orders. The lieutenants, the platoon commanders, those who are still alive after the first couple of days, will have to very quickly learn on the job and will by then know infinitely more about battle than any of their superiors giving them orders. Captains, majors, lieutenant-colonels, generals of any intelligence will realize this and will deliberately go forward into the leading platoons to gain the battlefield knowledge that they *must* acquire as quickly as possible lest they continue to get their soldiers killed stupidly. No doubt, in going forward like this, some of the senior officers will be killed. This will be all to the good: it will open the way for promotion of platoon commanders. *They, and they alone,* will have acquired the experience needed to command in battle.

But when these lieutenants do get promoted and become company commanders, they must *not* then act as though they think that their fighting days are over, that they never again have to risk their skins as a good platoon commander does every day. *All* commanders must constantly go forward, far forward, to ensure that they *never* give an order that their reconnaissance would have shown them could not be carried out. At Borodino in 1812, although Napoleon was technically victorious, forcing the retreat of the Russian army, the French lost *forty-eight* generals killed or wounded. In those days, generals *led*. They still should.

On page 345 of the *Histoire du Royal 22e Régiment* one reads:

On New Year's Day (1945)…Lieutenant Pope was wounded in the arm
on emerging on the summit of the embankment (of the Senio).

I was never closer than six feet from the summit of the
embankment of the Senio and that occurred at 0410 hours 31
December 1944 during the failed attack of my platoon. On New
Year's Day, the bullet that fractured my arm came from the summit
of the embankment but I was 100 yards distant from it.

It was Lieutenant Aimé Desrosiers who was hit "on emerging
on the summit of the embankment." He was killed by a *faustpatrone*
(a rocket) on 3 January 1945 during the attack of "A" and "C"
Companies on the embankment.

The death of Lieutenant Desrosiers brought to 13 the number
of lieutenants, platoon commanders, out of 12 rifle platoons, killed
by the enemy since I had arrived at the regiment nine months earlier.
Taking account also of the lieutenants too seriously wounded to
return to the front, I had thus become the senior lieutenant after
the IO, Muck Richard, designated to replace him if ever there should
be promotions within the regiment.

Chapter Five

Out of Action and End of War

I spent seven weeks at military hospitals with my left arm in plaster. I started off at our regimental aid post (RAP), where a couple of our stretcher bearers satisfied themselves that the two bullet-holes – in and out – had been bound tightly enough and gave me an anti-tetanus shot. Considering that I had not had a bath since before swimming chest-high through liquid manure on 14 December, this was a useful precaution. A trip sitting next to the driver in a 15-cwt (hundred-weight) truck got me to 4 Canadian Casualty Clearing Station (CCS), where I sat quietly in the admitting room for a few minutes while a nursing sister was busy with her papers. Finally, she hit one that surprised her: "GSW!" (Gun Shot Wound), she exclaimed. Apparently this gave me priority over the half dozen others sitting there, some of whom seemed to be nursing New Year's Eve hangovers or the resulting falls.

Soon I was on an operating table, with an undoubtedly competent surgeon over me. Since I have not had the slightest trouble with my left arm in well over half a century I must assume that the surgeon knew his business and got out all the bone fragments (the bullet had made a half-inch gap in the ulna), tidied everything up, and put on a correct plaster cast to keep the two parts of the ulna in alignment as they grew back together. Also, I owe it to this surgeon that my flannel R22eR badges (far preferable to the issue canvas flashes), my britches, and my puttees were all rolled up together and travelled with me to the hospital in Rome, where I was first able to dress as a soldier again.

But the operation was the high point of my treatment. When I came to after the operation, I was in a large, unheated room lying on the floor on a canvas stretcher, wearing a thin cotton robe and covered by a single thin woollen blanket. There were about 20 others similarly laid out. When I opened my eyes, the medical major in charge noticed this at once and ordered: "He's awake, into the ambulance with him!" It was by now late on the night of 1-2 January 1945, and the medical major no doubt had better things to do with the rest of his night than ensure that those who had just awakened from an operation and anaesthesia were not in shock or in any other way unfit for a bumpy, several hour ride in an unheated ambulance at the beginning of January.

The utter callousness of the man was without limit. Even if our corps had been in the middle of heavy fighting with casualties pouring in, (and we were not, the nursing sister had been surprised that there should have been even a single solitary GSW awaiting her attention), his lack of concern for us was unpardonable. But lately, having received a copy of my army medical records, I note this entry for 2045 hrs 1 January 1945:

> P.O. [post-operation] orders
> 1. Sulphathiazol routine
> 2. Evac. lying when conscious.

It seems that it was standard procedure at this CCS to get rid of wounded soldiers without in any way checking on their post-operation condition. So, maybe the medical staff was merely following orders, the type of orders that only a damn fool would obey.

I do not know whether any of us developed pneumonia on that night. But that medical major must have been directly responsible for several deaths during that winter.

Like the other three in my ambulance, I was desperately cold, but that shortly became a lesser problem. I had not had a bowel movement since the day before, since I had been shot shortly after awakening. And now, in that ambulance, after the pentothal, the operation and all, I *had* to go. Above my stretcher was a cupboard, and in it I found a small bowl, just about the right size for a lieutenant with the runs. I filled it and put the bowl back where it belonged. But, as I said, it was a bumpy trip. The door of the cupboard flew open, and my bowl landed upside down on the left handle of my stretcher. Not a word was said by my three fellow wounded. No one even said, "Well, ain't that the icing on the cake."

Arriving at 1 Canadian General Hospital (CGH), I heard the Italian orderlies come to carry us into the hospital. Well, he found out. What could I say except, *"Scussate me?"* After a startled exclamation, he did his duty and got me to my ward, already occupied by five or six lieutenants.

When I learned that I was going to be given sulphathiazol to prevent my wound becoming infected, I told the staff that I was allergic to it. The staff gave it to me anyway. My temperature hit 102.4, and my pulse rate 115. And, because I was still bathless since the liquid manure swim of 14 December, I began to stink. I was told that I should head for a bath. "I'm not staggering over to the bathroom with a temperature over 102." Once I got on penicillin (a shot every three hours), I at last had a bath.

About this time, I noted that my arm was bleeding under the cast; indeed, the wet stain was now a circle two or three inches across. Thinking that this might indicate that the stitches had come out, I pointed out the stain to a nursing sister. Her reply? "When it starts dripping on the floor, let me know." The two wounds (in and out of the bullet) had *not* been sewn up. I understand that this is a perfectly sensible medical procedure: it gives time for any debris, any foreign matter, to work its way out.

After eight days in No.1 CGH, I went further down the line to the No.14 CGH, where my arm was at last to be sewn up. Apparently, the maximum delay between initial operation and sewing up is ten days. My arm hurt like hell: the skin and flesh had got rather used to the gap, and the stretching to pull everything together took a day or two to settle down. Moreover, the angle of the new cast (from my wrist to halfway between my elbow and my shoulder) also took a couple of days to get used to. Finally, coming to, I was sick as a dog for 24 hours. I had told the surgeon that I reacted very badly to ether, while pentothal was fine; he poured on the ether. The surgeon sent me to No.5 CGH in Rome, with a note to the receiving Medical Officer (MO): "This man will probably be found to be a bit *uncooperative* as his demeanor and attitude here to the staff has been that of a series of complaints. [signed] W.S. Archibald." However, my two gashes healed so well that the scars are hardly worth showing off.

In Rome, I got a new battle-dress uniform and set to work sewing my two pips on each shoulder and, for the first outing, the R22eR flash on one shoulder. With only one free arm, I found sewing slow going, and so I contented myself with one R22eR flash, and no Canada, and no 1st Division red patch. By the next day, I had got properly dressed. But the medical authorities considered Rome altogether too pleasant for the likes of us, so down the line went the walking wounded.

Arriving on 19 January 1945 at No.15 CGH in Caserta, the end of the line and not far from Naples, I was perfectly able to walk. I visited my distant cousin Taschereau Major Nick Cannon, R22eR, who was town major somewhere (maybe at Avellino). When he learned that I had not asked permission to leave the hospital, he suggested to me that I cut short my family visit.

A little over three weeks later, with my arm deplastered the day before, I decided to celebrate my 22nd birthday in Naples. Since it was the 22nd day of the 2nd month and I was in the Royal 22nd, that made seven 2s. How could I miss? So there I was in a bar with a redhead whose father (or her husband) was a colonel with Mussolini in the north. When I said to her *"per l'amore"* ("for love"), the little devil replied *"cinque mille lire."*

I came to on the sidewalk at 0300 hours. Back in the hospital the nursing sister had helpfully pointed out to the MO, "Lieutenant Pope didn't sleep here last night." Thus the doctor-colonel-commanding wished to see me. After mentioning a court-martial, he told me that I would not have a two-week holiday at the rest and recuperation centre; instead, he was sending me directly to the reinforcement depot at Avellino, precisely what I wished. However, demonstrating tact out of necessity, I assumed a saddened air, comforting with my right hand my poor wounded left arm: there was no point in inciting renewed desire to talk of a court-martial, especially missing a night in a hospital.

After a couple of weeks at the depot, I left it with all the other Canadians in Italy, heading for Marseilles. There, by pure good luck, the reinforcement depot arrived on the same day as the regiment, 17 March. Moreover, the tent lines of the depot were up against those of the regiment. I at once went to find Colonel Allard to ask him to get me back in the regiment as quickly as possible, without bothering with the usual bumph. The colonel agreed, and my kitbag was in the lines of the 22nd two minutes later.

In Holland with the regiment, I ended the war as IO. My mother being Belgian, I had female first or second cousins all along the regiment's route in Rouen, Paris, Brussels, the Hague. Naturally, at each stop, I asked permission (initially Allard, then Turcot) to go visit them. And never got permission. Finally, arriving in the Hague, Turcot told me that if ever we reached Berlin, on arrival there he did not wish to hear any more about my female cousins.

Getting out of hospital at the beginning of March 1945, I had become the senior lieutenant and therefore the battalion's IO as soon as I got back, just in time for our move to Holland and our advance from the Ijssel to the Eem.

At the beginning of May, R22eR was part of 1st Canadian Corps, facing west, since the corps had encircled a German army, which was occupying western Holland.

I believe that it was 4 May 1945. I was busy explaining what I knew about the enemy to a company about to enter the line. I explained to the hundred men in front of me that the mass of the German army to the east was going to seek refuge in its last fortress, the mountains in the south of Germany, and that therefore the war would last another couple of months. I was in full oratorical flight when one of the men of my little intelligence section who had been listening on the radio tapped me on the shoulder. "Lieutenant," he said, "The whole German army in Holland has capitulated without condition. The war is over."

Next day, I left for the 3rd Brigade commanded by Brigadier Bernatchez to act as a liaison officer (LO) because a fourth battalion had been placed in the brigade to aid in the occupation of our designated area in southwest of Holland.

Soon after my arrival, a Dutch partisan came to see the brigadier to tell him that the Germans intended to blow up all the food dumps under their control and thus deprive the Dutch people of what they needed to survive. Since the advance in strength of 1st Canadian Corps into the German positions was slated only for the next day or the day after that, Bernatchez ordered me to return to R22eR with the partisan and with the Carrier platoon (13 lightly armoured 5-ton tracked vehicles), go through the German lines, find the German commander, and tell him that if he blew up the civilians' food, he would be shot.

Delighted thus to have the opportunity to say something like that to a colonel, I left at once, with the partisan seated behind me on my motorcycle. Now, the village that 3rd Brigade HQ had had many canals and bridges. Thus it was impossible to take the direct route to R22eR. I left it to the partisan to tell me which bridges to take. And when we were at last out of the village, I realized that the partisan had not understood that we were first to go back to my battalion. We were heading directly towards the German lines.

Obviously I could have – I should have? – turned around and headed for my battalion. But my motorcycle was acting up. The damned machine was burning as much oil as gasoline: the blue smoke that followed me everywhere was impressive. I said to myself: "This bastard is going to die soon; maybe as soon as we get to my battalion. Therefore the Carrier captain will act towards me as I would if an imbecile arrived from brigade with a broken-down motorcycle; he'll leave me there and go with his gang without me to amuse themselves among the enemy." I did not have to slow down from my 60 miles an hour to decide to continue towards the enemy lines.

When we arrived there, the partisan explained to the German soldier at the check point that I had a message for the sector's commandant. We were allowed to pass. And that is how I personally liberated at least two Dutch villages, because we had to pass through several to get to the German HQ.

The villagers were celebrating, as I was the first Allied soldier whom these people had seen. It was pleasant being the conqueror, to bound up on to platforms to the cheers of crowds delirious with joy! But I was sorry for the German soldiers in the vicinity, still armed but no longer daring to maintain their hold over the people, an often cruel domination that had lasted for almost five years.

But I had spent only eleven days under German rule a year earlier in Italy. And during those eleven days, I was treated with respect. I believe that I behaved in the same way towards the defeated German soldiers with whom I dealt in May and June 1945.

Arriving at the German HQ, I met one of the officers to whom I said that it would be viewed extremely badly by my army if the German authorities destroyed in any way whatever food, material, and so on, that remained in occupied Holland and that could be useful to the civilian population. I do not believe that I spoke of firing squads. It would have been insulting to make such a menace to the *Oberst* through one of his subordinates. Besides, alone and ten miles from our lines, surrounded by several thousand armed enemy soldiers who did not in the least look defeated, I would not have been wise to talk of shooting.

In any case, the German officer came out of the *Oberst*'s command post after a few minutes to assure me that no one had the slightest intention of blowing up anything. And they kept their word.

I got back on my motorcycle and, with the partisan sitting behind me, we left in a cloud of blue smoke, leaving the whole German HQ wondering how the hell the Allies won the war with vehicles like that.

Back at 3rd Brigade, I reported to Bernatchez. But I do not believe that I mentioned to him that the Carrier platoon had not been in the party.

The 22nd arrived in the Hague on or about VE Day, 8 May 1945. Being the battalion IO, I had a Jeep, and I at once went in search of my wealthiest relative, my great-uncle Joh de Kuyper, my grandmother's brother. In the middle of a large square, I stopped to ask for directions. A very good looking girl said that she could help me but needed to look at my city map. To do so she had to lean over me and press her body, hard, against my right arm and shoulder. Later, too late, it occurred to me that she might have accepted a proposal of marriage on the spot. But I was thinking only of my great-uncle.

I did not smoke, but I had with me two 300 cigarette parcels that my parents had sent me. Each parcel cost $1 in Canada but was worth $120 in Europe, since *one* cigarette was worth 40 cents. I gave them to my uncle. "*Mais c'est une fortune que tu me donnes, mon enfant.*" ("But it's a fortune you're giving me, my child"). And in exchange he gave me a couple of bottles of de Kuyper gin.

Now it so happened that the R22R was responsible for managing "Eclipse Dumps" full of German booty. Our job was to see to the orderly transfer of all this to the Dutch authorities. But one of the dumps was full of gin in 40-litre flasks. German soldiers worked for us in moving the flasks around. Once while I was watching, a couple of very youthful and small members of the *Wehrmacht* dropped one of the flasks and 40 litres of gin spread across the concrete. The poor lads looked at me in horror, fully expecting to be executed on the spot. But I laughed. I did not especially like gin, and we were engaged in flogging a few flasks of the stuff in exchange for beer to other units that were busily guarding boots and socks and things of that nature. Of course, these other units had to *buy* the beer that we demanded in trade. We then *gave* the beer to our own men.

I was promoted to captain around the middle of May 1945, effective 1 May 1945, the effective date being conveniently just before the war ended in Europe – convenient, that is, for retaining rank when peace broke out.

Chapter Six

At Peace – In A
Manner of Speaking

Having volunteered to fight the Japanese, I returned to Canada in July 1945. The Japanese surrendered in August 1945 without our army becoming involved. VJ Day occurred while I was still on disembarkation leave in Ottawa. The fact that we no longer had an enemy could not stop our mobilization in an instant. Thus, my leave over, I arrived in Camp Debert, NS to become camp commandant of the brigade being assembled under the command of Brigadier Bernatchez, who had commanded the 3rd Canadian Infantry Brigade in Italy and Holland. Impressive as the title may sound, a camp commandant is simply a low-level administrator, responsible for the signalers, cooks, batmen, drivers, vehicles and equipment and for whatever else is needed to keep those running the brigade – the commander, the brigade major, the Intelligence captain, and the three liaison officers – unworried about getting their three squares a day in an area not an obvious target for enemy guns and heavy mortars.

In choosing me for the job (not knowing the war was about to end), I suppose Brigadier Bernatchez was trying to keep me out of harm's way for a while, as had Lieutenant-General Burns in Italy. Had the war continued, I have little doubt I could have convinced Brigadier Bernatchez to let me return to R22eR as soon as we got close to Japan.

But as camp commandant, I learnt that in peacetime conditions – such as at Debert – it is wise to carry out a detailed "marching-in inspection:" on leaving, the Camp Debert engineers presented me with a bill for every broken window and other barrack damage of a similar nature within our lines. Without doubt some of the damage went back to before the war. Since I had no proof, the bastards had me. Finally, we reached a saw-off: they would supply the glass panes and all other material required; we'd repair everything in sight. With no war on, we had nothing better to do anyway. But the Camp engineers came out ahead.

By the end of November 1945, NDHQ had figured out what to do with us and the R22eR assembled in Camp Valcartier, I as a company second-in-command. In December, a vacancy existed on a three-week vehicle mastership course in Camp Borden. I applied for it. Had I been sent on the course, I might have learnt how to change the oil filter correctly and thus not burn out the engine of my MG a few years later. But I was told my services were needed in Valcartier. Shortly thereafter, we had a mess meeting at which the battalion second-in-command, Major Georges Sevigny, DSO, presided. General Crerar, who had commanded First Canadian Army in Europe, was on a farewell tour of our camps and it had been decided that in our eastern Quebec district (MD 5) all officers would donate a dollar or two for a present for the General plus another 50cents for a cocktail party for him at the A-13 (Advanced Training Centre) officers' mess.

I do not recall who was the first to object but certainly I was not the last to point out that it was contrary to KR(Can) – the King's Regulations for the Canadian Army – for juniors to give presents to their seniors. Moreover, we could not be assessed so much as one cent for an event in any mess other than our own. It was agreed that the officers of R22eR would not pay. Hardly surprisingly, the CO, Lieutenant-Colonel Gilles Turcot, called another mess meeting for early the next morning, before the first parade. "Who refuses to co-operate in the farewell gift and party for General Crerar?" demanded the Colonel.

Shortly after I, alone, had stuck up my hand, I found myself on the way to Camp Borden for a one-week hygiene and sanitation course. Thus I missed the Crerar party and presentation. Moreover, I got a "D" on the course – "D" for distinguished. But even this got me into trouble. Whenever we came out of the line in Korea, I insisted on perfection in my company's latrines:fifteen feet deep, minimum. So deep no self-respecting fly would go down to check them out – before landing on our food for its dessert. But while "C" Company was digging its superlative latrines, the other companies were lining up the guy ropes of their tents and whitewashing every rock in sight within a hundred yards that could be lined up with something else. My last annual confidential report in Korea – after a year and a half in action! – spoke disparagingly of my guy ropes and lack of whitewashed rocks. But not a word about my pride and joy: my latrines.

In January 1946, General Eisenhower made an official visit to Ottawa – and the Chief of the General Staff, Lieutenant-General Charles Foulkes, had to bum a ride with his guest because none of the three officers on his staff, a lieutenant-colonel, a major, and a captain, all members of the Corps of Military Staff Clerks, had thought of getting the staff car of the CGS to the right place at the right time. Obviously, the CGS needed an aide-de-camp (ADC), one with experience, and preferably bilingual. Who else but me?

Thus in early January 1946 I was posted to the CGS staff in Ottawa. In an office adjoining the CGS, I manned a two-line telephone exchange, one line for the CGS, another for the VCGS. It was important not to get the toggles confused: horizontal for the CGS, down for the Vice Chief. One day, the CGS told me to get the Chief of the Air Staff (CAS), Air Marshal Leckie, on the line. I got through to his office and his assistant, a female flight lieutenant, told me to be sure to get the CGS on the line *first* – since, as we both knew, Leckie had been appointed CAS before Foulkes had got to be CGS. Of course, I'd be damned if I'd have the CGS waiting on the line for a blue job. So, I waited until I heard "Leckie here." I then pressed the buzzer for the CGS and heard "Foulkes here." But they couldn't hear each other: I'd phoned the office of the CAS on the line of the VCGS. I had to hang up on one of them: naturally, it was the CAS that got the chop. When I tried again – with the toggle utterly horizontal – I didn't argue: the CGS got buzzed first.

Another day, the CGS told me to get Mr. Rabbit in Montreal on the line and to be sure that he, the CGS, would be on the line first. Always willing to amend orders that don't make much sense, I said to myself, "damned if I'll get the army's boss on the line before a Rabbit." Pretty soon, with the CGS in blissful ignorance of my amendment, a voice came in loud and clear from Montreal: "Abbott here." The Minister of National Defence. I leaned heavily on the CGS's buzzer. And awaited my summons. The CGS surprised me by mildly stating, again, to make sure he was on the line before the Minister. I decided not to mention the Mr. Rabbit business. I was at zero already: why try for negative territory?

The CGS had his visitors' book in my office. Lieutenant-General Guy Simonds was not happy when I asked him to sign it. I think he believed that *he* should be CGS (which he later became). Nor did General Simonds cheer up at all when, as one ex-cadet to another, I volunteered the information that I was one of his centuries, his RMC number being 1596 and mine 2796. I got the impression that had we been together in France a year earlier, he would gladly have given me directions into the nearest minefield.

One morning a brigadier I did not recognize came in. When I suggested he sign the CGS's visitors' book, he exploded, "Damn it, I'm the Deputy CGS and I've been talking to you on the phone every morning for the past two months. I will *not* sign the visitors' book."

In May 1946, shortly after I was promoted from ADC to the CGS to ADC to the Governor General, the RMC Annual Meeting took place at RMC in Kingston. Because of the war, this was my first meeting. Unfortunately, I suppose, the evening before the general meeting, I was talking in the mess to an old brigadier about the re-opening of the College. (It was closed from 1942 – when I graduated with my class from the two-year war course – until 1948.) The brigadier had two sons whom he wished very much to see graduating from RMC. "What units do you expect they would join on graduation?" I asked. The brigadier was astounded. "Of course they're not going into the Service," he replied. No idea of service to the country. What did count was the prestige of being an RMC graduate, getting an inexpensive education, and then making bags of money on Bay Street or as a corporate lawyer. "To hell with that," I said to myself – and was well primed for the general meeting the next morning.

When all my seniors had had their say – as a member of the last war class I was junior indeed – I said: "It seems to me that all the preceding speeches have viewed the tragedy of the closing of the College from a personal rather than a national point of view. If the responsible committee at NDHQ – which included ex-cadets – has recommended the closing of the College to cadet training, how then could the ex-cadet body, without the facts and figures before it, recommend its re-opening? The national interest should have priority over sentimental attachment. All that matters is what is best for Canada: if it's best for Canada that the College be re-opened, then it should be re-opened; if it's best for Canada that the College stay closed, then it should stay closed." And my seniors, to a man, generals and all, booed. What especially angered my brother ex-cadets was the fact that I was recently ADC to the CGS and he was *not* an ex-cadet and was believed, probably not unfairly, to be opposed to the re-opening of the College. My remarks, then, were viewed as letting the side down, if not as downright treasonable. And so Brigadier W.A.B. Anderson expressed himself to me in the mess that evening. Brigadier Anderson had been the senior cadet, the Battalion Sergeant-Major, before the war and ended his career as a lieutenant-general. Not a good man to upset. Years later, in the famous letter in which my father set out my military indiscretions – as he saw them – my RMC speech figured prominently.

Many years later, I got my copy of the ex-cadet November 1997 Newsletter. Included in it is the "Commandant's Message" of the new RMC Commandant, Brigadier-General K.C Hague, half in English, half in French. The following is one of the French paragraphs, which I have translated.

"It goes without saying that RMC's most important mission is to produce subaltern officers that meet the operational needs of unit commanders. With regard to this, RMC never ceases being the object of criticism. The high rate of failure that the Centre for combat training has recently experienced during phase 3 of the elementary formation of armoured and infantry officers, forces us to ask ourselves if our officer cadets are motivated to make a career in the CF [Canadian Forces]. One can see a direct correlation between their lack of motivation and the military formation they get at RMC in the framework of their university programme composed of four disciplines (leadership, studies, bilingualism and physical ability). While we have not yet received concrete information from operational commanders on this subject, I have ordered a complete revision of our programme of military formation. The result sought must be a progressive and coherent cycle of formation during the whole of the four years that the officer cadets spend at RMC, so that each of them acquires the knowledge, the competence and the enthusiasm needed to permit integration into a unit of the line on leaving the College. We intend to send the draft of our plan to the training centres and to the operational commanders so that they may send us their comments and help us find the right way."

It is understandable that the Commandant wrote this paragraph in French: much less chance of it making headlines in the press of English Canada. I wish the Commandant every success in trying to make combatant officers out of what the recruiters for RMC have sent him. He will not succeed with them all; probably not even with most.

It is dead wrong to recruit for RMC – to send officers across the land begging Grade 12 and 13 students to come visit RMC and see all the benefits of a free RMC education. And, moreover, getting paid for it. Why on earth expect someone that signs up under those conditions to somehow wish to serve in tanks or infantry on graduation? The brand-new ex-cadet will immediately head for civvy street and look for a job in the trade learned at the College. Only if the job cannot be found will the Army be considered tolerable... until something better turns up.

Entrance to RMC should be restricted to those that apply and give every appearance of wishing to make a career in the armed forces and, insofar as the Army is concerned, in one of the five combatant arms: armoured, artillery, engineers, signals, and infantry. Cadets should be trained to fight and kill enemy soldiers – and to lead those they will command by their proficiency in doing so. There should be no place at RMC for those that wish to learn a trade. Civilian colleges and universities are the place for that – and that's where those who wish non-combatant commissions should go.

All this will cut the size of the cadet body down to probably a quarter of its present strength, quite possibly even less. But Brigadier-General Hague will then have cadets all of whom are highly motivated to pass their phase 3. I can hardly expect what I've just written will become the order of the day between now and 2010. But I can foresee some movement in that direction. I was much encouraged by the after-dinner speech of General Ramsey Withers, CMM, a former CDS and an ex-cadet, to the annual dinner of the Toronto Branch of the RMC Ex-Cadet Club on 24 April 1998. General Withers made it clear that the committee he heads that has been examining RMC will recommend that the emphasis in recruiting on all the *benefits* – being paid while getting a degree – will be dropped. Instead, the emphasis will be on service to one's country. It's a start.

And it's a start that can't come soon enough. In 1998, the Environics Research Group Ltd. did a survey of our officer training. It asked 671 cadets in the Regular Officer Training Program (ROTP) about the program and how it could be improved. The *National Post* of 21 October 1999 had this extraordinary headline above its report on the survey: "Military training irks RMCC cadets, poll shows." (The extra "C" on RMC stands for Canada.) What on earth did cadets at RMC expect if not military training? The survey gave the answer. Forty-five percent stated they did not intend to make the military their career. Nearly a third stated they only enrolled at RMC to get a free education. There are others, thank God, on whom public money is not wasted.

One of them said: "Unfortunately, this pride [in being at RMC] is not shared by most of my peers here. To them, RMC is merely a springboard into business or politics. They care more about a fully subsidized education than what it means to be an officer cadet, not to mention an officer. They are what is wrong with RMC." Another cadet said RMC should be tougher: "If you want to fix this place, make us proud of what we do, instead of having to be a kinder, gentler army. We joined with the promise of dying for this country if necessary. At least give the majority of us credit of having integrity, discipline, and honour." I wish these two cadets – and their like – all the success in the world. May they rise to high command in our armed forces.

ADC to the CGS lasted until April 1946 when I became the Canadian ADC to the incoming Governor-General, Field Marshal Lord Alexander. There were also two British ADCs, Squadron Leader Tony Tollemache, George Cross, of the RAF, and Captain David Lloyd-Thomas of the Irish Guards (Alexander's old regiment).

With a Harold Alexander (called "Harry" by Her Excellency) and the second most senior, Major-General Harry Letson as Private Secretary, it was decided that I would be one Harry too many. Owning up to my full name of William Henry, I became "Willie" at Rideau Hall - shades of the "*Guglielmo*" of two years earlier with the Italian partisans.

ADC at Government House was a most pleasant job. The ADC-in-Waiting for the week was in attendance on the Governor-General, which usually meant being off duty before dinner since Their Excellencies dined en *famille*, with no staff present – unless, of course, there was a state dinner, in which case, all three ADCs would be on duty to get everyone lined up in the correct order for presentation to the Governor-General. A second ADC would be the ADC-Next-in-Waiting. During his week, he would be in attendance on Her Excellency on the rare occasions when she needed a man along in addition to the Lady-in-Waiting, Lady Bridget Vesey. The third ADC would have the week completely off, unless there was a state dinner, as mentioned, or the annual Garden Party.

We three ADCs lived at the front of Rideau Hall, on the third floor, each in his own bedroom and each with a footman to act as his valet. The valets, like all the rest of the domestic staff, were British. I rather got the impression that my valet felt rather put upon having to be valet to a Canadian. But he never let me down.

One of our many perks was use of a car with licence plates 9A1 (9A being for the diplomatic corps. The "1" that ended our "9A" meant we were pretty close to the Deity.) One fine afternoon, I was ADC-in-Waiting but with His Excellency away (in London, I believe, for the Victory Parade) I was having a quiet drink or two next to the swimming pool of the Country Club (of which we three were all automatically honorary members). The Country Club was on the Quebec side of the Ottawa River. (And so remained until 1999, when it closed after 91 years). Then I looked at my watch and started to figure out how much time I had left before driving back to Rideau Hall, changing into my uniform, boarding the vice-regal limousine that would be waiting for me at the main entrance two floors below my window, driving to the Supreme Court Building, bounding up the stairs to the office of the Administrator of the Government of Canada, the Chief Justice of the Supreme Court of Canada, Thibodeau Rinfret, and ask him to accompany me to the Senate entrance of Parliament, where the Prime Minister, the rest of the government, senators and MPs would be awaiting his pleasure to enter, proceed to the throne, seat himself on it and then nod each time he was asked, regarding a bill, "*le Roi le veult?*"

My belated time appreciation informed me that I had cut it exceedingly fine. When 9A1 and I arrived at Rideau Hall, the limousine was in its place with the driver looking worried. Getting to my room, I found my uniform laid out in precisely the manner Jeeves would have done it for Bertie Wooster after a hard night at the Drones Club. My trousers were *not* folded: that would have wasted time. They were laid on a chair, open, so that in one bound I could get both legs into them. With my trousers secured, I grabbed cap, Sam Browne belt, shirt, tie, socks and shoes; and thus half-naked I boarded the vice-regal limousine. The driver didn't need any suggestion from me about not sparing the horses. By the time we got to the Supreme Court, I was fully dressed. When I entered the Chief Justice's office, Thibodeau Rinfret said, "*Vous êtes en retard.*" ("You are late.") "*Je ne crois pas, Excellence.*" ("I don't believe so, Your Excellency.") Which was true, provided the Chief Justice didn't start fiddling around. But he did. After about thirty seconds of this, I said I thought we should go. We arrived at the Senate entrance precisely as the Peace Tower clock began striking six o'clock. The whole group standing at the entrance waiting for us looked a little nervous but then Mackenzie King never did look especially happy and possibly on previous occasions of the giving of Royal Assent, the assenting party may have got there a little ahead of time, just in case.

Though it was mid-summer, I was wearing my heavy winter woollen service dress. I could have worn my Indian Drill but since my brother ADCs did not have any summer dress, I decided to suffer along with them in the heat. But standing at attention to the right and behind the throne while the Chief Justice nodded at each appropriate moment, I regretted my fraternal courtesy. The sweat never stopped running down and dripping from the end of my long nose.

* * * * *

In the mid-summer of 1946, I was the ADC-in-Waiting accompanying the Governor-General and the Viscountess Alexander on their cross-country train trip. Somewhere on the Prairies, Her Excellency went to an evening function leaving His Excellency to dine alone on the train with me. This seemed to me to be a good time to ask him how he liked the French translation of his speech that I had made flat on my back. "Well, Willie," he replied, "it wasn't one of your best efforts."

Having got that settled, I next asked him about the speech to the Boy Scout Commissioners that I had been asked to prepare – for no better reason than I was the only one of the three of us that had been a Boy Scout (2nd Class!). "Willie, you didn't really expect me to make a speech that had in it a reference to the Hitler *Jügend*, to

French-English divisions in Canada, and to the religious affiliation of Scout troops, did you?"

Strangely, Alexander seemed to like me. He was always kindness itself to me, both while I was on his staff and later, as we will see. For myself, I loved him and Lady Alexander. Had I not known my own parents, I have often thought I could not have done better than having Lord and Lady Alexander as my parents. And I have never remotely felt the same about any other couple.

But to return to our cross-Canada train trip. When we arrived in Vancouver, the Governor-General disappeared on a private holiday on one of the coastal islands, not even one ADC being needed. I was then put up at the Vancouver Club. Two weeks later, back with his Excellency, I wrote the Club Secretary on 28 August 1946 on the letterhead of the Governor General's Train:

> On arriving at the Vancouver Club on the 11th August I asked the hall porter to have my tropical worsted uniform pressed. When it became time for me to leave the Club, on the 13th, I found that instead of pressing the uniform on the establishment, it had been sent to Liberty Cleaners, 436 Hornby Street.
>
> When I asked for my uniform at the desk, I was referred to these cleaners whom I found had managed to burn a hole in the back of the tunic. I have my uniform back now, patched after a fashion. In my position such a uniform is useless, and I shall have to have another one made.
>
> I consider that in this matter your Club has been negligent and that the services rendered me were below the standard I would expect from a gentleman's club. You will therefore remove my name from the list of Honourary Members of the Vancouver Club.
>
> [And I signed it] W. H. Pope, Captain ADC.

When the Vice-regal car reached Ottawa, I was given permission to leave (and not go on to the Quebec Citadel with the Governor General). I was supposed to be best man at the wedding of Lieutenant François Richer (Fritz) LaFlèche, MC, (son of Major-General Léo LaFlèche, a deputy minister) to Suzanne Cloutier (daughter of the King's Printer). (Suzanne later married Peter Ustinov. At Fritz's second wedding, I was an usher. At the third - the one that lasted 'til death - I was not invited.)

Since the train was late - so that I missed the wedding, but *not* the all night nuptial party - I got off in a hurry, leaving a copy of my letter to the Vancouver Club face up on a desk. A few days later, I dropped in at the Citadel to see what was going on in the Regiment. I also dropped over to the vice-regal quarters. (The life of an ADC was easy: during the summer of 1946, I, like other ADCs, was on duty only about a quarter of the time. In the vice-regal quarters, I encountered Captain Edson Sherwood, RCN, the Senior ADC, who was looking very embarassed. "Willie," he said, "I just happened to glance at this letter of yours that you left lying on a desk on his ex's train. I didn't mean to read it, but since Major-General Letson was secretary of the Vancouver Club some years ago, I couldn't stop myself. Now, Willie, you simply can't write letters like that. You must write them and apologize."

I replied that the facts were as stated in my letter: the services rendered me by the Vancouver Club *were* substandard. I would not withdraw the letter. Captain Sherwood then said, "Willie, you can't remain an ADC and write letters like that. Even his Ex wouldn't write a letter like that." To which I replied that the life of an ADC was altogether too easy and, though I had been greatly honoured to be on the Field Marshal's staff, I would prefer to return to my Regiment. When I told Lieutenant-Colonel Gilles Turcot, CO of R22eR, that I was leaving His Excellency's staff, the Colonel replied that he would like me to be the regimental adjutant and that I should so tell the Director of Infantry, Colonel Dollard Ménard, DSO, on returning to Ottawa. Colonel Ménard accepted the information and replied, "Well, Harry, there are three other adjutancies open at the moment that might suit you better: the Royal Canadian School of Military Engineering in Chilliwack, British Columbia, the jump school in Shilo, Manitoba, and Fort Churchill, Manitoba. I replied that I didn't see much point, as an infantryman, being adjutant of an engineering school. "So, I'll take the jump school." Colonel Ménard then said that he thought my career might be better enhanced by Churchill. "Well, if you think so, I'll take Churchill."

A few days later, in Montreal as an usher for RMC classmate Jean-Paul Wilson Ostiguy's wedding to Michelle Bienvenue, I dropped in uninvited to a cocktail party at the province's Army HQ on Atwater street. It was in honour of Major-General "Bunny" Weeks, the Adjutant-General. Going up to him and proud of having landed the plum adjutancy in the Army, I said, "You know, Sir, I had the choice of my Regiment, Chilliwack, Shilo, or Churchill, and I chose Churchill." The Adjutant-General replied: "Pope, you had no choice."

Four days by train from Ottawa, Fort Churchill was about as far as one could be sent in 1946 and still be in our Army. Through the study of the two handbooks provided adjutants, four days on the train were enough for me to learn my new administrative trade. Just as well: as orderly room sergeant, AHQ had sent a pleasant young man who had spent the war in Ottawa as a clerk typing out honours and awards; and instead of three clerk typists, Prairie Command had provided one clerk non-typist. Yet camp HQ worked efficiently. Of course it was six-day work weeks – but what else was there to do in Churchill? And the experience of working understaffed – and with an incompetent one at that – showed how grossly overstaffed all Army HQs are. Thus in the five subsequent times I was appointed an adjutant before finally getting a rifle company in Korea in August 1952, my first act was to send back to the rifle companies all the extra bodies in the orderly room my predecessors had thought necessary.

I was adjutant Fort Churchill from 16 October 1946 to the end of August 1948 – a double tour for a single officer. At about the halfway mark, there was a conference in Ottawa for adjutants, to which I was summoned. I was happy to obey the summons and headed as soon as I could to the La Touraine bar in the basement of the old Roxborough apartments, now demolished, bar and all, by vandals. I had hardly hoisted my first beer when Captain Edson Sherwood, RCN, still the Senior ADC, noted my presence in the restful gloom of the place. "Willie," he said, "I must tell His Ex you're back in town." A couple of days later, I was having lunch with Their Excellencies, two new British ADCs, and a new Lady-in-Waiting. After lunch, these new British arrivals told me their predecessors – Tollemache, Lloyd-Thomas, and Bridget Vesey –

had impressed on them the importance of not annoying high-ranking Canadian Army officers. "Or you'll end up in Churchill like Willie." Also, my former colleagues had handed their replacements a little rhyme. Unfortunately, I can recall only a couple of lines, of which I can be absolutely sure only of the rhyming ending:

"Cold, cold as the tip of an Eskimo's tool,

But not as cold as Willie, for he's in Churchill, poor fool."

There was also a line along the lines of "Cold, cold as a polar bear's bum." I know I must figure in the next line but I can't find the rhyme for "bum."

I got out of Churchill once more during my two-year exile. It was a trip to Winnipeg. In those days, messages to HQ Prairie Command had to be headed "GOC" (General Officer Commanding) even when, for instance, I was curtly telling the DAAG (Deputy Assistant Adjutant General), a major, that, dammit, I wish he'd get it right and quit adding to my work. The GOC, Brigadier Penhale, took such messages – and there were many – as personal insults. So that northern SOB was summoned to Winnipeg.

On arrival around noon, I recalled that my mother, wife of an Army officer, always spent the first few weeks of a new posting calling on the wife of everyone senior to my father. Well, I had a supply of visiting cards, which certainly were not getting any use in Churchill. So I said to myself, "What the hell, since I don't have a wife (the lack of which I didn't properly rectify until I'd left the army, thus not running afoul of Napoleon's dictum, 'a married soldier is only half a soldier'), I'll call on Mrs. Penhale myself this afternoon. With luck, she won't be in and all I'll have to do is fold over the top left corner of two of my cards, indicating I had called personally, place the cards on the small silver tray that should be just inside the door – and then get the hell out."

It worked as I had hoped: Mrs. Penhale wasn't in. That evening I was at the bar having a beer, when in charged Mrs. Penhale with the Brigadier in tow. "Captain Pope," she cries, "how delightful of you: you're the first officer to call on me since before the war!" And Brigadier Penhale never did get around to telling me he didn't like my telegrams. Possibly he thought that if he did, I'd tell his wife.

And possibly I should have learnt from this that a little tact can go a long way. But, of course, I didn't learn: this was simply a one-off.

Shortly before my time in Fort Churchill was finally up, Major MacKinnon, in command of the camp in the temporary absence of the Commandant, Lieutenant-Colonel Tedlie, told me they would hold the customary farewell party for me in the mess. I replied that I would prefer there be no party since it would be attended by women none of whom was mine, they all being the most faithful bunch of other officers' wives I'd ever had the misfortune to meet in my entire life. I added that if the party went ahead, I'd make a speech based on the paper I'd shown Major MacKinnon: "The Problems Involved in Maintaining Canadian Sovereignty with Particular Reference to Canada's North."

Major MacKinnon did not take me seriously.

After all the usual nice things had been said about my long service in Churchill, I made my speech, ending with: "History will record as our darkest hour the time when our leaders, both political and military, showed they lacked the courage to refuse the demand of the Americans to establish troops in Canada's north. In time of peace, I'd just as soon see Russian troops here as American."

Though these lines may make it appear I did not get on well with the American unit stationed in Fort Churchill for arctic training, this was not the case. During the summer of 1948, for instance, I worked evenings with the American assistant adjutant, Lieutenant Rufus Garrett, a 1946 graduate of West Point, to help him build a house (a shack, really) for the young lieutenant's bride, Mary Jo – who, incidentally, was at the landing strip with her husband to see me off at the end of August. They gave me a note: "Here's something to munch on your trip. Best of luck, and maybe will see you in Texas some day." The present was a box of chocolates, on which I did *not* munch as the plane bounced its way south.

Courtesy, kindness, consideration for friendly allies, fine; abasement before the demands of an overweening imperial power, no.

Certainly not to my surprise, the Adjutant-General, Major-General W.H.S. Macklin, did not see it that way and in a letter dated 31 March 1952 to me he wrote:

> We next find you in trouble when you made a very stupid speech at Churchill which strongly offended certain Americans who were in the audience. This incident showed, in my opinion, a want of good judgment and common sense and was so badly regarded here at Headquarters that a special report was rendered on you and your posting was changed.

The "special report" contained some memorable lines: "I strongly recommend that he not be employed in any capacity which entails relations with civilian agencies or the forces of other friendly countries." And my score for tact was 3 out of 9.

Before the "special report" had made its way up and down the military bureaucracy, I spent two months on leave in Berlin during the Blockade at my father's Canadian Military Mission to the Allied Control Commission (for Germany). Here I met and escorted around Berlin for two days the CCF Leader, M.J. Coldwell, MP, and the CCF Premier of Saskatchewan, T.C. Douglas. Thus began my interest in social democratic politics.

But politics would have to wait - the Korean War had begun.

Chapter Seven

The Korean War

It seems Brooke Claxton, Minister of National Defence, was outside the Montreal army recruiting centre for Korea in mid-summer 1950, saw the line up, did not like it, and ordered that everyone be enrolled *immediately*. And they were. "*Vos noms, adresse? Signez ici.*" ("Your surname, first name, address? Sign here.") And no one up to and including the adjutant-general had the courage to tell the Minister that enrolling all in the line including the unfit was sheer bloody nonsense.

Of course, the adjutant-general, Major-General Macklin, was aware of these matters and did bring them to the Minister's attention. But his manner of doing so was entirely inadequate. The AG was responsible for enrolling *fit* soldiers. As soon as he heard of the minister's interference, he should have countermanded the minister's order and placed his resignation on the minister's desk, and then let the government handle the political fall-out. Quite possibly, Claxton would have run for cover, blamed the recruiting officers in Montreal for misunderstanding his instructions, and refused Macklin's resignation. But in handing in his resignation and taking the risk that it would be accepted, Macklin would have acted honourably, and allowed those of us who were preparing the Special Force for war to get on with our jobs without having the dead weight of hundreds of unfit men in our barracks.

The outbreak of war in Korea and the Canadian government's decision to send combat troops meant another chance to get into action. The Canadian Army Special Force of 1950 was quickly recruited with little attention to details such as a medical exam. As Adjutant of the 2nd Battalion, Royal 22nd Regiment, which was to go to Korea, I was the first officer to deal with what Montreal had enrolled earlier in the day. Most, of course, would go on to become good soldiers. To the occasional riotous drunk piling out of the buses I would point out that we had a guard-room for intoxicated soldiers, where I could easily have them spend the night, none of them having noted on entering the camp, I assumed, that our guard-room could barely hold more than six. I noticed one man with his right arm bent at an awkward angle. Not caring that he could not salute me but wondering how he would hold his rifle, I asked him about this. He replied that he had been born that way: his elbow was fused; it would not bend. Another man was limping badly. He too told me that he had been born that way, with splayed toes on one foot. These men, all of them, had been enrolled to become combatant soldiers in an infantry battalion without the slightest attempt at a medical examination. Indeed, in the cases of fused elbow and splayed toes, it took an utter fool of a recruiting officer in Montreal to ask them to sign to become soldiers.

And I, more than anyone else, was stuck with this imbecility. Very quickly we had an H-hut full, with 148 soldiers waiting discharge as medically unfit. But while the idiots in Montreal could enrol blatantly obviously unfit men in five seconds each, it took us months to get authority to send them back for discharge. In the meantime their pay documents had not reached us. Not getting paid, having in many cases families to support, and bored stiff doing nothing (in preparing a brand-new battalion for war, we had no officers, no NCOs, to spare for social work), these unfortunates took off for the woods and their farms in droves.

Thus one evening at about 2330 hours when I was in bed sleeping after another hell of a day trying to sort out the mess that Montreal had dumped on us, I did not snap to attention when the camp's orderly officer (Captain J.C.P Hardy, and normally a friend) woke me to tell me that a ministerial inquiry needing my immediate attention had just come in. I replied something to the effect that if Brooke Claxton did not know why we had so many absent without leave (AWL),then he was a flaming idiot and so were all his Ottawa advisers who had not told him the results of enrolling absolutely anyone walking in off the street. I concluded by saying that I hoped to find time to make a more formal reply in the morning, provided that he would get the hell out now so that I could catch up on the sleep that I so desperately needed.

I woke in the morning to find a neat little note beside my bed: "I am directed to advise you that you will consider yourself as being under arrest by Order of the Field Officer of the Day until legally relieved. AA [Army Act] 45(3) & KR [King's Regulations] refs. JCP Hardy Capt" And the date and hour of delivery of the note was given as 0335 hours on 1 October 1950. At least my friend Hardy did not wake me to tell me that I would have something to read in the morning!

Since a man under arrest must be hatless and beltless, so that he has nothing to throw at his CO who is judging him, I went to breakfast carrying my hat and belt. On meeting the CO of 2R22eR, Lieutenant-Colonel Jacques Dextraze, I passed him the little note. "*Arrêt de faire le fou* (Stop playing the fool), and get properly dressed." And he wrote across the note, "Relieved from arrest by myself 1030 hours 21 Oct 50. Jadex." I heard no more about it. But I can easily imagine that word got to Ottawa by administrative channels (*not* through Dextraze) that Pope was being his usual unco-operative self and that what he had to say about the minister would not even be said about him by the Opposition.

On Sunday, in those days, everyone in 2R22eR in camp paraded to Mass. There were about 1,300 troops in the drill hall, since we had our first-line reinforcements with us. The colonel having taken all the other officers with him on a training exercise, I was the only officer on parade when a couple of staff-sergeants came in (they had skipped the parade somehow) and tried to make me understand something by their urgent whisperings. Being already partly deaf since Italy, I could not grasp what the trouble was. Finally, they practically dragged me outside to tell me that one of our recruits had shot himself while seated on his bed in his H-hut.

Deeming this a worthy reason to miss the rest of the service, I followed the two NCOs to the H-hut. The soldier had placed the muzzle of his rifle under his chin. His beret was stuck to the ceiling with part of his skull in it. His brains were spread on the floor where his body lay. Although many of our new soldiers were war veterans, most had never seen violent death before. I ordered an immediate clean-up and had the body carried out on a stretcher. Mass over, the young soldiers could return to their quarters without getting a premature experience of what awaited them in action in Korea.

The next morning I was in my office when a provost corporal entered, saluted, and then, while telling me that he had some questions to ask me, took off his gloves and dropped them on my desk, expecting thereby to intimidate me, in the manner of the tough cops whom he undoubtedly admired in the movies. I said, in French, "The first thing you are going to do, Corporal, is take your bloody gloves off my desk. And the next thing you are going to do is get the hell out of my office." Which he did. I heard no more from our military police although I did hear rumours of the usual unhappiness up the line.

At the civilian inquest that followed, the coroner explained to me that in Canada the police were responsible for bodies found lying around. In future, would I kindly not touch them? Still, it was ruled a suicide, and I was not accused of being an accessory after the fact of murder.

About this time, another of our recruits killed himself but, thoughtfully, at home. But both suicides, like all deaths outside of a theatre of operations, required that I set up committees of adjustment, and spend about eight hours of work on each one. All because the idiots in Montreal, apart from enrolling the halt and the lame, and sending them to me, also favoured me with unfortunate, unstable lads who were suicide prone.

My deafness started with all the noise that my friends and I created in Italy. I think that it was in 1949 that I first had my hearing checked by an army doctor. This resulted at my next year's medical examination in the MO's expressing some concern. It took no more than that for me to realize that I was in danger of having my medical category downgraded to reflect my hearing loss – probably H-3 instead of the H-1 required for service in action. Luckily, in those days, *all* personal documents were kept by the adjutant, which, as usual, I then was. When next my personal documents moved to another unit's control, there was absolutely nothing in their medical component to indicate that I suffered from any hearing loss at all. And then somehow or other, I was able to bluff my way through the annual medicals so that my increasing deafness never again got a mention.

My deafness got worse in Korea, especially after I played spotter for our tanks with a twenty-power scope, giving my ears full benefit of the resulting muzzle blasts. I cannot hear high-pitched tones, and this apparently leaves my ears free to pick up low-pitched tones better than most, a gun firing, for example. As I was not allowed to make any patrols in Korea, my deafness was not a disability. On the contrary, I seemed to demonstrate more *sang-froid* than I probably felt: being always the last to hear the high-pitched scream of the incoming mortar bomb or shell, I was always the last to duck.

I had been at R22eR's St. Jean Detachment from the beginning of January 1949 until mid-August 1950, when I went to Camp Valcartier to take part in the formation of 2R22eR. In mid summer 1949, I went down the St. Lawrence to spend my leave *en famille* with my mother. Thus I met a young debutante from Montreal who spent the summers at her parents' summer cottage at the same place, about 400 miles from Montreal and St. Jean. Every subsequent weekend of the summer of 1949 that I could get away, I would drive those 400 miles to arrive late Friday evening to see her. We would swim and dance together on Saturday and be together all day Sunday until I would leave around 2100 hours to drive all night all the way back to St. Jean. And then put in a full day's work on Monday.

But we had a falling out at the end of the summer.

I did not allow the fact that I was in love with her and that she was now in love with me to have the slightest bearing on my desire for active service – and so leave her, as I did. But I did not wish the manner of my leaving to be as cruel as it was. When 2R22eR left Camp Valcartier by train for Fort Lewis, Washington (en route to Korea) at the beginning of November 1950, I, as adjutant, knew that the train would pause in Montreal long enough for a last good-bye in the station. The colonel arranged for Mme Dextraze to meet him there. I did not do the same. My reason was simple and cold-blooded: the men had not been told that there would be an opportunity in Montreal for a last hug, and I was not going to take for myself so very great a privilege that was denied them. Some time after we had arrived in Fort Lewis, Dextraze told me that his wife had run into my girlfriend in Montreal. She mentioned having met her husband in the station. *Of course* I should have phoned and told her of the train pausing in the Montreal station and explained to her that while the CO could have his wife meet him there, it would be most unfair to the troops for the lowly captain-adjutant to do so also. After all, the company commanders – majors – with wives in Montreal would not be met by their wives.

I know that she married after two or three years, but I do not know whether she ended up as happily as I did. She deserved that *infinitely* more than I.

The Second Battalion, R22eR arrived in Fort Lewis in Washington State to complete its training in the late autumn of 1950. When the RSM handed the 1,300 men on parade over to me (as adjutant), and I had fallen in the officers, I about-turned to hand over to Dextraze. Finding him not there, highly unusual, I wheeled around again, stood the reinforced battalion at ease, and marched smartly off the square to get behind the nearest hut where I promptly lost my breakfast, having had far too much to drink the previous evening. Then, moving even more smartly because I could see the CO approaching, I got back in front of the reinforced battalion just in time, brought it to attention, about-turned again and, sweating profusely, handed his battalion over to the Colonel. Later Dextraze told me that he could see that I was having a little trouble, and that was why he had delayed his entry on to the parade square.

On 1 December 1950, Colonel Dextraze appointed me to command support company, with my relinquishing the appointment of adjutant the previous day. On 13 December, HQ 25 Canadian Infantry Brigade (CIB), acting on Dextraze's request, recommended my promotion to acting major effective the date of my being given command of support company. On 18 December, Colonel T.A. Johnston, D Pers (Director of Army Personnel), noting that I was recommended as ready for immediate promotion on my last confidential report, asked the army to give favourable consideration to the recommendation. But things soon turned around.

On 21 December, the director of infantry in Ottawa, Colonel R. Rowley, wrote the director of personnel requesting that "the proposed promotion of this officer should NOT be concurred in." He pointed out that I was "a very junior captain in the RCIC with a total of 98 officers senior to him. The following bilingual officers are senior to him, have been recommended for immediate promotion and are considered suitable for regimental duty in the rank of major." The blacked-out list that followed contained two names, one of which I could make out, that of an R22eR captain who was promoted to that rank on 1 May 1945, the same day I was.

The AG's message of 28 December was clear: "Reference promotion of ZD 220 Capt WH Pope. This promotion is not repeat not concurred in. Capt Pope is a very junior captain in the RCIC [infantry] [with] a total of 98 officers senior to him." Then another officer, not then with 2R22eR, was recommended to be promoted in my place.

On 9 January 1951, HQ 25 CIB's answering message stated CO 2R22eR preferred not to have the officer whom Ottawa recommended and then added:

> OC R22eR considers Pope has necessary qualifications to command Support Company and again requests promotion to the acting rank of major be considered. This Headquarters concurs in the recommendation of the Officer Commanding R22eR.

Colonel T.A. Johnston replied for the AG on 15 January:

Because of the seniority of Capt W H Pope and after study of reports on this officer it is regretted that his promotion cannot be approved at this time. He has not previously been recommended for accelerated promotion and it is normal to secure confirming recommendation from sources other than the first before taking promotion action.

Then Ottawa came up with another captain whom it considered more suitable.

HQ 25 CIB made a third attempt on 23 January. After stating that CO R22eR preferred not having Ottawa's second suggested officer under his command, the message continued:

Recommend Pope be carried [on the battalion's establishment] as Support Coy Comd in rank of capt for 6 months and recommendation for promotion to A/maj be considered at that time.

Ottawa replied on 26 January by noting again that this was the first recommendation for my accelerated promotion and then adding: "Promotion to acting rank of major or appointment to cover major vacancy will not repeat not be made at this time in view of low seniority." And the message concluded by stating that the second captain whom Dextraze had turned down was being promoted to major and was being posted to 2R22eR to take over the company that I had been commanding for two months.

But before Dextraze had to give up his attempts to get me promoted, my two-month appointment as OC Support Company meant that during January 1951, which 2R22eR spent under canvas in the field, I was swanning around in the Bren-gun carriers of the Mortar, Anti-Tank, and Carrier platoons. Since it was cold and wet all the time and the MO's tent was warm and dry, support company very quickly had about 30 men reporting to the company orderly corporal at reveille to go on sick parade. Just as quickly, I told the company that for the sick parade I would be the COC. But no one wished to see me at 0600 hours, so I never did get to fill in the sick parade forms. And support company's sick parade dropped to zero.

AHQ having posted in a major to fill the vacancy Colonel Dextraze had wished me to fill, I relinquished command of Support Company and reverted to second-in-command "A" Company under

Major Roland Reid, MC. At the same time I was named mess secretary, an administrative job that did not please me at all. But when the Colonel told me 2R22eR would hold a mess dinner to which we would invite the Brigade Commander, Brigadier Rockingham, I decided at least the wines would be done properly. So I shoved off on my motorcycle in search of a liquor store and came back with enough brandy, port, Burgundy, and sherry to look after the hard drinkers of the 2nd Van Doos. I also arranged with the American staff-sergeant running the local officers' club for the use of the premises for the night of the mess dinner.

I knew that in the US Army, unlike in Commonwealth Armies, a staff-sergeant or other NCO in charge anywhere can tell an officer of any rank to lump it and get away with it. I was to be given a good demonstration of this. But on first meeting this staff-sergeant, when he suggested to me that he would supply the waitresses, I at once gratefully agreed. Damned if I was going to train a half-dozen or more of our infantrymen how to wait on tables: they hadn't joined the Special Force for that.

The big night arrived and before the soup had been drunk and the second course brought in, I noticed somewhat more camaraderie between the subalterns – practically all of whom were not Regular Army but had joined for Korea – and the servers than had occurred at our previous meals. The fact that this evening's servers were attractive nubile young women made a difference – as anyone except a mess secretary who didn't want the stupid job could have foreseen. In any case, it was about now I decided that if anyone was going to stay stone cold sober this night, it had better be me.

Suddenly, the mess president, Major Gilles Lamothe, got on his hind feet and gave the command, "Mr Vice, the King." At which the mess vice-president would be getting to his feet and loudly saying, "Gentleman, the King." At which everyone would stand and drink the Sovereign's health. But as soon as Gilles Lamothe had given his command, I bounded to my feet and shouted in French, "You damn fool, we don't drink the King's health in Burgundy!" For that's where we were in the meal, long before the dessert, after which the table would be cleared of everything but the port glasses and decanter.

My remonstrance was quite without the effect I desired, for the Colonel said, "*Pope, assieds-toi!*" ("Pope, sit down!") The trouble was the Brigadier, the Colonel, and the rest of the head table wanted to smoke and this can't be done before the Sovereign's health is drunk. That's the only bit of protocol that went right that evening.

Dinner at last over, someone got the juke box going and the subalterns started dancing with the waitresses. This not being part of the drill for mess dinners, I went around parting the partners telling the waitresses that they should make dates for the next evening; but dancing with the officers as part of a mess dinner? Well, no. One waitress told me she would dance with me first – to which I replied she wasn't supposed to dance with anyone. Another waitress told me the next night wouldn't do since she had a date with her fiancé then. I did not then know that this fairly casual attitude to being engaged was going to be helpful to me quite soon.

Suddenly, the lights went out. I at once went to the staff-sergeant's office to see what the trouble was, pointing out to the staff-sergeant that I had reserved the club for the night. "I'm not going to hang around all night watching a bunch of drunks," he replied. The Colonel now having arrived, I passed on this bit of information. The CO grabbed the phone to talk to the American Brigadier-General commanding Fort Lewis. The staff-sergeant, who had already phoned for the U.S. Military Police to come and clear us all out, then pulled the phone wires off the wall to prevent Colonel Dextraze getting through to the Camp Commander. I went in search of another phone, found it, and got *our* Military Police to arrive just as the American crew turned up ready to do their duty. It was an interesting confrontation in the middle of what had been the dance floor: each Army's Military Police lined up in a single rank, facing each other, night sticks drawn, waiting for the signal for the Battle of Fort Lewis to begin.

But it didn't. Somehow Colonel Dextraze got through to the Camp Commander who gave us until 0100 hours. The lights then went back on and the MPs, both sets, stood down and marched back out side-by-side.

I don't recall any subsequent remarks by Colonel Dextraze concerning my organization of our one and only Fort Lewis mess dinner. No congratulations at any rate.

While we were in Fort Lewis, the *Ballets de Paris* turned up in Seattle. Since they were as *splendide* as in Montreal in February (when I went with young X), I had no trouble getting Major Muck Richard to go with me this time around. It was, in fact, the two prima ballerinas who were truly *splendide, magnifique* – sexy as hell, to get to the point – namely Jeanmaire and Colette Marchand. Thus, as soon as the curtain came down, Richard and I were backstage and into their dressing-room. A fellow was there, whom I ignored. I later found out he was Roland Petit, the owner of the ballet company and husband of either Jeanmaire or Colette Marchand. It made no difference: both refused to go out with me – *un Français comme moi* (a Frenchman such as I). I had hoped, of course, that the famous *fraternité* of *La Marseillaise* would have done the trick. It didn't and as we left the theatre, without a cat in sight, it occurred to me – too late, as usual – that I might have done better making a play for one of the *corps du ballet*. I couldn't have done worse. On the other hand, who else has gone into the dressing-room of the two prima ballerinas of the day and asked each in turn to go out with him?

At about this time, on 11 January 1951, my father wrote me as follows:

> I just had a letter from Brigadier Harold Cameron, at Army Headquarters, part of which reads as follows:
>
> 'I understand that the Minister [Brooke Claxton] has told you of the very fine work which your boy is doing with 2nd Bn of the Royal 22nd. I saw the unit on parade with the Minister and in the opinion of all those I spoke to it was the smartest and fittest looking unit there. Brigadier-General Watson, the Commander at Fort Lewis, particularly mentioned it to me, and the officers of the 22nd both 1st and 2nd Bns give the most credit to your boy for this state of affairs.'
>
> This is very nice indeed for your parents to read and I congratulate you most heartily.

About this, I wrote my mother on 20 Jan 1951:

It is agreeable to receive so much praise from the Minister and Brigadier Cameron through the agency of my parents. But don't forget that when I disappeared in May 1944 you then also received high praise concerning me. Really one would have said I was the lieutenant the most esteemed for bravery at the Front in the whole Canadian Army. However, when I returned two months later, only the British thought of mentioning me in despatches. [My second MiD was, it seems, for my services in December 1944. And was published in the London Gazette long after the war was over, on 4 April 1946. Talk about an afterthought!]

So, don't believe a hundredth part of it. I know what I'm worth because I know what I do. The Minister is a politician and it's his business to be flattering about sons when he meets their parents. Brigadier Cameron is a friend of my father's: it's not necessary to say more. When something about me arrives at AHQ, it's a rule that it must go to the Adjutant-General himself. So it was General Macklin that said no to my promotion – and he's a friend of Papa.

I don't say this with bitterness. Quite the contrary. Only understand well that when you hear praise concerning me, it's done to make you happy and not because the flatterer is convinced I deserve his praise. As for me, I don't give a damn what people think of me. I have my aim in life clearly before me and I will arrive thanks to my own efforts.

I was right to discount the Minister's praise. No account whatsoever was taken of it and my service in action from 17 May 1944 to 1 January 1945 when Ottawa now got all upset over the following episode. It was simply mentioned in passing that I had served in Italy and Northwest Europe. For all the good my service in action and with 2R22eR did me, I might as well have been running the officers' club in Rome.

I should at least have spent an hour or so in church on Good Friday 1951. Instead, I spent a good part of the day in a Seattle Rathskeller. On re-entering my hotel (a second-class one, the first-class hotels were full of automobile conventioneers), I passed a meeting room with about 50 people in it and with a big sign up on the wall: "HANDS OFF KOREA." Being slated for Korea in about three weeks, I asked the man at the door if this was a Republican meeting, the Republicans being very critical of Truman's war.

"No," he replied. "It's Socialist Workers Party of America, Trotskyist." Not having had a good political discussion in a long time, I asked: "May I sit down with the proletariat?" "Yes, for thirty-five cents."

After about two hours of Comrade Joe Hansen's speech – he being the leader and a secretary to Trotsky when the latter got a Stalinist icepick in the back of the head in Mexico a decade earlier, I turned and noticed a very young blonde with glasses sitting at the back of the room. "A beauty with brains!" By now having had more than my fill of Comrade Joe, I switched all my attention to the young beauty. The only way to get to know her was to stick around.

At midnight, sitting in a restaurant with about a dozen Trotskyists, all of them seemingly a little uncomfortable at having a soldier in uniform in their midst, I was not able to get Colleen's address and could not do better than find out where the Trotskyists would be meeting the next evening: a Saturday-night social in a black woman's house.

For the Trotskyist social, I polished the buttons of my service dress and turned up, Sam Browne belt and all. As the evening wore on Colleen and I were in the pantry looking sufficiently happy with each other that our hostess suggested that we might be yet happier upstairs. Agreeing, we had hardly got there before we heard a loud voice downstairs asking for Colleen. "My fiancé!" It seems that the wretched band in which her fiancé played the drums quit at 0100 hours. Hearing his footsteps on the stairs, Colleen got behind the door while I sat at the window as though I had just come up for a breath of fresh air. "Have you seen Colleen?" he asked. I replied, "Who's Colleen?" "Beautiful blonde with glasses and long hair." "Oh, yes, I've seen her around." The lad shoved off to continue his search, followed, at a discreet interval, by his fiancée.

Of course, with all this, I still had not obtained Colleen's address. Nothing for it but to go to a Unitarian church next morning, Sunday, to hear Comrade Joe's lecture, "The Agrarian Reform Movement in China," this being Mao Tse-tung's takeover. This paid off: Colleen agreed to a date the next Saturday evening, when her fiancé's band had another gig.

Next morning, back in Fort Lewis, I said to the CO, Colonel Dextraze, "I'd better tell you what I've been doing over the week-end before the FBI tells the Adjutant-General. Ha-Ha." The most prophetic joke that I ever made in my life.

Two days later, Colonel called a mess meeting and told the officers that the mess would throw a thank-you party on Saturday for our American hosts in view of 2R22eR's imminent departure for Korea. "All officers will attend," concluded the CO. *"Tous les officiers?" ("All* officers?") I asked, horrified. "No, no, all except those that have a date with a Trotskyist blonde."

The U.S. mail service seems to have had my complete confidence, for in the six days from Sunday to the next Saturday when we had a date, I wrote Colleen to ask her if we could meet at 6:30 p.m. rather than at the 8 agreed on. She replied on 29 March:

> I do not have time now to argue the political questions you raised in your letter. I would like, however, to dwell briefly on your rather erroneous conception of Marxist morals. If Marxists had no sense of moral values, why would they devote themselves to the cause of socialism? Marxists reject absolute moral and ethical values; the idea that such values are valid for all times and all peoples and classes. One does not find universal agreement when it comes to the *concrete* application of certain abstract moral concepts which are regarded as universal principles. If you ever get around to it, read Trotsky's *Their Morals and Ours*, which, I understand, takes up this very question. (It is rather presumptuous of me to recommend a book I have not yet read myself.)
>
> More of this Saturday. It is rather difficult to carry on a political discussion via the U.S. mails. I am sorry, but I'll not be able to meet you at 6:30. 8:00 will have to remain the hour.
>
> I trust you are not offended by my crass breach of etiquette in writing in pencil rather than ink. I set very little stock in rules of etiquette (and besides I have lost my pen). Some people make a fetish of such rules and lose sight of the original purpose of them, which is simply consideration of other people, and the rules become an end in themselves.
>
> *Auf Wiedersehen*, then, until Saturday

The date went well. But I never saw Colleen again. I had her address, of course, but I had no wish to tell her of the events of the next few weeks and months.

Two or three days after my date with Colleen, Dextraze told me that he had been told by Brigadier Rockingham, Commander of 25 CIB, to parade me to him immediately. "I think you're in trouble."

Although most of 2R22eR – all the officers certainly – had heard of my two Trotskyist week ends, Rockingham was learning of it for the first time. "I think you've been a little indiscreet," he said, "I'll phone the Adjutant-General and see what can be done." However, the AG had not yet heard of it either: it had been handled at ministerial level.

I was ordered back to Ottawa to become adjutant of No.1 Army Administrative Unit, the clerks who handled the personnel administration of the AHQ staff. Before I left, Dextraze and I agreed that the affair would probably cost me my commission. "Come back as a private," Dextraze said, "and I'll keep a Company-Sergeant-Major's vacancy open to which I'll promote you as soon as you get back." Years later, General Dextraze told me the Americans really were not concerned by my Trotskyist episode. Maybe he was joking, maybe not. If not, it seems that the FBI has more of a sense of humour than it is usually given credit for.

On arrival in Ottawa (with enough duty-free booze to get me to all the best Ottawa parties for the six weeks that I was there), I was at once up before the adjutant-general. Before I had had time to salute, Major-General Macklin had let fly: "God dammit, Pope, when I used to work for your father I never thought I'd have his son parading up before me like this." The next ten minutes were no better, ending with: "Get out." Colleen was not mentioned. It might have lightened the atmosphere had she been. But probably not.

After a couple of weeks, on 25 April 1951, I wrote Lieutenant-Colonel McClelland, CO 1 AAU:

> I have the honour to request that I be returned to the 2nd Battalion of the Royal 22e Régiment, CASF.
>
> I was posted here on 9 April 1951 as a result of my having openly attended public political meetings in Seattle during the week-end of the 23-25 March 1951. Although I did not disobey KR(Can) 429, I acted without discretion in view of the Leftist character of the political

meetings and the deep concern with which the United States' authorities view the adherents of Leftist doctrines.

I made a full report of my actions during this week-end to my Commanding Officer on 26 March 1951. Since the latter was fully aware of my political opinions, he viewed, rightly, my actions merely as a search for knowledge, and he felt no action was warranted. However, an independent report was made by the responsible United States' agency to Army Headquarters.

It is my understanding that my removal from the Special Force was made necessary by American concern as to my political affiliation. I also understand that as soon as an investigation has revealed that I have no subversive tendencies, there will be no objection to my rejoining the Special Force. I cannot believe that it should take long to establish my loyalty.

My Battalion is en route to Korea. From newspaper reports of the battle now going on there, it is obvious it will have a hard and bloody fight. I feel that being removed from my Battalion ten days before it sails for the Front brings dishonour upon me. I can only be vindicated by serving with my Battalion, and that as soon as possible.

I therefore request that I be reposted to the 2nd Battalion Royal 22e Régiment immediately – if at all possible before it makes contact with the enemy. If it is felt that my continuing interest in political questions renders me a liability in my present rank, I am willing to serve His Majesty in action in whatever inferior rank that may be decided upon.

In the German army my raising the question of honour would have overridden any other consideration. I would have been sent back to 2R22eR as a private immediately, and there, in battle, proved, or not proved, that I was worthy of regaining my commission.

But not in our army. On 8 May 51, the adjutant-general, in his own hand, wrote to the colonel who was director of personnel:

1. I discussed Pope's case with DMI (Director of Military Intelligence) and CGS (Chief of the General Staff).

2. Pope must understand that his status vis-a-vis the Americans is such that it would be an error to send him to Korea in any rank. Nor do I think he can go to the US Zone in Germany. He will have to serve in Canada pro tem.

3. He is to be posted to 1st Bn R22e and should be told to get to work and mind his business in future.

Both of those things I had been doing, as always.

Adjutant 1 AAU was a typical AHQ administrative job with very little to do. I had a lieutenant records officer under me. Either of us could have been let go with not the slightest harm. I soon had my job organized so that I was doing two hours of work a day. My desk was *always* clear at night. One afternoon a file came in at 1600 hours. I completed work on it by 1715 hours, by which time I had been visited by security, unable to understand what an officer could possibly be doing after the 1630 hours quitting time. I spent my considerable free time reading von Clausewitz *On War* and sitting for and passing the captain to major promotion examinations. Also, my friends, after lunching in the Naval Officers' Club, found my office a convenient halfway point to stop for coffee on their way to the La Touraine bar.

In June 1951, I left 1 AAU to go on a six-week summer geography course run by McGill University at Stanstead in the Eastern Townships, before going to the Citadel to join 1R22eR. My room-mate at Stanstead was Captain Reuel H. Pietz of the U.S. Marines. Since our four hours of classes were all in the morning, my MG was useful for investigating pubs in the afternoon. One day we came in for supper later than usual. There were only two seats left at one table; all the other tables were full up. We took the two empty seats, naturally from my point of view at least. When we were the last two left at supper, Reuel suddenly said: "I sat down here to see what it would be like." "What do you mean?" I asked, "There was nowhere else to sit." "But didn't you see the coloured girl at our table?" said Reuel. "Yes, and so what?" I asked. "I've never sat at a table with a Coloured girl before." "Well, Reuel, how was it?" Looking puzzled, Reuel replied, "No different than with anyone else!" Reuel, of course, was from the U.S. South.

On arriving at 1R22eR, I became second-in-command of a rifle company and then, on 11 October 1951, I became the adjutant - my sixth time in such an appointment. As usual, I emptied the orderly room of the extra bodies over establishment whom my predecessors had thought necessary. These extra bodies I sent back to their rifle companies. I also had an assistant adjutant, a militia captain, "called out on active service" from the provincial government, where he was paid $5 a month less, which was why he preferred "being called out." His job was to handle proceedings of any and all boards of inquiry. Within a week of my becoming adjutant, after my assistant had gone home at 1700 hours, I emptied his desk of the five or six proceedings reposing there. I spent about four hours preparing the CO's recommendation on half the proceedings for their transmittal to area HQ, and on the other half I wrote notes to the presidents of the boards telling them what they still had to do to complete their work before I could prepare the CO's recommendation. At once securing the CO's approval, I greeted my assistant next morning with the news that his job was done and that he would be going to the area depot two days hence for release.

Having cleared up the outstanding proceedings of boards of inquiry, I did my damnedest to ensure that no new boards would be needed. I always tried to cut down on useless bumph so that all our energies, especially in the rifle companies, could be spent preparing for war. So I was not a bit happy when I learned that one of our privates had jumped that morning *without* having the benefit of his main chute developing as he went out the doorway of the Dakota: the tape that he had hooked to the static line along the ceiling of the plane had been cut. I know that I was not in his stick but I do not recall if I had jumped earlier or was down for a later one. Thus I missed his free fall of several hundred feet before he pulled the rip cord on his reserve chute (worn tight up against the belly) and ended up coming down nice and easy like the rest of us. Those who had seen it all believed that the soldier had cut the tape himself so that he would have the thrill of a free fall, a bit of an extra risk at our jump height of a thousand feet: without a parachute, you hit the ground in ten seconds. This means that you must pull the rip cord within five seconds to get the chute to open completely before the ground comes up.

Now, our friend had patted his reserve chute before boarding the Dak as though to say that this was what was going to get him down safely. So I had the private in, told him that we thought he had cut the tape himself, told him that I did not wish to set up a board of inquiry, asked him to *please* fess up and say that he had cut the tape, and that would be the end of it: he would not be charged. But the lad was not a fool.

I tried for a week to get the lad to admit that he had cut the tape. No luck. And when the colonel asked me how the board of inquiry was coming along and I had to tell him it was not, I then set up the board. I do not remember the results, except that our free-faller was not charged. The only possible result, then, after a long investigation working all the way back to Rivers where ordnance packed the chutes, was that the tape was cut somehow, somewhere, by someone unknown, with no one suspected.

In the Regiment we weren't worried: we *knew* what had happened. Of course, without our quasi-certitude we would have been very concerned. The drill in going out the Dak's door was to count three seconds ("one thousand, two thousand, three thou…"). If you got all the way to "three thousand" without your chute opening, you looked up. If you saw nothing there, you pulled the rip cord on the reserve chute at once. If you had a streamer (an improperly developed or opened chute) you tugged at the cords for a second or so. If that didn't work, you pulled the rip cord on the reserve chute and tried to guide it so that it would not wrap itself around that damned streamer. The whole point was not to panic but follow the drills. Of course, if the reserve chute *did* wrap itself around the main chute, you could go ahead and panic as much as you liked: whatever you did in the next three or four seconds made no difference. In any case it was: "Good-by, Charlie Brown."

Since I had been told that I would have to serve a full tour, two years, in Canada before I could again be considered for overseas service, I wrote the CO, Lieutenant-Colonel L.F. Trudeau, as follows on 19 October 1951:

> I have the honour to set before you certain facts which I think have bearing on my future employment.
>
> Since the end of the Second World War I have many times asked for posting to areas outside of Canada where I could serve His Majesty more actively than permits peace-time soldiering within my own country. I have been motivated by the conviction that service in action is the highest privilege and duty of citizenship.

However, my interest in military service is equalled by my interest in politics. I see no contradiction in this. I use 'politics' in its highest sense: the art of government. If I had not thought that eventually I would again have the opportunity of serving in the field, I would have quit the Army in 1945. To remain in the Army merely for the sake of a comfortable job and a secure pension is a miserable fraud upon one's country. As my hope of active service wanes, my desire to serve my country in a political capacity grows.

It is ironic that my attending political meetings so shortly before I was due to sail for an active theatre – when my interest in political affairs should certainly have been at an ebb – should result in the denial to me of my long awaited opportunity for action. Be that as it may, it now appears that American displeasure with and distrust of my openly attending Marxist meetings in uniform carries more weight with the military authorities of my country than my own record of complete loyalty to the Sovereign.

I have stated that to me so-called military service without prospect of action is dishonourable.

With my military career blocked, I propose to continue in my hope of serving my country, but in other fields. However, my formal education is inadequate at present. With the object of improving it I attended McGill University Summer Geography School three months ago. I have now made arrangements to attend Laval University during the evening. But this is too slow. It is too late for me to attend McGill University full-time this year. But I do wish to attend the Summer School again next year and then to attend the University itself starting in September 1952.

I therefore request that I be granted indefinite leave of absence without pay and allowances effective the 1st July 1952. Leave rather than outright release would permit my recall at any time that it was thought the possibility of full-scale war with the Soviet Union and a revised estimate of my military usefulness outweighed the suspicion of the FBI.

If the privilege of leave without pay is not to be granted me, I request that I be transferred to the Reserve Force, or failing this, to the Supplementary Reserve. If it is not felt that I should be granted one or the other of the three alternatives I suggest, I request that His Excellency the Governor-General's consent be sought to my outright release from His Majesty's service.

I would deeply regret thus temporarily quitting the service of my country, but I think that the academic training I would then be able to obtain in full measure would, in three years, increase greatly my usefulness to my country in any political or public capacity.

Within a month my letter reached the adjutant-general within, which moved him to write his old friend, my father, on 20 November. After listing my indiscretions, the AG wrote: "Since then he has agitated to get to Korea and even wanted to revert to the ranks to get there. This is a great pity because, except for these incidents his career in the Army has been a successful one. He has done good work and had several really excellent reports. His brains and leadership are not in question. His C.O. [Dextraze] released him under protest." Macklin consented to my going to Korea.

Harry Pope, aged 14 at Blackfriars School, England, 12 April 1937.

Harry Pope as an RMC cadet, summer 1941.

The Royal Military College Class of 1941.
Harry Pope is in the third row, sixth from the left.

Harry Pope with his father (left) and mother (above) in Washington, Spring 1943. Harry's father, Maurice, was Vice Chief of Staff of the Canadian Army in the Second World War.

Corporal Lachance being carried on a door by five of the POWs captured by 17 platoon, "D" Company, Royal 22e Régiment, 17 May 1944.

Above left: An October 1998 view of the château of Campiglioni, abandoned some years after 1944.

Above right: Signora Georgio Garabelli being presented with a silver tray from my father, by a Canadian Lieutenant-Colonel in the Fall of 1944. She provided invaluable help during my escape from German captivity.

Right: A memorial to some of the victims of the Nazi retaliations at Montemignaio. The boy, Raffaello Mugnaini, aged 15, is at the top of the list.

Below: The altar of the church in Montemignaio. On these steps were laid the bodies of the ten men and one boy massacred by the Germans in reprisal on 20 June 1944.

Left: The path we took coming down from the woods on 10 July 1944. We took our boots off and crept very quietly in our stockings since there was a German field kitchen on both sides of the path. The shrubs hid us.

Below: The end of the path we took on 10 July 1944. On the left of the photo can be seen the top of the monument. It was on the road, in front of this spot, that I placed the bomb – 10 pounds of explosives.

After Lieutenant-General E.L.M. Burns, GOC 1st Canadian Corps, learned that I had rejoined my regiment, he invited me to lunch at his headquarters. He asked me if I wished to be his aide-de-camp. I said, "No, sir, I wish to remain with my unit." Five days later the order arrived for me to report to Corps HQ. Here I am in the passenger seat of a staff car with Burns (wearing beret) and Lieutenant-General Sir Oliver Leese, GOC 8th Army, August 1944.

After I'd returned from the German side of the lines and was back commanding 18 platoon, "D" Company, R22eR, I'm telling Colonel J.L. Ralston, Minister of National Defence, that we are short of men. Oct. 1944.

This photo was taken at No.15 Canadian General Hospital in Caserta, Italy while recovering from a broken arm caused by a German bullet. Having read that in the Great War officers dressed like their men so as not to be obvious targets, I went the opposite route and wore britches and puttees.

Another photo taken at No.15 CGH, on 10 February 1945 with some fellow wounded officers. Left to right: D.B. Davidson, 48th Highlanders; Pope; Claude Bouchard, R22eR; Claude Gagnon, R22eR.

"Willie" Pope during his time as Canadian aide-de-camp to the Governor-General, Lord Harold Axexander. Photographed on the steps of Rideau Hall, Pope is in the back row, far left, with the other two ADCs, Squadron Leader Tony Tollemache, GC (next to Pope) and Captain David Lloyd-Thomas, Irish Guards (back row, far right). Lord Alexander is seated, third from the left, while Major-General Harry Letson, Private Secretary is seated second from the right. April 1946.

Pope leading a guard of honour from the 2nd Battalion, Royal 22e Régiment for Field Marshal Lord Alexander at the Québec Citadel, September 1950.

Pope escorting Alexander during an inspection.

Above: The clan McClusky in regimental garb for a Saturday night party: (l. to r.) Captain W.H. Pope, Adjutant, Fort Churchill; Mr. Kissick, US technologist studying permafrost; Major R.C. Faylor, CO, US Army Detachment, Fort Churchill; Inspector A.W. Parsons, RCMP (he was on board the supply ship *Nascopie* when it sank at the north end of Hudson's Bay and was with us for several weeks until Ottawa heard about the sinking).

Right: A McClusky (Pope) indulges in one of the clans favourite pastimes – chewing a mukluk to soften it, just like the Eskimos. Captain Crumlisch, US Army, sits with Pope.

Above: Fort Churchill,
Winter 1948. (l. to r.)
Lieutenant-Colonel James
Tedlie, Commandant;
Garrison Sergeant-Major
M.J. Gallon; Captain W.H.
Pope, Adjutant.

Left: Getting my
parachutist's wings, Shilo,
Manitoba, May 1950.

Top: In Korea at "A" Echelon, 1R22eR, May 1952: (l. to r.) Captain G. Vaugeois, 2ic "D" Company; Captain Pope, Adjt; Lieutenant W.E. Ismnd, A/Adjt.

Above: Field Marshal the Earl Alexander of Tunis inspecting 1R22eR guard of honour commanded by Captain Pope, in almost his last job as adjutant (before getting command of "C" Company. Korea, August 1952.

Right: Pope in the CO's caravan in reserve, shortly before re-entering the line, August 1952.

Three views of the "C" Company, 1R22eR position on Hill 159, September 1952. The photo at the top shows a bunker destroyed by an enemy shell marked with the sign "TERMITES."

Right: This photo shows me wielding a shovel helping to build the strongest command post in the Commonwealth Division. I had nothing better to do at that moment and why shouldn't the company commander work like everyone else? As the French say: *"Il n'y a pas de fous metiers."* ("There are no foolish – unworthy – jobs."). October 1952 on the crest of Hill 210.

Below: The enemy being out of range of my 60 mm mortars, Lieutenant Bruce Rutherford allowed me to be his gunner and shoot at the Chinese working on a tunnel across the Sami-chon, Januvary 1953.

Above left: Out of the line in Korea, 20 February 1953. Infantry-tank co-operation exercise.

Above right: Demonstrating a trip flare to some members of a patrol course. HQ 25 Canadian Infantry Brigade, June 1953.

Below: An observation post of "C" Company, 3R22eR, at the beginning of August 1953 (after the armistice). Left to right: Major Pope; L/Cpl A. Martel; Pte. Hochey; Pte. G. Guenette; Lieutenant J.H.A Berard.

Getting the Military Cross ribbon pinned on by Major-General Michael Alston-Roberts-West, GOC 1st Commonwealth Division, 2 June 1953. During the presentation, he said to me, "This is the best one you'll ever get!" I replied, "It is, sir."

Arrogant to the last! This photo was taken in July 1959 after I had resigned, but before its effective date of 15 August 1959.

Left: Harry and his son Richard playing hockey on the pond at Uxbridge, Winter 1986.

Below: Harry and Sheila Kathleen, along with Brigadier-General Marcel Richard, at a R22eR reunion, July 1989.

Chapter Eight

Company Commander

As captain-adjutant of 1R22eR, I arrived in Korea with the other elements of the advance party on 29 March 1952. I spent four months looking after bumph at "A" Echelon.

On 12 August 1952, with the battalion short a major, Colonel Trudeau entrusted command of his old company in Italy, "C" Company, to me, an act for which I will always be infinitely grateful. I continued to command "C" Company (as acting major from late March 1953) until the end of September 1953, since I had asked to stay in Korea until the war ended. When the 3rd Battalion replaced the 1st in April 1953, I transferred from the 1st to the 3rd, while keeping my company, now made up mostly of men who had just arrived with Colonel Poulin.

In mid-August, "C" Company entered the line for a couple of months' stints. For the first two weeks, we faced the enemy to the north with four platoons in line, the fourth being the pioneer platoon commanded by Lieutenant Paul LaFlèche, youngest brother of Fritz, who had commanded 17 and 18 platoons, alternating with me, in Italy eight years earlier.

In March 1939, having just attained the age of 16, I had joined a militia field artillery battery. Now, in August 1952 I was proud to have in hand my own battery: my four 60 mm mortars. So, shortly after our arrival in line, when Lieutenant LaFlèche on patrol at night told me on the wireless that he was facing a small enemy group, I was delighted to have my battery join in by ordering it to fire on one of the DF/SOS (immediate defensive fire) tasks that I had already registered. Having done this, I corrected the fire as LaFlèche requested the changes. The skirmish lasted a couple of hours, with no losses on our side; as for the enemy, I have no idea, except that it must have got pretty fed up with 60 mm mortar bombs.

Naturally, it did not take two hours for Trudeau to wonder why all this noise was coming from "C" Company. But, unfortunately, I had learned that when an artillery FOO was busy giving fire orders to his guns, all he had to say was "On fire orders, Out!" so that even the field-marshal C-in-C had to leave him in peace to carry on with his job. Also, in the situation facing LaFlèche, I saw no role for our 81 mm mortars or for our 25-pounder guns – the enemy was too close. Finally, I did not wish to miss a single request for support from LaFlèche. So, for two hours Trudeau heard nothing from me and all that my well-trained signalers would say to him was: "The captain is on fire orders. Out!"

It is perhaps understandable that after two hours the CO began to find that answer boring. So, when everything had quieted down, the enemy back home probably sufficiently deafened by the explosion of our bombs, I phoned the colonel to make my report. He demanded to know: "For whom do you think you're working?" "For 'C' Company, Sir," I replied. "No, you're working for me!"

It continued more or less like that for several months, until the battalion got all its seven majors back on board. At that, I became much more polite: the CO could have replaced me at the head of "C" Company far too easily! Because my date with the Trotskyist blonde in Seattle in March 1951 upset the FBI, I had lost 14 months seniority and did not get promoted to major until March 1953. But it is essential that I insist here on the enormous esteem that I had then, and have always kept, for Colonel Trudeau. I was fortunate in having had as my superiors these five colonels of R22eR: Allard, Turcot, Dextraze, Trudeau, and Poulin. Much more fortunate with them than with the brigadiers and generals with whom I dealt, or rather, I suppose, who dealt with me.

A few nights after LaFlèche's skirmish, a corporal in the outpost of my platoon farthest to the left (or west) asked me for mortar fire, since he believed that he was being approached by an enemy patrol. I asked him if he was certain that the enemy was there. On his "yes," I ordered the firing of his outpost's DF/SOS. After a short time, the corporal told me that he was satisfied.

It was always in the afternoon that I made the daily round of my platoons: we were all up the whole night through, and we slept in the morning after sunrise. So, that afternoon following the affair of the outpost, I discussed it with the corporal. He reproached me for having asked him the previous night if he was certain that the enemy was there. He was right to do so, and I do not believe that I insulted one of my subordinates the same way again. The corporal was infinitely more polite than I would have been in similar circumstances. If my superior had asked me what I had asked the corporal, I believe – I hope – I would have replied: "******, if you think the enemy isn't in front of me, come and have a look here yourself instead of sitting on your arse in your CP safe from bullets and shells!"

But I too had a reproach to make to the corporal – though, granted, much less serious. In Korea, there were only two French-speaking battalions, ours and one from France. So that the enemy would not know that it was facing either of us, it was forbidden to speak French on the wireless. Well, the corporal had spoken to me in French. "Why?" I asked him. "I didn't have time to find the English words," the corporal replied. Then he added, "but I spoke with an English accent!"

Almost half a century too late it has occurred to me that I was far too passive in merely defending my outposts with 60 mm mortar bombs. What I should have done was to have my reserve platoon commander take over my CP and control of my mortars while I went at once to the area of suspected enemy presence. And then gone forward from there to attempt to get behind the enemy patrol, if it existed. I would, of course, have told the platoon commander there what I would be doing and have him ready to join me with a section should I find any enemy and decide how best it could be attacked. Granted, my deafness would have placed me at a disadvantage but I would have had surprise on my side: the enemy would not have been expecting an active defence: we had never done it. The enemy certainly did defend actively. And it is my experience of this that shows me, belatedly, what we should have done when the enemy approached us.

But in August 1952, I had had no experience in defence: in Italy we were attacking and advancing all the time until we got to the Senio, and within a couple of days of reaching that obstacle I was on my way to a couple of months in hospital. Of course, the previous paragraph may appear to be the nostalgia of an old man dreaming of what might have been. But there *is* a principle involved: never forgo an opportunity to inflict the maximum possible casualties on the enemy with the least risk to one's own troops. And surely it is obvious that attacking a small enemy patrol close to one's own lines is far more likely to be successful, *costlessly*, than would be an attack on the superbly well-constructed enemy positions themselves.

After a couple of weeks in the line, the CO decided to have "C" Company replace the company that was occupying the most advanced position: the famous Hill 159 (metres). "C" and the company that had been occupying 159 for two weeks switched positions, not the easiest manoeuvre, given that both were already on the frontline.

Thus on the September evening of the relief of the company on Hill 159, at dusk, I was in the communication trench that led to the most advanced position, which 7 platoon of Sergeant Bruno Bergeron, MM, was to occupy for the next month. All was going well, and I thought that the whole platoon had gone forward, when the platoon's laggard arrived. Seeing me, he announced: "I'm not going any farther."

Fortunately, I was in good humour, and I had nothing better to do at the moment than to engage one of my soldiers in a long discussion concerning his responsibilities towards his comrades-in-arms of 7 platoon, which was already reduced to half strength.

Unfortunately, it was the rainy season and the dialogue had barely begun when it started to rain. Papasan, the old Korean who helped out in our kitchen (receiving food in exchange, and ten or so real American dollars from me from time to time) had just finished washing and pressing the uniform that I was wearing.

Obviously, after a half-hour of solid Korean rain, we looked like a couple of drowned rats. I could have placed the man under arrest for having refused an order from his superior officer in the face of the enemy – a capital offence at the time, I believe. Certainly, it would have cost him 90 days in the clink: the British "glass-house" in Seoul, which was not a place of rest. But I have always preferred to settle matters in-house.

Thus, after a half-hour, the laggard must have realized that he was dealing with an idiot ready to spend the night chatting amicably with him in the rain. So he said to me: "I'm going forward."

It was *his* decision. I did not force him to go by hitting him with my fists or by threatening him with my Luger, either of which I would certainly have done rather than send him before a court-martial. And because it was *his* decision, he could rejoin his platoon without feeling humiliated, without having in the back of his mind for the rest of his life the belief that he had acted in a cowardly fashion.

So, when a few days later, the company needed a storeman at "A" Echelon he was the one whom I sent back. He had lifted himself up once and he had done his duty. Everyone has a breaking point; his was lower than most. It would have served no purpose, either for the company or for the soldier, to force him to that point.

But the way in which one deals with a soldier lacking a little in courage must be totally different from the way one treats an officer also so lacking. And by that I do not mean that the officer is sent on leave or on a rest cure as an instructor somewhere in the rear. Even less do I mean that the cowardly officer should be returned to Canada to become an instructor of recruits, with a promotion because of his battlefield experience! That is what happened regularly during the Second World War.

Compare that to the fate of 7 platoon's laggard. If I had wished to behave stupidly with him and gone by the book: minimum of 90 days, very hard detention, followed by an ignominious discharge from the army.

The officer who cannot do his duty in the face of the enemy must be kicked out immediately, either by court-martial, or, if one wishes to be soft-hearted, by forcing him to resign his commission. Nothing is worse than to give such an individual a second chance: the cowardly lieutenant will become the cowardly company commander and the cowardly battalion commander. At each higher level, he will do more and more harm.

I know that one does not wish to be cruel towards a fellow with whom one has often had a drink in the mess. Perhaps he is perfectly charming and has a ravishing wife. Neither factor is of the slightest importance. The fundamental task of the infantry officer is to lead his men against the enemy. If he is not ready to do that at all times, he has no business being in the army. A cowardly infantry officer is a menace for the army and an insult to the troops.

The principle is clear: one encourages the private soldier to do his duty in the face of the enemy; from the officer, it is demanded.

Hill 159 was the most forward of our company positions. The hill made a sort of salient between enemy positions that half surrounded it; they were to the north and to the west. Since the enemy position to the north was on Hill 227, it dominated ours.

We could expect 30 to 50 155 mm or 210 mm shells every afternoon, when the sun was behind the enemy and in our eyes. The enemy was firing on our two tanks, which were on the crest of Hill 159, with my OP between them and my dug-out a few paces down on the reverse slope, but still in view of the enemy on 227.

One day I was brushing my teeth, when it suddenly seemed to me that there was an extra swish mixed in with the one that I was making as I rinsed my teeth. When a mortar bomb exploded a half-second later six feet from me, I realized that I was right. I was not touched, while a few days later, when my runner left my dug-out, he was killed by a mortar bomb landing in the same spot.

Yet I preferred my new position to the one that I had just left. In the old position, as I said, all my platoons were in line, with my CP in the same line. In the event of an enemy attack, I could do nothing except stay in my dug-out, order my mortars to fire, and ask the colonel for the support of the other arms. Certainly, I would not have been able to go to the area being attacked in case another part of our line was attacked in its turn.

But on 159, I had two platoons with me, encircling the hill. And my forward platoon, 7, (about 200 yards closer to the enemy to the west) was commanded by Sergeant Bergeron; in him I had absolute confidence. Therefore, in the event of an enemy attack, I would be able to do more than stay stuck in my OP.

When the enemy would send us our daily ration of shells in the afternoon, I would go to my OP in the hope of being able to determine from where the enemy was firing. After the enemy shelling, I would often go to the dug-out of the senior of the two Lord Strathcona's Horse (LdSH) NCOs commanding the two tanks in locality on Hill 159. These tanks were not under my command, nor were they even, officially, "in support." They were simply there, "in locality," doing what they or their troop commander on another hilltop thought that tanks in hull-down positions should do. Of course, however, since we were all working for Betty, we co-operated. Sergeant Jack (his surname) was the LdSH NCO in charge on 159. And it was precisely because he was not under my command that I liked having my daily single bottle of beer with him: I did not have to concern myself about his morale, as I certainly did about the morale of my lieutenants and every man in their less-than-half-strength platoons. In short, chatting with Sergeant Jack allowed me to put out of my mind my responsibilities for a 1/2 hour out of 24.

One afternoon, the enemy shelling of our two tanks began while I was in my OP. The tanks were all from "B" Squadron and were each given women's names that started with the letter "B." Seeing where the shells were landing, in front of "Bonita," Sergeant Jack's tank, and thinking him in his dug-out, I picked up the field phone and said, "Sergeant Jack, I've got news for you: they're shelling Bonita." "I've got news for you, Sir," Sergeant Jack replied: "I'm inside Bonita." They missed Bonita that day, but a month or two later, when Sergeant Jack was again in Bonita (and "C" Company and I were on Hill 210), a shell stove in the front of the tank, wounding Sergeant Jack in the legs, requiring his evacuation.

As platoon or company commander at the front, my primary preoccupation was always the morale of the soldiers whom I commanded. I was never sure that I was successful in keeping their morale high. However, I think that I did a good job of hiding my worry about this.

I do not believe that I ever thought about the best way of keeping up the morale of my soldiers. Without thinking about it, I always believed it best to tell them the whole truth; to give them always all the information that I had, except during September 1952, when we were on Hill 159. I have already mentioned that I knew that in the event of an enemy attack, the position could not be held with the 50 or 60 men of a "C" Company reduced to less than half its regulation strength. Since my orders were simply to hold the hill, it would have been idiotic of me to tell anyone that the hill could not be held. I took it for granted, since retreat or surrender never entered my mind, that a serious enemy attack meant annihilation.

So, instead of scaring everyone with my knowledge, I spent the daylight hours with my platoons, especially the 7, the forward platoon of Sergeant Bruno Bergeron, when the enemy was dropping its mortar bombs there. Also, from time to time I went on patrol in the daytime, normally alone, forward of our lines, to assure myself that the enemy had done nothing crooked during the night, such as building caves to shelter its assault troops.

One fine afternoon I was strolling thus on one of the salients descending from Hill 159 towards the north when I noticed that an enemy shell was arriving on my salient every two or three minutes. It would fall no closer than 100 yards from me, but close enough to dispose me to go down to the valley floor so that I could then climb up the neighbouring salient. When I noticed shortly thereafter that the shells were now landing on my new salient, I decided that I had seen enough for that day. I thought that it was a bit much to be sniped at by a 105 mm! After all, I passed all the days outside my dug-out not only to keep up the morale of my men but mostly to keep up my own. And I was convinced that a 105 mm exploding next to me when my stroll could wait until tomorrow would not help my morale at all.

When the enemy fired on 7 platoon, usually with mortars, I always went there, thus obeying the lesson that I learned from my father when he took me to Waterloo when I was thirteen. One of Marshall Grouchy's subordinate generals uttered: "*Marchez aux canons!*" ("March to the guns!") - something Grouchy did not do, allowing the Prussian Blucher to turn the day for Wellington.

But one must not think that I found it much fun to be in an open trench with mortar bombs landing around us. Once one has seen what a mortar bomb does when it lands in a trench already occupied by a soldier, one has to be raving mad to find that funny.

One day I was in a trench of 7 platoon with one of its corporals when a mortar bomb landed on the parados two feet from our heads (which had ducked, of course!). In lifting his head, covered with dust and enveloped in smoke, the corporal, grinning, said to me: "That was a close one, Captain!" No doubt, the corporal judged that it could not be very dangerous if the company commander was there with him!

But if the corporal had never seen me in the afternoon during the enemy bombardment, he would not have found it at all funny. His morale would have been low, and he and his comrades would have said to each other: "That ******* of a captain who we have is fine hiding in his dug-out back there, while we get mortared and shelled every day here." And they would have been right to say it.

Since I always liked knowing what was happening on my front, especially whether the enemy was preparing an attack or doing anything else crooked under my nose, one afternoon I invited Bergeron to accompany me on a patrol in front of his platoon. Sharing my curiosity, he did not have to be invited twice.

Both of us armed with rifles, we started down 7 platoon's forward slope facing the enemy. Obviously, because the sun was shining brightly and we were in full view of the enemy and within easy range of its 60 mm mortars, we moved either on all fours or crouched. Both of us, working separately, were looking for signs of the enemy, when I saw directly in front of me at a distance of hardly more than ten yards a rifle slowly appearing from behind a bush.

I aimed a couple of feet behind the rifle of the unknown individual, at the centre of the target, of course, that was the said unknown individual. But since I could not possibly miss at ten yards and since it was certain the enemy had not the slightest chance of firing first, I decided to wait a second before firing. Good thing. The second up, the unknown individual presented himself before the muzzle of my rifle. It was Sergeant Bergeron.

I did not deem it helpful to tell Bergeron that I had been seriously thinking for a second or so of killing him. Our little stroll continued without further incident.

In the afternoon when the sun was in our eyes, the enemy would amuse itself by firing 155 mm or 210 mm shells at us in the hope of hitting one or other of the two tanks that were hull-down on the top of 159. I would then go to my OP, into one of the tanks or into a trench alongside one of the tanks. In each case my aim was to try to sight the enemy guns or at least to choose any enemy target to allow our tanks to reply "by the mouths of their canons." Even if we hit only air on the enemy side, it was more encouraging than to remain at the bottom of our trenches or in our dug-outs, which, in any case, were not proof against heavy shells. In fact, during the month that we were on 159, "C" Company lost on average one man killed or wounded every three days.

The tanks had ten-power scopes. The telescope that I used in my OP or in the trench alongside the tank was 20-power. Therefore, being able to choose targets better than those in the tanks, I often directed the tank fire.

One fine day, Sergeant Bergeron joined in the game and was directing the tank fire while I was in my OP. But he was a little too close to the tank. The muzzle flash burned his eyes. Despite that, he returned to his forward platoon, completely blind, a bandage covering his eyes. He remained thus for two days, commanding his platoon as though nothing unusual had happened to him. But after a couple of days, realizing that he still needed to have his eyes bandaged, I had him evacuated to the RAP. Although I needed him, especially with my company already reduced to less than half strength, I judged that without medical treatment there was a danger that he might become permanently blind. Besides, in remaining completely blind at his post for two days, he had already demonstrated quite extraordinary courage and devotion to duty, and his example continued to inspire his platoon even during his temporary absence.

I was most happy to be present in 1954 in Rideau Hall, when Vincent Massey conferred the Military Medal on Sergeant Bergeron. Later, having attained the rank of RSM, he received his officer's commission and was simultaneously promoted to the rank of captain.

As I have already said, Hill 159, which "C" Company 1R22eR occupied for September 1952, faced the enemy to the north and to the west. Thus we were a salient in the enemy positions which dominated ours, especially from the north, where the enemy occupied Hill 227. The enemy could very well see all my company HQ, which was placed on the reverse slope, just below the crest of 159, between the two tanks that were on the crest itself.

The shells that came our way every afternoon were big ones, either 155 mm or 210 mm, all missed the tanks during this month. But they did not miss the company. The shells landed on the forward trenches in front of the tanks, on my HQ, and at the bottom of the hill, where I would have placed our kitchen, had I wished to find new cooks at the end of each afternoon. The shells also landed in the garbage dumps where we put our empty food tins, because, without a kitchen, we ate only "C" rations. Finally, the shells that did not land in front or on the crest of 159, or again completely at the bottom of the reverse slope, landed in the Rosebowl.

This Rosebowl was a circle of sand, maybe 60 yards in diameter, surrounded, except to the south, by two of my platoons and my HQ. No one strolled there during enemy shelling.

We started our month on 159 with maybe 60 men, half the regulation number. Apparently in the great Ottawa HQ (NDHQ) no one had realized that the departure from the battalion during the summer of the last Korean Special Force volunteers would leave gaps in the autumn. Since the company was losing one man killed or wounded every three days, after a month we were down to 50.

I was perfectly aware that, in the event of an enemy attack, my company would die in place: the position could not be successfully defended by a company at less than half strength. Of course, I did not tell my platoon commanders of my "appreciation of the situation," or the battalion commander. It was not his fault that the imbeciles of Ottawa were unable to count.

There was nothing to be done except to do our duty the best that we could. Among other things, this meant 100 percent stand-to in the trenches all night long: no one slept at night. So, at about 0600 or 0700 hours, after a tin of Spam, it was bedtime. But there again it was the hour of the grand visit of the generals, who all seemed to prefer spending a few minutes at the front line when the enemy had the sun in its eyes and therefore offered no fire.

I was not happy about these visits, probably because the generals always found the same things to criticize in my command: my men had not shaved, there were empty food tins scattered all over our famous Rosebowl, I did not have a steel helmet.

I told them that my whole company, like civilized men everywhere, shaved on getting up early in the afternoon, to the sound of the start of the daily enemy shelling. As for the empty food tins, the generals would have to ask the enemy to stop shelling our garbage dumps. My steel helmet of 19 May 1944 had saved my life on the Hitler Line, but I suppose in Korea I had decided that it was worth it to take a small risk if that made my men a little happier: "It can't be very dangerous, if the captain doesn't wear a helmet!" Or possibly it amused me to be different. Probably mostly that!

Well, one day after another grand visit that had interrupted our breakfast, I decided to settle the matter of the garbage and also indicate to the big chiefs the proper visiting hours.

The next morning, at about 0700 hours, consternation at battalion HQ: Hill 159 is on fire! Is it a surprise enemy attack? I was called to the phone (signallers relaid the wire in the evening after the enemy shelling).

"No," I replied, "everything's fine here."

"And the smoke, then?"

"Yesterday you ordered me to clean up my hill. I'm doing it with my three man-pack flame-throwers. I've torched all the garbage dumps."

"But you're giving away your position to the enemy!"

"It's the enemy that put his ****** shells in our ****** garbage dumps in the first place. The enemy knows well, too well, where we are."

In these days also, I sent a request to the pioneers to make me up a whole pile of signs. I was very happy when they arrived during the night. Early one fine afternoon, with all my signs under my arms, I was standing in the middle of the Rosebowl trying to decide where to place them, the better to annoy our high-priced visitors, when the enemy, who could see me, decided to start the daily shelling.

Exactly as on New Year's Day 1945, when I saw coming the tracer bullet that got me in the arm, I noted that one can think far faster than one can act. On hearing coming the first shell of our daily ration, I had time to think that it was not brilliant of me to get caught like that in full daylight, smack in the centre of where half the enemy shells landed. I hit the ground with such force that I got sand in my teeth – and the shell went down the hill.

I did not wait to see if the enemy would have better luck with its second shell. So, I left the signs where they had followed me to the ground. Happily, the enemy had no luck that afternoon: the signs came through the afternoon untouched, and I had them all in place before dark.

Unfortunately, I can find only one of the photos taken of my signs. It is a dug-out destroyed by an enemy shell. My sign reads: "TERMITES." You understand: I was joking. Next to it was another dug-out destroyed by a shell; my sign read: "MORE TERMITES." (All my signs were in English for the edification of unilingual generals.)

Another indicated where the front was: it had three arrows: one pointed northeast, another northwest, and the third towards the southwest. Didn't I say we were a salient? The one pointing towards the position of Sergeant Bergeron was marked R & R Centre (Rest and Recuperation Centre).

Finally, the biggest and best was aimed precisely at the big chiefs. Very formal, it stated the visiting hours: 1400 to 1600 hours only. Moreover, the sign guaranteed a grand show: large calibre shells and mortar bombs as much as could be desired. Also, it was suggested to the visitors not to be cautious about showing themselves to the enemy: the enemy had a daily ration of shells and bombs reserved for us that we were going to get and that was all there was to it.

I do not believe that my signs had much effect on the generals! But one day while chatting with one of my platoon commanders, I think it was my distant cousin Lieutenant Taschereau, I asked him how it was in his platoon. He replied that it was all right but that his men were concerned that I so much liked making war on 159 that I wanted "C" Company to stay there until the armistice!

On occasion, the signals officer, Lieutenant Ramsey Withers, RC Sigs, accompanied his linesmen when they relaid the telephone line to Hill 159. Extraordinary how even one shell fired at us, although it might do nothing else, would cut our line! Ramsey seemed to like seeing what I was up to and I liked receiving him in what the sign at the door claimed was "A" Mess, shades of my enforced 50 days at corps HQ in the summer of 1944. In fact, it was my dugout with double-deck bunks. The top bunk the sign at the door designated as belonging to the FOO, who, possibly because he realized that a shell landing on my dugout would have spread him in bits halfway across the Rosebowl, preferred sleeping with another company. My sign also indicated that "A" Mess was not quite up to the standard found at corps HQ: guests were advised to bring their mess-tins and their own "C" rations.

Ramsey was a good friend, a graduate of the first RMC class (1948-52) on the reopening of the college. He was kind enough to draw up a citation for me awarding me the HS II (Hot Shit Class Two), "Insufficient Boxtops Submitted for Class One." I was happy that, while I was at the Staff College in 1954, Ramsey invited me to his wedding, which of course I attended. Ramsey eventually became

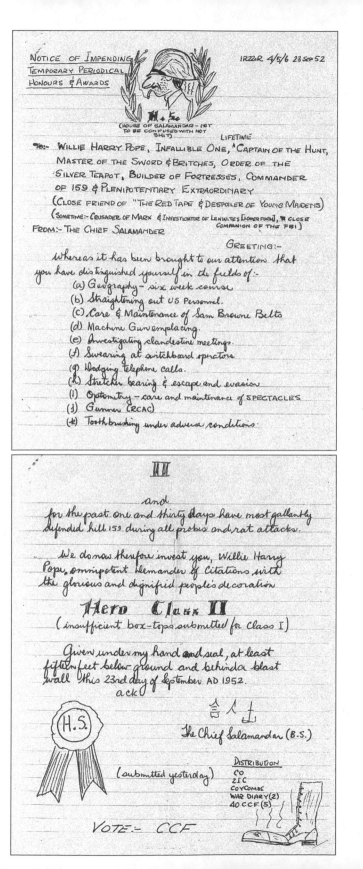

NOTICE OF IMPENDING
TEMPORARY PERIODICAL
HONOURS & AWARDS

IR22&R 4/5/6 23 SEP 52

H.S.
(HOUSE OF SALAMANDER — NOT
TO BE CONFUSED WITH HOT
SHIT)

LIFETIME

To:- WILLIE HARRY POPE, INFALLIBLE ONE, CAPTAIN OF THE HUNT, MASTER OF THE SWORD & BRITCHES, ORDER OF THE SILVER TEAPOT, BUILDER OF FORTRESSES, COMMANDER OF 159 & PLENIPOTENTIARY EXTRAORDINARY

(CLOSE FRIEND OF "THE RED TAPE & DESPOILER OF YOUNG MAIDENS)

(SOMETIME:- CRUSADER OF MARX & INVESTIGATOR OF LENINITES [LOWER FORM], & CLOSE COMPANION OF THE FBI)

FROM:- THE CHIEF SALAMANDER

GREETING:-

Whereas it has been brought to our attention that you have distinguished yourself in the fields of:-

(a) Geography – six week course
(b) Straightening out US Personnel.
(c) Care & Maintenance of Sam Browne Belts
(d) Machine Gun emplacing.
(e) Investigating clandestine meetings.
(f) Swearing at switchboard operators
(g) Dodging telephone calls.
(h) Stretcher bearing & escape and evasion
(i) Optometry – care and maintenance of SPECTACLES
(j) Gunner (RCAC)
(k) Toothbrushing under adverse conditions.

III

and

for the past one and thirty days have most gallantly defended hill 159 during all probes and rat attacks.

We do now therefore invest you, Willie Harry Pope, omnipotent Demander of Citations with the glorious and dignified people's decoration

Hero Class II
(insufficient box-tops submitted for Class I)

Given under my hand and seal, at least fifteen feet below ground and behind a blast wall this 23rd day of September AD 1952.

ack

The Chief Salamander (B.S.)

H.S.

(submitted yesterday)

DISTRIBUTION
CO
2 I C
COY COMDS
WAR DIARY (2)
40 CCF (5)

VOTE:- CCF

Chief of the Defence Staff (CDS). I like to think that his beginning his Regular Force career with 1R22eR set him off on the right track!

On 20 September 1952, I wrote my mother from Hill 159:

> All goes well here. I'm still commanding "C" Company on the front line. We're still occupying a forward position but we'll be going soon to a position a little more in the rear. I'm quite happy, as my men are also. I haven't eaten fresh rations for four weeks and I haven't had a bath in a month and a half.
>
> I don't believe I've been chosen for the Staff College course beginning in January 1953 despite being one of the rare French-speaking officers that passed his entrance exams. This doesn't bother me at all. I hope only that the Adjutant-General doesn't again send a major from Canada to take my company as he did in February 1951.
>
> The war in Korea isn't very amusing. We only hold our positions and send shells on the heads of the enemy and get shells back in revenge. Naturally, we work on our positions to improve them; that's to say to make them more proof against an attack and more comfortable. Trench warfare reveals war in all its futility, especially when we know that it's not us that have the initiative and that this war will not be decided on the field of battle.

The proof of my new-found belief in the underground dugouts is to be found in a photo taken two months later on the crest of Hill 210 (i.e., 210 metres in height), a reserve position, where I organized the construction of the most solid company CP in the whole Commonwealth Division. Above my head is visible a railway rail, procured in the dark by *le système D* ("the make-out system").

I sent the company's quarter-master-sergeant with a truck to find some rails somewhere in the south to serve as rafters for our CP, which I wished to be the masterpiece of my defensive constructions, my father having been a lieutenant with the Royal Canadian Engineers at the front in France in 1916. Did my rails come from a railway being used by the American 8th Army? I know nothing.

But the building of my CP exacted a terrible cost. The spoil from digging the pit was high enough that those working on the rafters laying the cross-pieces were completely out of sight of the enemy. But I was not. At a distance of several hundred or even a thousand yards, I knew that I was out of range of sniper-rifle fire, at least I never heard a bullet whistle by me in Korea. I knew that every shell or mortar bomb that the Chinese sent our way had to be carried on some poor bastard's back all the way from the Yalu River (because of our total air superiority). I much preferred that the enemy waste them one by one by taking pot shots at me than saving them all up to shoot them by the hundreds per minute on my company (including me).

So, one fine afternoon, as on-site, I was standing on the spoil outside the pit, while my batman, as foreman, was supervising three Korean workers. Then, the merest fraction of a second before it landed, I heard the scream of a shell.

Later that afternoon, the enemy fired three more shells at my company. Each time, I ran to where the shell had landed, each at least 50 yards from my CP, to take the compass bearing of the groove made by the shell before it exploded. The artillery asked us to do this, although I am sure that their own instruments gave them far more precise indications of where the enemy gun was. Probably the artillery figured that it would be good for the infantry's morale to think that it was being of some use in counter-battery work. Never in my life had I more desperately wished to kill every enemy soldier servicing a gun.

Being half-deaf, I heard the scream of the first shell when it was too late to jump into the pit with my four men. I therefore dropped where I was on the spoil, completely in the open, and where I expected the shell to land. Thus I saved my life: the shell landed on the rafters among my four men. I jumped into the pit pulling at the shell-dressing that we all wore on our belts, meeting on my way in one of the Korean workmen who came charging out covered in blood, presumably not his own, for he did not appear to be wounded. It was different for the remaining three. One look, and I saw that we were beyond the shell-dressing stage. I jumped back out of the pit and got my morphine ampules from my dugout.

One of the Korean workmen was lying on his back on the rafters, screaming and pointing at his feet: both had been severed at the ankles and were dangling from bits of flesh and skin. The morphine immediately quieted him. Next, I jumped to the bottom of the pit. There the other Korean workman, in deep shock, was moving on the ground, dragging himself by the jagged bone sticking out from the top of his arm. His forearm was gone, as were both his legs, severed at the hips. One arm only remained to him. The morphine quickly knocked him out. God is merciful: the man died shortly afterward.

For my batman, nothing at all could be done. He was lying on his back at the edge of the rafters, practically cut in half: his entrails were hanging halfway to the ground.

Always in the past, I had left the tending of my wounded to stretcher bearers, if any were there, or to my NCOs. I had never felt that I had ever come anywhere near to my breaking point, but I saw no reason why I would not have one like everyone else. My job was to kill and to lead my men in killing. I did not wish to reduce my efficiency in these duties by dealing with the results of the enemy's counter-strokes. However, on this afternoon, I was the only one who had experienced the full horror of what this single enemy shell had done. I did not wish others to share it. So I got the minimum number of stretcher bearers to help me carry the wounded Korean on a stretcher to the Jeep-ambulance at the bottom of Hill 210. And then I had the same minimum number help me carry the two bodies down the hill, while, in the case of my batman, using one hand to keep his entrails from dragging on the ground.

The rest of the afternoon, apart from my three attempts to take bearing on the enemy gun, I spent going around with an empty sandbag to pick up all the pieces of flesh and bone that I could find. I was not entirely successful: later that day one of the LdSH tankers in locality next to my CP, in an aggrieved tone of voice, told me that he had found some flesh stuck to his tank. My last task was to spread bleach paste on all the blood stains I could find.

The battalion CP was behind a small hill a couple of hundred yards from the foot of 210, so I usually ate there, since, in my Jeep, I could be back where I belonged in a minute or less, should an enemy shell or mortar bomb land on my company or anything else unpleasant happen. Of course, I never left my company close to or after last light. Well, late in the afternoon that we are talking about, supper was meatballs and spaghetti with tomato sauce. I remember wishing that the cook had thought of a different menu this particular day. But I ate my supper.

Usually, about 30 Korean workmen arrived in my company area at last light to help in the digging of trenches. On this evening, however, their lieutenant came to me to tell me that his men were very upset by what had happened to two of their comrades and to ask if the others could be excused from working this coming night. I had no difficulty in giving permission.

But it's worth noting that the reaction to disaster of these Orientals was identical to that expected of those of European extraction. There is a myth among whites that Orientals are callous, a myth partly derived from pictures of Chinese fleeing famine areas walking by those that have fallen and can go no farther. Well, if you're all starving, it would be useless to try to drag granddad any farther than he can go on his own steam. In Naples, in 1944, more than one starving unfortunate was left untended where he or she fell. And no one would call the Italians callous.

My dead batman had been glad when I offered him the job, figuring that the company CP would be a safer spot than being with a platoon. After that afternoon, I decided that I would not risk the life of another of my soldiers by asking him to replace my dead batman. But we had Korean civilians about who asked nothing better than to work for us in exchange for food, and a dug-out somewhat further back than mine. So, my next, and final, batman in Korea was Kim, one of the millions of that surname. About all that he did was my washing, for which I paid him five real American dollars (not soldiers' scrip) from time to time. Since he had little to do, and there were no women at all in our battalion area, Kim would sometimes wander further to the rear. And then, since he was from the north and had no South Korean identification papers, he would get himself picked up by the military police. At least once I had to spring him from the clink.

The time when Lieutenant-Colonel Louis-Frèmont Trudeau ordered me to command a raid on an enemy position in Korea, I did not have men of my "C" Company. I suppose that the Colonel had given me the task because after a month in the most exposed position of 1R22eR Hill 159 "C" Company was now much more comfortably installed on Hill 210. But the two lieutenants and the 40 men came from other companies. Since the commanders of the companies having to supply the soldiers did not wish to change complete sections from one spot to another in the FDLs, only three men of one group were known by the lieutenant who had to lead them in the attack, with only eight known by the other.

The two lieutenants and the 40 soldiers had undergone no training together in preparation for the attack, had had no rehearsal on ground similar to the enemy position, had not even had time for the two groups to begin to think and act as teams.

Before organizing the raid, I thought it necessary to learn all that could be learned about the enemy position, in other words, to make one or several deep recces. Now, on New Year's Day 1945 in Italy I had learned, to my great surprise, that I was not proof against enemy bullets. Therefore I was no more enthusiastic about going into the enemy lines than anyone else. However, if I was going to send two lieutenants and forty men against an enemy position, it seemed to me that I should risk my skin just a little bit also. So, I asked the colonel for permission to do a lay-up patrol of at least 24 hours duration around the enemy position. The colonel refused.

However, he said that I could do a recce by plane. So, there I was one fine sunny morning in a two-seater plane piloted by an artillery sergeant. I am not an infantryman for nothing: I suffer from sea-sickness, air-sickness, the works. With both feet solidly on the ground or on all fours, I am fine. Otherwise, no. So, very soon after we were over the enemy, I could barely see the ground. Even at my best, I would have seen nothing useful.

I was just about to tell the sergeant that we should go home, when I heard knocking outside the plane. At the same time, I saw an explosion and smoke a few feet away. "Ack-ack," said the sergeant, at the same time starting the evasive action proper to all little planes that do not wish to meet a 40 mm shell. Evidently, I could no longer tell the sergeant that we should go home. What would he have thought of the 22nd? It is also evident that the evasive action of this damned little plane, for the shells did not stop knocking at the door, did not at all help my air-sickness. I would have been glad if one of the shells had connected, for then I would have had an excellent reason for parachuting out of there. Knowing that the sergeant-pilot would have found it unhelpful if I had lost my breakfast on his back, after ten minutes I told him that I had seen enough. (for 15 minutes I had not seen anything.) "Good thing," the sergeant replied. "We're out of gas."

I honour safe and back on the ground as soon as I got out of the plane, I immediately lost my breakfast. And the recce was completely useless.

Since it was a patrol of two platoons and since the colonel had put me in charge, I told him that obviously I would command it in the valley with the two lieutenants and the forty men. He replied that I would command from my CP in the middle of my company on the top of Hill 210.

Not being used to making war sitting on my arse, I then said to the lieutenant responsible for leading the assault against the enemy position: "You will command the patrol. You know that the aim is to take at least one prisoner. If once the assault is launched, you think you can do it, fine. If you think you cannot do it, you will be the sole judge. I have no orders to give you, neither now, nor certainly when you are with your patrol forward of our lines. I will give you advice should you ask for it. In addition, I will give you all the necessary support, from afar, especially by the fire of the two tanks that are next to my CP on Hill 210. Also, since I will have a Chinese with me who will be listening on the enemy radio frequency, I will probably be able to tell you what is happening on the enemy side while you're in the valley with your gang."

So the two lieutenants and the forty soldiers went into the valley leaving me comfortably seated in the OP of my CP, where I would be able to see the gun flashes that would be occurring around the enemy post a half-mile away.

"*On y va!*" ("We're off!"), cried the lieutenant to his men, and to me by wireless, when they were 100 yards from the enemy post. An instant later a machine-gun opened fire on the patrol. An instant after that, on my order, the two tanks opened fire on the enemy position. I had, of course, had the targets registered beforehand. The enemy machine-gun did not fire again.

And that is all. The lieutenant and his 20 men threw themselves on the ground, a good idea, really, when you have an enemy machine-gun firing at you practically at point blank and your own tanks are firing ten feet over your head. And they stayed on the ground. After about 30 minutes, maybe more, my Chinese listening in on the enemy radio frequency told me that the enemy was preparing a strong patrol, probably a company – to go into the valley to encircle ours. I at once passed this information to the lieutenant. At the same time, I asked him if he saw any chance of renewing the assault on the enemy position. He replied, "No." Then I told him that it might be a good idea to bring his men back into our lines.

And that is what they did. No score: no losses on either side, unless our tanks got someone from the other side.

For the raid to have been successful, the enemy would have to have been sleeping until our patrol was actually in its trenches or cave, or whatever its position consisted of we did not know! Since all preparatory recce patrols had been forbidden me, we had no exact idea of where the enemy was. Therefore a frontal attack was necessary. And that no longer worked as soon as the enemy machine-gun opened fire. Not one of the 42 officers and men in the valley had previously taken part in an assault.

In my first attack, that against the Gustav Line on 17 May 1944, almost everyone else in 17 platoon had faced the enemy previously. I was backed by excellent corporals such as Colas and Lachance. My sergeant was the incomparable Maurice Careau (killed six days later). And my company commander was the man without fear, the unforgettable Major Ovila Garceau (dead seven days later from wounds sustained from the same shell that had killed Careau).

Compare that to the situation of the two lieutenants and the 40 men, each facing the enemy for the first time in his life, with the captain supposedly in command sitting on his arse in a shelter proof against the heaviest shell! I am still ashamed. Yet, I did not lose a single man, and I had a perfect example of the way not to conduct patrols to present to Brigadier Allard when he ordered me to teach the brigade how to patrol.

The moral: if the aim (to take a prisoner) is worth risking the lives of two lieutenants and forty men, it is certainly worth it to throw another into the pile, a captain or a major. And if he is killed, that is far from a dead loss: it will open up a promotion for a lieutenant who has the only valid experience for a senior officer: having commanded a platoon in action.

* * * * *

Have you ever seen a brigadier resting on his neck and shoulders, feet in the air? And, moreover, you are under his command. It is your fault he finds himself stuck like that and he doesn't find it at all funny?

It was during the winter of 1952-53 in Korea. 1R22eR was at rest out of the line when one of the two British brigades in the Commonwealth Division with 25 CIB got the order to replace American troops on the left of our normal divisional sector. The position was called the Hook. It was not at all a restful sector: the enemy was only 100 yards distant from the allied positions. There was not there as elsewhere on the divisional front a nice big valley in which patrols could play hide-and-seek with the enemy. On the Hook there were constant attacks by one side or the other: each side wanted the Hook for itself alone.

The British had decided that the battalion that was to replace the Americans would need five companies: four on the Hook itself, the fifth on the right of the line in a little island of tranquillity, separated from the enemy by a valley a mile wide. "C" Company of 1R22eR was this fifth company.

Thus one fine afternoon I was ordered to report to the HQ of the British brigade because the brigadier himself wished to take me on a recce of the position that "C" Company would occupy one or two days later. Believing in the principle of conservation of effort, I did not bring my driver with me. Or maybe, I liked floating around in a Jeep as though I were still in Canada in my MG convertible.

In any case, the brigadier was not happy to see me arrive alone, as he told me, since he wished to discuss matters with me on the way. "Well," he said, "I will drive my own Jeep and my driver will drive yours."

Everything went well until we arrived at my new position, where there was a fine little hill. The brigadier was not much of a driver: halfway up the hill, he stalled the motor. What he should have done then was to go slowly backward down the hill and then try to go back up, giving it a bit more gas this time. But no, to avoid going backward, he gave the wheel a sharp turn. It was splendid: the Jeep turned completely upside down in the middle of the road. Seeing no advantage in remaining on board a Jeep that was going to end up with all four wheels in the air, I rolled clear before the manoeuvre could be completed.

But the brigadier stayed at the wheel. What saved his life was that the windshield was in place. Without that, he would have had his neck broken for it could not have carried the whole weight of the Jeep. But all the same, since he was six feet tall, there was not all that much space for the brigadier at the wheel under his Jeep. He did not look happy.

So, with the aid of his driver, we got him out of there. The driver looked quite worried but I do not know whether this was because of the state of his brigadier or of his Jeep, which had left the brigade HQ all shiny and now would be returning with a broken windshield and the brigadier's pennant looking like a rag.

"I'm sorry, Sir," I said, "it was really my fault." "Yes, it was," replied the brigadier, "what shall we do with you?" Judging that there was absolutely no profit for me in continuing this conversation, I helped the driver put his Jeep back on its four wheels.

Our reconnaissance of the position continued without further incident. Back at brigade HQ, the brigadier took refuge in his caravan to loosen up in a hot bath, leaving me alone with his staff, with whom I had exactly the same unfruitful conversation that I had had with the boss 30 minutes earlier. I never went back to the HQ of that British brigade, nor, for that matter, did I ever get to see the HQ of the battalion under whose command I was. For practically all intents and purposes mine was an independent, detached command, with which no one wished to have anything to do.

In October 1952, I was comfortably installed with "C" Company of 1R22eR on Hill 210. 1RCR was immediately on our right (to the north) on Hill 355. The enemy was also on Hill 355, but not on the crest, which 1RCR occupied. Thus the only enemy positions that I could reach were directly in front of and much closer to 1RCR. Now, when I amused myself by having my 60 mm mortars fire on the enemy positions, 1RCR complained to Brigadier Bogert that I was endangering its patrols. One more bomb coming from me and I would be paraded to the brigadier. 1RCR desired no co-operation from me, 1RCR was content to make war as though its allies on the left did not exist.

On 23 October, the enemy attacked, with success, the positions of 1RCR on Hill 355. At the same time, an impressive number of shells and bombs were landing on my own company. I do not recall getting any orders that evening (23 October), but I did not need any to see what was happening to 1RCR. Therefore I had the two tanks in locality with us, my Browning machine-guns, one of which I fired myself until its barrel glowed red-hot, and my four 60 mm mortars, which I always kept brigaded under my command, all open fire. These 60 mm mortars, under the orders of CSM H. Dussault, fired 400 bombs that night. Even if this had been his only feat of arms, Dussault certainly earned that night the mention-in-despatches he subsequently received.

The next morning, I phoned 1RCR to express my regrets that I had not been able to support it with more precise enfilade fire the previous night. Would it now permit me to do what I always did with my own forward platoons and outposts: register my 60 mm mortars 35 yards in front of its positions? "God, yes!" was the answer 24 hours late.

I think it was my first or second bomb that landed smack on 1RCR's OP. Greatly embarrassed, I at once tried to reach someone there by phone to apologize. Impossible to contact anyone. "[Expletive deleted], I've killed the whole bloody lot," I said to myself. But after a few minutes, the OP phoned to tell me that my bomb had cut its phone line and that, apart from that, all was well, "Please continue zeroing in your mortars." Not a single reproachful word from them! The day before, it would have cost me a court-martial.

Maybe that bomb saved the lives of one of my lieutenants, one of my corporals, and my own. One of the times I was registering my mortars, I was with these two in a forward trench. My first bomb landed 50 or 60 yards ahead of us, as far as I was concerned, too far for an immediate DF. So I phoned a correction to the mortars.

During the 30 seconds before the bomb reached us, perhaps I thought of the bomb that had landed on 1RCR's OP. So I said to the lieutenant and the corporal, "I think we'd do well to take cover for this one," for in the communication trench there was a piece of tin covering about four feet of trench. Seconds later the bomb landed in the back of the trench that we had just left. Rather than giving the order to the mortars, "Check your bubbles," I told them to revert to the degrees, minutes, and seconds of the first bomb.

A couple of days later, "C" Company was in its position under British command. We spent two very quiet weeks like that, too quiet, in fact. So one day I suggested to Sergeant Bergeron that he accompany me on a recce towards the Chinese position directly in front of us.

About a mile from our position and thus about 500 yards from the presumed Chinese position, we saw what looked like a white spot in the middle of what looked like the entrance to a cave. Having a rifle with us, as well as an SMG, naturally, either Bergeron or I fired at the centre of the cave. The white spot disappeared, which indicated to us that it had been one of our enemies who had been watching us.

Since, as usual, I had not advised the battalion CP of our stroll in the valley, which meant that we were without support if the enemy decided to come see what we were doing on its side of the valley, Sergeant Bergeron and I agreed that we should return whence we came.

Back with "C" Company, I phoned battalion, to be told by a British major that we had come damned close to having the fire of the 24 guns of the divisional artillery regiment come down on our heads. Apparently, one of its OPs had seen us, and it was only at the last minute that they had realized that it was a couple of Van Doos strolling like that in the fresh air and not the Chinese.

I replied that our recce had been worthwhile because it showed that the enemy defended very badly this part of his front. Therefore, I proposed to the major that I make further recce patrols in front of my company to determine exactly the enemy positions, so that I could then lead a strong fighting patrol into the enemy lines to take prisoners.

The reply? Come and make your patrols on the Hook where the enemy is one hundred yards away! It was impossible to make him understand that it was far more intelligent to make war where the enemy was not expecting it and that it was precisely by harassing the enemy in front of my position that I would force the enemy to reinforce its own position in front of "C" Company and thus reduce its pressure on the Hook.

The major replied that his battalion already had enough to do to defend itself on the Hook. "Don't go waking them up in front of you." It was impossible to make him understand that the tactical advantage in front of "C" Company was entirely ours: if the enemy tried a counter-attack across a valley that had no cover and was a mile wide, it would be a massacre. Our artillery, our mortars, our tanks, our air power (complete air superiority) would permit none of the enemy to get out alive.

There is a principle at play here, not merely a particular method: defend yourself where the enemy attacks; attack the enemy where it gives no indication of wishing to make war. Why leave to the enemy the choice of the field of battle?

Our next patrol together was not there. It happened at the end of 1952 at Christmas-time, starting from a much more tranquil position along the Sami-chon River. "C" Company was in reserve, and 7 platoon, still commanded by Sergeant Bergeron, was in company reserve. I had a tank hull-down on the crest of the hill where I had my command post. The tank belonged to the Lord

Strathcona's Horse troop commander, Lieutenant Bruce Rutherford, with whom I got on well.

We were occupying a very quiet position, apart from a few shells fired at our tank every two or three days, with the loss of two or three of my men. To fire back at the enemy I had only Rutherford's tank, because the enemy position was out of range of my 60 mm mortars. Thus I was often glad to assume the role of tank gunner. I was even happier when one of my signallers, Private J.A.A.F Deschenes, proposed to me that he go in broad daylight with another signaller to the enemy side of the Sami-chon to see what was to be seen there. I admired this aggressive spirit and the example that it gave to the rest of the company. I warned the adjoining companies and asked the FOO to hold himself ready with his 24 guns to massacre any enemy soldiers showing a disposition to annoy the patrol; I asked Rutherford to follow the patrol with his tank gun, ready at any moment to fire 100 yards in front of it. In effect, I did everything except tell the CO, for I knew that he would not authorize the patrol.

There was no reaction from the enemy, even when Deschenes and his colleague, on the other side of the Sami-chon, 200 yards from the enemy position and 2,000 yards from ours, put down a NAAFI box. We had written on it "To replace your wheelbarrow" (which Bruce and I had destroyed with his tank gun when we saw spoil being emptied out of it from a Chinese tunnel), and stamped out "Merry Christmas from 'C' Company" in English in the snow. Yet no response!

But because the total lack of enemy reaction was useful military information, I phoned in a report to the battalion CP. The IO, Lieutenant J.M. Fournier, transmitted my report with all the other patrol reports (no doubt all authorized, these) to Colonel Trudeau on his entering the CP that evening. I soon learned that I was to be paraded to the brigadier. In another of our companies, a couple of soldiers had got themselves thoroughly sloshed and had gone out on an unauthorized patrol. My defence was thus easy to predict: because I encouraged my soldiers to act against the enemy, they did it stone-cold sober and supported by all our arms. They did not go stupidly into the valley loaded to the eyeballs.

That night, I was busily congratulating myself yet again on my genius, when the phone rang from the lance-corporal in command of my outpost. "Captain," he said, "Corporal 3N of 7 platoon has just gone through my outpost to go to the enemy side to take a prisoner. He's sloshed." After giving the lance-corporal hell for not having arrested the corporal, I phoned Bergeron.

In my gentlest voice, I asked him: "Sergeant, where is Corporal 3N?" "With his section, Captain," replied Bergeron. "No, Sergeant, your imbecile of a corporal is in the valley loaded to the gills. You and I are going to go down to the outpost immediately in my Jeep. From there we'll go into the valley looking for this [expletive deleted] imbecile before he's got the whole 40th Chinese Route Army mad at him."

Before leaving, I told my signaller to tell the Battalion what was happening. Being already in the soup because of the unauthorized patrol, I thought that it would be pushing things a little too far now to go on patrol myself without letting the Battalion know in advance. But I made sure that I was out in front of my outpost before the CO could be informed.

Also before leaving, I told Lieutenant Rutherford to turn off the lights on the Christmas tree that we had installed on top of our tank. Battalion was not aware of the tree, and I judged that it would not help my case at all if the colonel chose that moment to send someone to see what was happening in "C" Company, someone not intelligent enough not to talk of Christmas trees. No doubt I would have been accused of revealing my position to the enemy, though the enemy saw our tank the whole day through, which is why we were shelled.

Bergeron and I went into the valley to within 100 yards of the Sami-chon. There, we sat down to await events – that is, the attack of the missing corporal on the 40th Chinese Route Army. Our idea was to run immediately in the direction of the firing in the hope of retrieving our corporal before the Chinese army launched a counter-attack with a force superior in firepower to that represented by the loaded corporal, Bergeron, and me.

After an hour, maybe more, looking to the rear I noticed that our Christmas tree was again shining in all its glory, a beauty that I was far from appreciating at that moment. "Damned Bruce," I said to myself, "There he's gone and got himself sloshed in turn, and he's playing the idiot with those [expletive deleted] lights." Not having learned as a platoon commander in Italy to think before leaping, I was in the valley without a wireless (or maybe I had judged that the best way not to get an order from the colonel that I would not wish to obey was to give him no means of communicating with me).

It seemed reasonable to go back with Bergeron to my outpost to find out what was happening in my company, with the object of returning to the Sami-chon if the errant Corporal was still lost somewhere in the mists. In fact, the corporal was already back, without an enemy prisoner, and Rutherford, fully as sober as I, told me that he had turned on the lights of our Christmas tree as a signal that our corporal was back safe and (more or less) sound, a signal that, naturally, I had neglected to plan for beforehand.

As far as I was concerned, the affair could have ended there, Bergeron being perfectly competent to explain to the crazy corporal that it was not wise to stroll around no-man's-land after loading up with half a dozen beers. But the colonel did not share my view, and he demanded that I parade the corporal to him. I tried to convince the colonel that a simple "admonished" was sufficient punishment. Instead the corporal lost his stripes and Bergeron and I, a good corporal, who had spirit. The Colonel asked him why he had acted as he had. "I went into the valley," replied the Corporal, "because Captain Pope had told us that if any one of us captured a prisoner, he would give that one his ration of a bottle of rye - and I was thirsty."

When Bruce Rutherford's tank and "C" Company were together on this hill, my company kitchen was a few hundred yards back in a valley behind another hill. From there, hot meals were brought up to the platoons. But since, apart from the occasional shell, our position was a quiet, reserve one, 2,000 yards from the enemy, I would invite Bruce at meal-times to come with me in my Jeep to inspect my kitchen. The five-second inspections over, Rutherford and I would sit down to our meals. I knew, of course, that I could always be back where I belonged in plenty of time should something happen – such as enemy shelling of my company.

One day, at meal-time, it happened. As soon as I heard the first shell land, I knew from its sound that the enemy had put it down on my company and would be putting down more. With our last mouthfuls gulped while my Jeep was already on its way, I decided to enliven things by making like a radio announcer describing what was coming next week on a western long-running serial: "Hair-breadth Harry rides again! Will he make it?! Tune in next week for the next exciting episode!" I kept this up as one or two more shells landed around Bruce's tank and thus also on my HQ.

As I drove my Jeep into its open bay behind the tank, I heard the boom of the gun that was firing on us. Another shell would be arriving in five seconds. Jumping out of the Jeep and diving under it, I yelled to Bruce, "Duck, Bruce, here comes another one." Bruce, having got out of the Jeep, stayed standing. The shell landed close enough to him that a fragment could have obliged me to ask the Strathconas to send up a replacement tank troop commander. Rutherford was not happy about this: "Dammit, Harry, I thought you were still joking!" "Sorry, Bruce," I replied, "But when I dive under my Jeep, I'm no longer playing radio announcer. I thought you knew that." We are still friends. Indeed, the friendship has extended down to his grandson, Lieutenant Jason Adair, who is interested in war stories. Bruce had told him that I was a reputable source.

In early January 1953, Lieutenant-Colonel Tony Poulin visited us from Valcartier to get an idea of what he would be bringing his battalion, 3R22eR, into, come rotation time in April. I was ordered to report to 1R22eR's CP to escort the two colonels, Poulin and L.F. Trudeau, to "C" Company's position. Shortly after I arrived, with the two colonels still busy in discussion, I heard a shell land forward of us. By the sound, I figured that Rutherford's tank and my HQ were on the day's hit list. I quietly got hold of a phone and called up my signaller on duty: "*Ça shell chez nous?*" ("We're being shelled?"*) "Oui, Capitaine.*" ("Yes, Captain.") "*Je reviens.*" ("I'm coming back.")

Getting the two colonels into my Jeep, I headed us up to my company. As we rounded the last corner, the enemy, rather embarrassingly, dropped one right in front of Bruce's tank. Startled, Trudeau asked me: "*Le char vient-il de tirer?*" ("Did the tank just fire?") "*Je ne pense pas, Monsieur.*" ("I don't believe so, Sir.") I replied quietly, too quietly, it seems, for my colonel to catch my drift. We arrived safely; but then the enemy had to fire another one at us that did *not* land anywhere near the front of the tank, somewhat closer to where we were grouped near my CP, as a matter of fact. "*Savais-tu que l'ennemi tirait avant que nous montions à l'avant?*" ("Did you know the enemy was firing before we came forward?") "*Oui, Monsieur.*" ("Yes, Sir.") The colonel looked a trifle pensive for a moment or two but seemed to conclude that I was not tryingto get him killed but simply doing my duty of always being with my company when it was under fire. I then suggested that we might start by inspecting CSM Dussault's dug-out, which was close to mine but of a considerably more solid construction. My suggestion was accepted.

1R22eR went into reserve with the rest of the Commonwealth Division on 30 January 1953 and stayed that way for the next two months. Of course, we used the time to train and work on the reserve Kansas Line south of the Imjin River. If the enemy were to break through the Jamestown Line, our present position, the "Kansas Line" was the last stop before Seoul. To get to the top of the hill where I had to develop a defensive position, we could, carrying our rolls of barbed wire, hike in several hundred yards from the north, or we could drive from the west directly to the position up a steep hill that ran through a US camp. But we never drove up that hill. The previous week, a British tank had got half-way up, slipped over the edge, and landed on a US tent, crushing the US officer inside it.

So, when I arrived and asked permission to use the hill, I met considerable hostility. My pointing out that a truck was not a 30-ton tank and that I would always give warning before trying the hill made no difference: the memory of the sight of the crushed officer was far too recent. After all, the man with whom I was dealing was not a front-line officer. The sight of the blood and guts of a friend spread all over the place was not in his usual scheme of things. So, added to the exercise that we got with pick and shovel, we got a whole lot more carrying barbed wire on our shoulders.

On 17 February 1953, I wrote my mother about being in reserve:

> life is quiet, training instead of digging. In fact, my last tour in the line [the Sami-chon] was much less interesting than the first [Hill 159]. The valley between us and the enemy was larger and very many fewer mortar bombs and shells were coming down on my head. I'd like very much to go to Malaya or Indo-China when my year here is finished. You have no idea how monotonous life is on a static front, even, one might say, useless.

But having a command in action for the past six months, my first since a German tracer bullet broke my arm on the Senio on 1 January 1945, I was determined to keep it. This was made clear in the citation for my Military Cross, which was drafted in March 1953:

> This officer has commanded a rifle company of 1st Battalion, Royal 22e Régiment, for the past seven months in the Korean Theatre. Throughout this period he remained continuously with his men, refusing periods of rest that were offered to him, despite the strain imposed on him due to frequent enemy shelling on his company area and the organizing and directing of patrols into enemy territory. He handled his company at all times in a most cool and efficient manner, particularly when it was subject to heavy stress. His calmness and competence under fire have gained for him the complete confidence of all who served under his command, and he proved untiring in his efforts to improve the positions that his company occupied. Through his own resolute manner and his eagerness to strike back at the enemy at every opportunity, he has developed a fighting spirit of the highest order in everyone under his command. And his unceasing attention to the welfare of his men and the needs of others have endeared him to both officers and men alike. Major Pope has shown qualities of leadership of the highest order. His enthusiasm, competence and coolness under fire have been an example to all, and have been reflected in the high standard of efficiency of his company and the indomitable spirit of its members.

From the Canadian Embassy in Paris on 2 September 1953, Major-General Georges P. Vanier wrote (translated) :

I have just learned that you have won the MC.

I send you my lively and affectionate congratulations. Bravo – your Honourary Colonel is proud of you.

I hope to have the pleasure of reiterating my congratulations to you in person. In the meantime I beg you to believe, my dear Harry, in my sentiments of affection and admiration.

Lieutentant-General Henri Tellier wrote me, "You finally were awarded the Military Cross [in Korea] after having been recommended for it, Gallantry for Service in Italy, as well. It also seems to me that you were wounded twice, a very brave soldier and leader, Harry."

Finally, Major-General W.H.S. Macklin, the Adjutant-General, wrote my father on 22 May 1953:

I am pleased to tell you that your son, Harry, has been awarded the Military Cross. I enclose a copy of the Citation.

He asked to have his tour in Korea extended. The new Brigadier, Jean Allard, knows him very well and agreed, but will send him home if he seems ready for it. I have just returned from Korea and Japan, and can say with assurance that it is a strenuous war. I do not want this young man to become overtired. I am confident that Allard will see that he doesn't. Unfortunately, I didn't get a chance to see him in Korea. It is a big front and very toilsome to travel around - nothing but hills.

From all accounts I have had, this Military Cross was earned the hard way. This I am sure will be very satisfactory to you.

With kindest regards,

Yours sincerely,

Mac.

Out of the line, on parade, I demanded that my company stand at attention as though they were the British Grenadier Guards before the Queen. However, I demanded the standing at attention as infrequently as possible. I preferred the stand at ease or the stand easy. And in "C" Company, in the stand easy all was permitted (speaking, smoking, everything except moving the feet). On the march, the same thing, practically always, march at ease. I demanded only that everyone keep in step. The rare march to attention, necessary when passing before the Colonel, was done as though we were trooping the colour in the Citadel or on the Plains of Abraham.

I had noted that whenever companies came out of the line, practically everyone declared having lost a whole pile of equipment because of enemy shells and mortar bombs. That did not cost anybody anything because the quarter-master replaced without charge all equipment lost in action. Obviously, the men were causing to disappear all the equipment that they found useless.

So, I had a company parade the eve of our re-entry to the line. Everyone was there with their equipment. I said to them:

> I require that you face the enemy with the weapons and the ammunition given to you. I require that each wear a helmet and trousers. As for the rest, I don't give a damn. Everything you don't wish to bring with you, place it in a pile in front of you and the company-quarter-master-sergeant will strike it out of your equipment booklets (MFM 800). If you lose anything at the front, you will report it immediately. On coming out of the line, there will be an inspection of your equipment. If you're missing anything at all and you have not reported it, you will be charged for it.

The company entered the line looking like a band of brigands. Two months later, at the equipment inspection, nothing was missing and "C" Company was able to make a nil return, no loss of equipment, while the other companies had losses in the thousands of dollars, as had "C" Company previously. Obviously, I made sure that all my men had their uniforms and their equipment complete again before the colonel came to inspect us! With the 3rd Battalion, "C" Company spent May and June 1953 at the front. We were one of the two forward companies. Therefore it was legitimate to think that if something happened, it would be the turn of one of the two companies that had passed two months in reserve to enter the line.

Well, something happened two days after we had come out of the trenches: the enemy launched a strong attack against the Republic of Korea (ROK) Army on our right. To provide reinforcement, the company on the extreme left of its army was sent into the battle. To fill the hole, I was ordered by Colonel Tony Poulin to take my company back into the line immediately.

Giving an order to the company-sergeant-major, Staff Sergeant Stewart, to put the company stand-to to go back into the line, I immediately left with my three platoon commanders to make a reconnaissance of our new position before the rapidly approaching dark.

On returning after a couple of hours, I found the company awaiting me in complete darkness, which permitted those who were in a bad temper, 100% of the company, to say loudly what they thought of our being sent back into the line when it was decidedly not our turn. I stood up on the hood of my Jeep and shouted: "All of you come around the Jeep! I want to speak to you!" Several helped me by shouting: "The Major wants to speak to us!"

I started by explaining what was happening at the front on our right and why a company of the Van Doos must go back into the line. And I continued: "The Korean company that we're replacing has left us a pig-sty. They shat everywhere. There's shit in all the trenches. There are live grenades lying everywhere. Our first job, because it's a very quiet reserve position, will be to pick up the grenades and bury the piles of shit."

I continued: "I know it's not your turn to go back into the line. The colonel did not tell me why he's not sending one of the two companies that spent the last two months in reserve. He doesn't have to tell me. He's sending us because we're the only company that's ready. On coming out of the line, you've spent two days cleaning your weapons, your grenades, and your equipment. The other companies have been on a drunk for the past two days." (I was exaggerating a little, maybe!)

"The war is ending, but it's not over yet. You, all of you, have acted like soldiers to the end. *Je suis mauditement fier de vous* (I am damned proud of you)."

I then took off in my Jeep with my company following in trucks behind me as we went back into the line, definitely not in our turn. And, so help me, the men were singing!

A day or so later, I was sitting on my company's forward slope trying to see what I could of the enemy positions all of two miles distant. Then I heard an explosion behind me that filled me with horror. I knew that it was not an incoming shell or mortar bomb. I knew that it was not the RCR firing an 81 mm mortar. I knew that it was not a shot from our artillery. I knew that it was not one of my 60 mm mortars: the teams were busy digging in their base plates; besides, they would not fire off a bomb without my orders; moreover, the enemy was out of range.

I sat a moment or two longer, hoping that I was wrong. Then, over the hill-top from the reverse slope, I heard, *"Major, major!"* I ran back. There on the ground lay two of my mortarmen: the spade of one of them had hit a grenade left hidden under the earth by the company that we had replaced. The blow had dislodged the safety pin that had been inserted carelessly. I phoned the RCR's Regimental Aid Post (RAP). "Doctor," I said, "two of my men have been very seriously wounded by a grenade that went off under their feet. They need the helicopter ambulance as fast as you can get it here." The MO replied, "The regulations are that I must see them first. I will send our Jeep ambulance for them and then decide about the helicopter." I protested, "I've commanded a rifle platoon or company in action in two wars for a total of two years: I know what a soldier looks like when he's close to death." It did not matter a damn. My men were taken in a bouncing Jeep to the RAP so that the doctor could satisfy his regulations. Eventually, the two soldiers were picked up by the helicopter ambulance. Within hours they were dead. Gladly would I have traded their lives for that of the cursed doctor.

I wrote the mothers of the two soldiers. Madame Malvina Gallant of Atholville, New Brunswick, replied on 27 September 1953 (translated):

I had in effect learned the sad news of the death of my dear son, SG57584 Corporal Jean-Moïse Gallant on 17 July last; a first telegramme told me he had been gravely wounded and a second, the very same day, told me he had died.

Today I wish in the name of all my family and in my own name to thank you for your delicacy in offering us your sympathy. It is true that the trial has been very great especially since we had already passed through a similar bereavement during the 1939 conflict. Another of my sons gave his life for *la Patrie*. But let the holy will of God be done because it is He who wishes it so!

Now I would be infinitely grateful to you if it were possible to give me some details of the last moments of my child. Since he lived for five hours, did he receive the consolation of the Faith, was a priest at his bedside? I would appreciate a photograph, or several, of his place of burial.

I beg you to receive, Sir, the expression of our profound gratitude for your devotion and I beg you to believe me.

A heartbroken mother.

This letter arrived at 3R22eR while I was in mid-Pacific on an American troopship. It finally caught up to me on 14 November 1953 while I was in Europe on leave. I answered at once. An Armistice was signed ten days after Gallant's death.

Chapter Nine

Patrolling

In late March I received an appointment as acting major. On 22 May 1953, I wrote my mother:

> I went back into the line recently with my company [now part of 3R22eR]. Everything was settling down to my liking when, a week ago, I got a call from the CO [Poulin] telling me Brigadier Allard wished me to go to his HQ for several weeks to organize several patrol courses. I replied that I did not at all agree to quitting the company I had been commanding for more than nine months, and I demanded to be paraded to the Brigadier. So the next afternoon Allard received me, smiling [he, not I!] and said he knew without asking me why I wished to see him and that he knew what my answer would be if he had asked me whether I accepted this new task. The end of the story is that I reported to Brigade HQ on 19 May to start getting things ready. The first course starts on Monday, 25 May.

> The idea, evidently, is that in static warfare, patrols become the only means of maintaining the local tactical initiative, and for a year and more now the Chinese have massacred our patrols with theirs whenever it pleased them. It's up to me to remedy this. Naturally, now that I've undertaken the task, I'm enormously interested in it, and I wish to go far beyond organizing patrol courses for the subalterns and the NCOs of our our three battalions in the line.

> I wish, in fact, to form a scout company, a band like 'Popski's Private Army,' formed by Lieutenant-Colonel Vladimir Peniakoff in North Africa and in Italy in 42-45. The Brigadier is not against the idea, but I don't believe the COs of the three battalions would like very much to see Pope's Private Army appear in front of their positions! But don't

talk of this to anyone except Papa. If the PPA is formed, I wish the first notice the Chinese get to be the disappearance of several of their outposts. Even the fact that I'm giving patrol courses should not be mentioned, for it's my aim to change our present system from top to bottom.

To complete the cadre of our school, I had two sergeants, one from the Royal Canadian Regiment (RCR), and the other from the Princess Patricia's Canadian Light Infantry (PPCLI), both wearers of the Military Medal (MM). Sergeant Prince, PPCLI, was a Canadian Indian. The other, Sergeant J.C. McNeil, RCR, won his MM commanding a patrol during the Chinese attack on "C" Company on the night of 23 May 1953.

Shortly after our school started, I wrote for Brigadier Allard a memo of 20 pages on patrolling. In repeating it now, I put my readers on guard against confusing principles of war and methods. Perhaps the most important thing for the soldier starting his second or third campaign is to distinguish clearly between principles of war, which never vary, and methods that may well apply only to his first battles. Without studying the differences that may exist between one campaign and another, it is dangerous to transplant to the second campaign a method that was shown to be useful in the first.

Moreover, it is fatal to continue fighting an enemy that is not in full retreat, routed, without often changing tactics. In war, the ideal solution is rarely the same twice in a row. When the enemy reacts against one of our actions, it is essential for us to react against its reaction. Better yet, we should react *in advance*, against what we believe *will be* the enemy's reaction. To summarize, it is necessary to conform to the principle *maintenance of the aim,* while often changing the method.

As we see below, this concept was often neglected in Korea.

This is the paper on patrolling that I submitted to Brigadier Allard on 2 June 1953.

* * * * *

For the past year and more, the enemy has held the tactical initiative in no-man's-land. He has raided our outposts and forward positions and ambushed our patrols at will. We, on the other hand, have not carried out any successful operations forward of our lines.

The object of this paper is to examine the reasons for our lack of success and to set out the methods by which we may regain the initiative, so that the security of our forward defensive lines (FDLs) may be assured while the enemy's forward positions are caused the maximum casualties at the minimum cost to ourselves. And by "minimum cost" I mean less casualties than we are suffering in our present very ineffective patrolling.

Why have we been unsuccessful for the past year and a half? In the first place we have been waging the war on the assumption that the peace talks at Pan Mun Jom were going to be successful from one day to the next. A humane desire of commanders to avoid risking lives in the possible last days before an armistice has led to a purely defensive patrolling policy of which more aggressive enemy commanders have taken full advantage. A defensive attitude on the part of commanders inevitably leads to a lack of aggressiveness, a strong desire *not* to close with the enemy, on the part of the troops. Since effective patrolling can only be carried out by troops imbued with an ardent wish to close with and destroy the enemy, it is obvious that from the morale point of view alone we have been labouring under an impossible handicap.

Before examining our own patrolling policy, it will be advantageous to examine that of the enemy.

The Enemy's Patrolling Policy
Outposts

It is not possible to determine definitely the enemy's manner of employing his outposts since only rarely have our patrols even gone within hearing distance of them. However, I think he employs them close in to his main defensive positions, usually at the end of spurs, and linked to his platoon positions by communication trenches. This system permits easy reinforcement of the outposts if they are attacked, with the platoons, companies, and battalions being reinforced from the rear in the same manner. The disadvantage to the enemy of having his outposts close in lies, of course, in the fact that a well-planned and determined raid by us on one of his platoon positions will probably achieve surprise and gain complete success before reinforcements arrive from the company position – provided the latter is sufficiently well neutralized. No doubt the enemy employs his outposts close in, thus exposing his platoon positions to a surprise attack, because of his confidence in our complete inability to mount even a successful platoon-sized raid. So far, we have done nothing to disillusion him.

I think the enemy may also at times use small (two- or three-man) mobile outposts in the valley immediately in front of his position. These outposts follow no set pattern (unless it be because our patrols fail to detect them). They are most useful to the enemy to let him know the routes of our recce and so-called fighting patrols. No doubt, many a successful ambush is a based on information given by these mobile outposts.

Recce Patrols

I think it is obvious that the enemy is most meticulous in his recces before a raid or an attack. Apparently all the commanders – up to regimental level – carry out lay-up recce patrols up to and behind the area to be attacked. His recce patrols move with extreme caution on crossing to our side of the valley – at least they never fall into our ambushes. The recce patrols undoubtedly never number more than three men and probably usually two or possibly one.

These recce patrols sometimes deliberately draw our fire by throwing stones into our barbed wire. Our answering machine gun fire into the wire is probably ineffective since it may be assumed the enemy is some 25 yards removed from where the stones fall. However, the enemy gains a picture of the positions of our automatic weapons. Our best answer to this particular ploy of the enemy's would therefore seem to be to throw grenades in the manner of a destroyer laying depth-charges.

Fighting patrols

Here also the enemy excels. He gets his information for aggressive action from his skilled recce patrols which NEVER make contact with us. However, when the enemy has decided on the time and place for his raid or ambush, he apparently always details at least a company for the job. Regardless of the size of the party he uses for his fighting patrol in the valley, he always has sufficient men standing by in the FDLs to bring his total force in the valley up to 100 to 150 men immediately upon contact. *He never risks contact in the valley*, that is, he never sends out more than one to three-man recce patrols, *unless he has sufficient men of a well-trained reserve or patrol company standing by to ensure control of the battlefield once contact has been made.*

To sum up then, the enemy's patrolling policy is as follows:

Outposts are of two types:

Static – These are close-in and easily reinforced from the platoon positions.

Mobile – These consist of 2 to 3 men and usually operate between the enemy FDLs and his side of the river.

Recce patrols consist of 1 to 3 men and are sent out to get information directly leading up to aggressive action by a fighting patrol or raiding party. The commanders of the troops selected for the aggressive action do the recces. Lay-up patrols are extensively used.

Fighting patrols The enemy never risks contact without ensuring that he will remain master of the battlefield. For this purpose, he does NOT use front-line troops for patrolling but instead uses specially trained patrol companies, which are kept in the rear echelons until a fighting patrol is ordered. Even if he only sends a small ambush of 20 men into the valley, he will keep the remainder of the patrol company standing by in the FDLs ready for instant action.

Our Patrols in Korea, 1952-1953

Our patrolling in the past eighteen months has followed the pattern and obtained the results described below.

Outposts

These have varied in size from 3 or 4 men to a complete section and have been placed on secondary features outside the platoon positions or in minefield gaps. They went out at last light and returned at first light. Usually they occupied precisely the same position for months on end and were dug in to form isolated posts. Normally telephone lines were laid to them – ensuring their rigidity.

Their distance from the FDLs varied from fifty to one thousand yards. In the course of time, their exact positions became well marked not only by the paths and telephone lines leading to them but also by the quantity of empty tins of self-heating soup and the occasional beer bottle around them.

Sometimes the outposts were supported by prearranged, tank, mortar, and machine gun fire from their company positions; but this was certainly not done more than half the time, if that. They were too weak and too isolated to withstand an enemy raid. Their sole chance of carrying out their object of giving early warning of the approach of the enemy lay in the enemy not knowing where they were. But because of their rigid employment, the enemy always did know where they were.

They have therefore furnished a most convenient source of prisoners to the enemy. Certainly they provided early warning of the enemy's approach but when the approach was merely to the outpost for the purpose of successfully raiding it, this early warning became a dubious advantage. That outposts are essential is indisputable; that our past techniques in their employment have been wrong is obvious.

Recce patrols

These usually consisted of a commander and two men and were sent out in swarms to the stream dividing the valley. Whenever the patrols crossed to the enemy's side, whether or not any attempt was made to penetrate behind the enemy's outposts, the patrolling was considered "aggressive." The great majority of these patrols' main object was to observe and report on enemy movement towards our lines. They were, in fact, mobile outposts. Recces leading up to aggressive action by a fighting patrol were usually inadequate, rarely, if ever, penetrating behind or even up to the enemy position selected for attack. Little use was made of the lay-up recce, and those that were made were not deep enough. Rarely was the officer selected to lead a fighting patrol allowed to do the preliminary recces.

Fighting patrols

These were ordered from time to time in an effort to redress the defeatist spirit. Their practically continuous lack of success served only to depress morale still lower and ensure further defeats. These patrols were of two types: the ambush and the raid.

The ambush would consist of a subaltern or NCO and five to 20 men. Usually they were sent out without regard to the fact that recce patrols had been reporting no sign of the enemy. In other words, the schedule called for ambush patrols and so they were duly sent out to places were it would be most convenient for us for the enemy to pass.

Rarely was provision ever made to reinforce the ambushes should they have accomplished their object, that is, of ambushing the enemy. And, of course, since ambushes were usually ordered from forward companies, the company commanders concerned were simply quite incapable of reinforcing their ambushes adequately without denuding the entire company position – an impossible risk. So on the rare occasions when our ambushes did fire first, the initiative quickly passed to the enemy, who alone had the power of quick reinforcement.

And the morale factor must not be forgotten: our men knew the enemy patrols were specially trained for their jobs and would be quickly reinforced whereas they themselves were simply out in the valley for a routine task that came round to their platoon every third night and was interspersed with other routine assignments of standing guard, cleaning up the area, laying wire and digging. In other words, "the basic sense of mission" was lacking. Our ambushes have been uniformly unsuccessful.

The fighting patrol numbered between 10 and 40 men (including the firm base) and was commanded by a subaltern or a sergeant. Sometimes their object was simply to sweep an area in search of the enemy and then to engage him. This woolly idea inevitably led to defeat when the enemy was met. A fighting patrol cannot operate as a recce patrol and then become a fighting patrol when the enemy is located: ten men cannot move as silently as two.

Sometimes the decision would be made to raid an enemy platoon. To accomplish the task, two groups would be selected, each of twenty men commanded by a lieutenant, one group to act as a firm base between the lines, the other to carry out the raid.

Having described for Brigadier Allard on 2 June 1953 the useless raid for which I had the responsibility (see above, pages 173-175), I continued by describing how to dominate no-man's-land.

To provide relief from this dreary chronicle of defeats, we should consider the successful snatch patrol pulled off by 1RCR in September 1952. This excellent feat, which earned the MC for Lieutenant Gardiner and the MM for Corporal Fowler, is a classic example of how to kidnap a Chinese soldier. This seven-man patrol was successful because of its preparation (a deep lay-up recce patrol inside enemy lines carried out by the leader of the snatch), its originality, its stealth, and, finally, its audacity. Most regrettably, this operation – our only success – has not been allowed to become a model for the Brigade.

Before I begin an exposé of what I think our patrolling policy should be, I think it would be advantageous to consider our minefields. In the first place, it must be borne in mind that no minefield is more than a temporary obstacle to the enemy: even a brand-new Commonwealth pattern (four mines to every yard of front) minefield can be breached by the enemy. Therefore it is sheer folly to consider a normal trip-wire minefield with one mine to every seven yards of front, planted 18 months ago, as being anything except a nuisance *to us*, not the enemy. Realization of this will ensure a more logical disposition of outposts. Further, I consider that all our patrols in addition to being told the location, the gaps, and the type of minefields on their route should also be told the density and date of laying of the minefields. This will allow the patrol commander to decide whether he should risk crossing a minefield or not if the enemy is lying in wait in the gap. It is worthy of note, however, that this additional information is not available from Brigade or battalion IOs.

Another factor to be considered is the choice of weapons. This factor transcends the terms of reference of this paper since it concerns army policy as a whole. However, it must be considered. Our present enemy uses masses of grenades and machine carbines on patrol and in his raids. Our single action rifle in the hands of the Old Contemptibles was a match for the German Army of 1914.

However, the Old Contemptibles were a very well-trained crew and they were shooting down Germans, also armed with rifles, by day at 500 yards. Our one-year soldiers facing Chinese with burb guns at ten yards at night are quite another matter. I consider the machine carbine (the Patchett or Owen gun) should replace the rifle in all operations of war. This most definitely includes patrols. (The solitary exception is sniping, for which the sniper's rifle should be retained.)

Still other factors to be considered to help us regain the initiative are the greater use of our overwhelming firepower, the use of dogs, the use of sniperscopes, and finally the use of special attachments on our wireless sets to reduce user noises. In other words, we should use on every patrol, recce or fighting, all the specialized equipment we have. Add this to a new policy aimed at ensuring that we at least have the same number of well-trained troops in the valley as the enemy and we will have a definite advantage.

In future, I consider the following should be our patrolling policy.

Outposts - These will normally consist of two men equipped with light automatic weapons and a wireless set, but no telephone. Their object will be to give early warning of the approach of any sizable enemy force towards our FDLs. They will accomplish this object in the following manner:

1. Normally they will go out at last light and return at first light.

2. They will occupy positions ahead and on the flanks of the company positions close to likely avenues of enemy approach. These outpost positions will NOT be prepared in any way but will simply be places chosen to afford good observation coupled with good concealment for the outpost.

3. An outpost will NEVER occupy exactly the same position on two successive nights. Its position should vary from night to night by as much as two or three hundred yards. There is NO objection to an outpost moving its position during the one night. If it is considered that an outpost should be relieved during the night (for instance, during inclement weather) then the relieving outpost must NOT occupy the exact position of the outpost being relieved. Physical contact between the two may, however, be effected, if this is considered desirable.

4. Since minefields have proven to be completely unreliable as long-term obstacles to the enemy, outposts must NOT be sited in relation to minefields or minefield gaps. It must always be borne in mind that the enemy is just as likely to go through the minefield as through the gap. An outpost placed permanently at the home side of a minefield gap will soon be detected by the enemy who will then at his leisure move through the minefield and attack and destroy the outpost from the rear.

5. An outpost should NOT necessarily be sited on a secondary feature leading off the platoon position since it will then tend to become static and take on the form of an isolated section post – a tactic eventually fatal to the outpost.

6. Outposts should adopt the technique of recce patrols, for, in fact, that is what they are: close-in recce patrols. Outposts, on the approach of the enemy, should rely on their small size and concealment for protection. They should try to remain in position or get behind the enemy, the while reporting his movements by wireless.

Recce patrols - These will normally consist of a commander and one man equipped with light automatic weapons and a wireless set. Their object will be to obtain sufficient information on the enemy to allow us to plan and carry out raids on enemy positions or ambushes of his patrols. Recce patrols will carry out their object in the following manner:

1. Deep penetration of the enemy's position will be effected. NO raid will be attempted on an enemy position until it has been observed from close range by a recce patrol or patrols both by day and by night and from front and rear. Normally the commander of the raiding party or ambush will make the recce.

2. Close-in recce patrols whose sole object is to add to the security of our positions by giving warning of the approach of any sizable enemy force will NOT be called recce patrols but will be called by their proper name: outposts.

3. NO recce patrol will ever be sent out except to find out definite information about the enemy, directly leading up to a raid or an ambush by us. Any recce patrol that does NOT bring back

information directly leading to aggressive action by us is a waste of time and energy. The ratio of recce to fighting patrols should be about 3 to 1. However, the bigger the fighting patrol or raid, the greater should be the number of recce patrols preceding it.

4. Much greater use should be made of lay-up recce patrols. In fact, to observe properly an enemy position from the rear – a prerequisite of any raid – the lay-up is essential. The technique to be used by a lay-up patrol in getting behind an enemy position will depend on the circumstances, as will the length of time to be out. Normally, however, it seems the patrol should close with the enemy line at first light, examine the position from the front during the day and get in behind at last light. The length of time to be out may well vary between 24 hours and 72 hours, or even more.

Fighting patrols - No fighting patrol will ever be sent out unless it has, in the first place, the remainder of the company from which it is found standing by in the FDLs ready to give it immediate assistance. Fighting patrols will therefore come from reserve companies or battalions. Normally a week of planning, recce-ing and training should precede every fighting patrol, be it ambush or raid. Since the object of a fighting patrol is to clash with the enemy, the plan should be so devised as to make contact practically inevitable. Once the enemy has been met, mastery of the battlefield must be gained and maintained. We, not the enemy must police the scene of the action, and if the length of the conflict makes this necessary, we must be prepared to continue after first light under cover of our preponderant supporting fire power. The supporting arms will have the role of interdicting the battlefield: for the enemy, there must be no chance of survival after first light.

Conclusion - This policy will not prejudice the security of our positions. They will be better protected by our mobile outposts than they are being at present.

This policy will ensure that when we go into the valley to fight, we will be fully prepared to do so. We will be sending out far fewer fighting patrols (ambushes or raids) – maybe not more than one every week or two to each battalion. But I am convinced that it is better to have one successful fight out of two attempts each month than to have 55 NTR (Nothing to report) fighting patrols and 5 unsuccessful ones out of 60 attempts each month.

Thus I ended my report to Brigadier Allard on 2 June 1953. The Armistice was signed less than eight weeks later, on 27 July.

* * * * *

During the six weeks when Brigadier Allard had removed me from "C" Company to run the brigade patrol school, a Chinese attack was expected on the front of the Commonwealth Division. I was then given permission to rejoin my company for the night of the expected attack. As always, I wished to make the rounds of all my trenches before dark. But Colonel Poulin had ordered that no one was to go down the road leading to my company before last light, since the road was in view of the enemy and any movement invited shelling.

When I arrived in broad daylight at the checkpoint manned by soldiers of one of our reserve companies, and finding my way blocked, I raised the barrier and told my driver to take off, and to hell with the dust. Halfway down the hill, I passed a couple of military policeman who had taken cover in the ditch. "Stay down! There's another one on the way." I yelled to them in passing for I had heard the boom of the enemy gun whose crew may have been encouraged by the sight of a new target: the Jeep, the driver, and me. At the same time, I told the driver not to take his foot off the gas. We made it, of course. And the shell did no damage. But Poulin was not amused and passed the word down that the next time Major Pope presumed to disobey orders and go through a closed barrier, he was to be fired on. I passed word back up that I always shot back.

In any event, I got to my company in plenty of time, asking each man how things were going. One replied, "Everything's fine, except that we don't see you often." A fully justified criticism: a commander's position is *always* with his troops, and as far forward as he can possibly be while still being able to control the battle. Captain J.P. Dufour, RSM of the Voltigeurs when I joined in 1942 and now of my company, second-in-command, was entirely competent to command the company in my enforced absence, but I was the commander, and it was the commander whom the men expected to have there to lead them. That night, the enemy attacked the Hook, well to the left of our position, and all remained quiet on our front. Still, I was happy to have been allowed to spend one night of my six-week exile with my command.

The Chinese questioned at least one of their new POWs concerning the brigading of the four 60 mm mortars that occurred when I was on Hill 123. This difference in their enemy's defensive arrangements seems to have worried them, which is good. The enemy may also have noted that my company's position had been ringed with 60 mm mortar DFs. Is this why it was not *my* company that was attacked?

Since the 1st Battalion had completed its year in Korea, we quit the front on 20 April 1953, to be replaced in the line by 3RCR. And it was this Battalion that was subjected to the Chinese attack on 2-3 May. I talk about this when I discuss our defences in Korea. (I transferred to 3R22eR on the departure of 1R22eR.)

Now, let us talk of the patrol that I did with Lieutenant Jefferies.

At this time, apart from continuing to make war like good soldiers, the enemy was trying to convince us that we should all become good friends; that is, the enemy was practising psychological warfare. Thus one night, Lieutenant Denis Joyal, who had taken over command of my forward platoon, no. 7, from Sergeant Bergeron, (who remained as platoon sergeant), told me that he had heard on the enemy loudspeaker on the other side of the valley that the enemy had some wounded allied soldiers that it would turn over to us if we would kindly go down into the valley at dawn in front of and to the right of our position, that is, near where the [destroyed] American outpost had been.

I asked nothing better than to go for a walk in the valley to see my positions from the enemy's point of view, and this at the enemy's invitation! So, I said to the commander of my reserve platoon (no.9), Lieutenant Frank Jefferies, "Jeff, you and I are going into the valley at dawn tomorrow with a stretcher." I did not think about a Red

Cross flag. Besides, with my Luger in its holster on my belt, I had no right to the protection of the Red Cross.

As I have written above, at Christmas 1952 Colonel Trudeau had paraded me to Brigadier Bogert (who commanded in Korea before Brigadier Allard) because I had permitted two of my soldiers to do a daylight recce to the enemy positions without telling the CO. It was clear, then, that Trudeau was not fond of patrols going out from "C" Company in broad daylight. Thus Jeff and I went off into the valley without telling him.

In a letter to me, Lieutenant Joyal wrote (translated): "I remember very well that you arrived early in the morning with Jeff. You borrowed my Very pistol with flares, in case of difficulty; you borrowed my stretcher; and you asked me to advise the Battalion CP *after* your departure (to avoid a countermanding order from the CO) and also to warn "B" Company (I believe) on our left and the battalion (Australian or PPCLI?) on our right."

Arriving at the foot of 7 platoon's position and in front of the abandoned right-hand outpost, abandoned by me because I did not hold with the view that the men in my outposts were expendable and served their purpose of early warning on being killed by the enemy. We found no wounded, despite the presumed enemy promise. "Now that we're here, we might as well continue," I said to Jefferies. Arriving in the middle of the valley, about 300 yards away from both our and the enemy's positions, I felt that it was going so well that I was beginning to think of strolling like that along the whole front of the Commonwealth Division. But then suddenly the man on duty at the Chinese loudspeaker woke up and threw this one at us: "What are you doing?"

Talk about a stupid question! "Jeff," I said, "unfurl the stretcher and show it to him." But that did not do us any good, for the next question arrived: "Are you just going for a walk?"

From bad to worse! "Jeff, that one over there doesn't seem to be aware of the affair of the wounded. Come, we'll go into the enemy lines to explain it to him."

But after two or three steps towards the enemy, I remembered that it was precisely on going into the enemy lines to rescue my wounded that I had spent eleven days in the bag nine years earlier. So I said: "I think rather that we'd do better by going home." Making an about turn, we quietly re-entered 7 platoon's position by the side opposite to our sortie.

At every instant, we were expecting a burst in our backs, but it seemed to me that to break into a gallop, as I had a very great desire to do, would certainly have brought enemy fire down on us. Better then to continue to stroll like a couple of idiots who had nothing better to do.

Since I now had proof that the Chinese attack on our position was not imminent, I phoned Trudeau to make my report. An advantage of the French language is that it is possible to say "*on*" ("one") when one should really say "*nous*" ("we"). Therefore, in relating the patrol, I started by saying that "one has gone between the lines looking for wounded." Only when the colonel had come to realize that "C" Company had once again made a patrol that he had not authorized did I introduce my "we." "Who's that 'we'?" demanded the colonel. "Jefferies and me."

Trudeau was one of the rare Van Doos who never swore, but if he had ever come close with me, it must have been that morning. But, in effect, without cause. In seizing the opportunity that the enemy was offering me to examine my position from the point of view of the enemy's position, I was precisely carrying out my mission: to defend my company position with the least loss possible. And precisely because it was abnormal to make reconnaissance patrols in broad daylight, I would have been ashamed to send anyone else to do it. Also, I wished to assure myself personally that the enemy was doing nothing crooked on our side of the valley: no caves being dug.

And, finally, my first company commander in action, Major Ovila Garceau, did as much on 18 May 1944 when he strolled in no-man's-land with me at the head of my platoon and of "D" Company.

Regardless of the nature of future war, we will be occupying defensive positions most of the time: when we're not attacking, we're necessarily on the defensive. Since we were on the defensive continually during two of the three years that the Korean War lasted, it is probable that we can gather from it lessons useful for the future – even though they may be how *not* to do things!

During the Second World War, the armies of the British Commonwealth, chastened by their experiences at Dunkirk and in the Western Desert, developed the technique of the all around defence. In our subsequent campaigns in Italy and in North-Western Europe against a weakened German Army, we found the all around defence still worked well even during the months-long winter halts. Convinced we now knew all about the art of war, we applied our all around defence technique without variation to the Korean hills we occupied in October-November 1951. As the enemy shelling increased – and with it nasty-minded probes – we remembered the stories of our fathers, and began digging in and wiring in the positions we had first occupied in the 1940-45 pattern. We were overwhelmed at our own sagacity in thus applying the lessons of the two world wars.

But had we applied the lessons properly? What were the basic defensive lessons of the Great War? I think that one was as follows: in non-mountainous country, a defensive line extending across the entire front must be developed in depth and not only must flanking units be able to fire in enfilade across each other's front but the second and third lines of defence *must be able to fire in front of the first line*. Depth does NOT simply mean that after hitting and breaking one line, the enemy must then hit and break a second and third line and so on. The reserve lines must be able to fire small arms in direct support of the front line. Their job is not simply to sit there waiting for the chop.

However, this technique of continuous mutually supporting lines was adequate in non-mountainous country only; and only then before the advent of tanks and planes which, by their mobility, increased the power of attack to the point that the impregnable continuous line no longer exists. Even on a perfectly flat plain, although we may appear to present a continuous front to the enemy, our infantry localities down to company level must be organised in all around defence. In hilly country the obvious thing to do is to occupy the hill tops and to guard against infiltration in the valleys by mobile outposts. This is what we did in Korea, but the trouble was that we occupied too many hills and in consequence did not develop the defences on any one hill to their natural conclusion.

We never stood back to look at our hills and ask ourselves what they were in essence. They were, of course, fortresses or castles. By simply developing our hills on the all around defence techniques of 1940-45 and on the dug-in techniques of 1914-18, we made the mistake of not extracting all the lessons of the Great War, and in particular the one of the mutually supporting lines. As a matter of fact, we could have gone back to the Middle Ages to find this technique revealed, for a castle did not base its defence on having another castle on the next hill behind but rather on having several lines of defence – each mutually supporting – within the castle, starting with the battlements behind the moat and ending with the keep.

During the last year of the war, 1st Commonwealth Division's platoon and company localities were successfully raided again and again by the enemy. I will show why by detailing the sequence of an enemy raid.

First the enemy increased his patrolling in front of the locality to be raided. Our routine recce and so-called fighting or ambush patrols would be engaged and defeated on our side of the valley by enemy forces of up to company size. Our static, night-time outposts would be raided or destroyed. Our reaction to this would either be to send stronger forces into the valley – but for some unaccountable reason never strong enough to defeat the enemy – or to withdraw our patrols and outposts and sit tight.

Either technique was disastrous. In the first case, on the night of the raid, the enemy would engage and defeat our routine recce, fighting, and ambush patrols on our side of the valley, while we hesitated to bring down our artillery, mortar, and MG DFs lest we hit the remnants of our patrols in the valley. The enemy was into our trenches before we even asked for DFs. In the second case the enemy was able to close with our trenches before the slightest alarm was given. In this case also, our DFs came down too late.

Secondly, enemy shelling and mortaring would greatly increase on the selected locality. We would call this harassing fire. In actual fact, it was more truly neutralizing fire since it was intended to keep our heads down, disorganize our defences, depress our morale, and, most importantly, discourage us from doing any daylight reconnaissances on our forward slopes where the enemy often prepared caves in which his raiding party laid up so that it might attack at last light without being bothered by our defensive fire.

The last stage of the enemy preparation was the registration of his guns and mortars on the target. This should – and admittedly usually did – provide sure proof that an enemy attack was imminent. However, we often did not put this forewarning to good use.

Now, what faced the enemy when he finally made his attack? The answer was always the same: a *single* circle of fire trenches, each with two soldiers armed with nonautomatic weapons, the trenches joined one to the other by a communication trench around the top of the hill.

Regardless of what Hollywood would have us believe, there is not a platoon in the world that can absorb a thousand shells and bombs in the space of a few minutes and then resist completely alone the resolute attack of fresh troops outnumbering them five or ten to one. The enemy was fresh because he had avoided our defensive fire and our troops were alone either because the rest of its company and the flanking companies were being neutralized by the enemy's intense fire or because their weapons were sited so that they could not fire directly in front of the platoon being attacked – the only place where our fire would have been of the slightest use.

In November 1951, 2R22eR repulsed an enemy attack on their positions on Hill 355. On 23 October 1952, the enemy carried out a successful raid on "B" Company 1RCR on this same Hill 355. On 2-3 May 1953, the enemy carried out a successful raid on the two forward platoons of "C" Company 3RCR, which was on Hills 123 and 97.

Far from me to wish to have it believed that the difference in the results of the Chinese attacks stem from differences between the R22eR and the RCR! On the contrary, I insist that in employing the same methods, the Chinese would have been successful against any company of the 1st Commonwealth Division (including mine!). Quite simply, the Chinese had realized why they were unsuccessful in 1951 and, in consequence, had developed new methods. We, on the other hand, satisfied with our successes of 1951, tried to defend our positions without the slightest major change of method for a whole year and a half....seriously!

This was one of our errors. In the reorganization phase of a battalion attack, the medium machine guns and the anti-tank guns are often placed under command of the forward companies. This is done so that the company commanders can, during the *initial* defence, beat off the enemy's immediate counter-attacks. Soon, however, the battalion commander takes back control of these weapons to give them battalion tasks. That is to say, the weapons are placed defiladed from the front and sited in one company locality to fire in enfilade in front of another.

But in Korea, especially in regard to our MMGs, in many cases they remained in the reorganization phase for a good 20 months! It was agreeable to have many of our .30 Brownings in the forward companies firing directly to the front on the enemy positions. Therefore, we could trace in chinagraph on our maps magnificent arcs of fire of almost 180 degrees, thus showing that these machine guns could fire in enfilade immediately in front of the company on the right as well as the one on the left, all the while being able to fire in front of our own company.

But these machine guns were in no way defiladed from the front. After a year and a half in the same positions, did we really have the right to hope the Chinese would not neutralize all these machine guns on attacking a neighbouring company? A 180 degree arc of fire is beautiful to see....but it's not war.

When I brought "C" Company 3R22eR into the line for the first time in May 1953, we occupied the position immediately to the right (to the north) of the position that I had occupied a month earlier with "C" Company 1R22eR – where "C" Company 3RCR was attacked on 2-3 May 1953. What especially interested me in my new position was a hole in the back of the trench where a Browning machine gun had been sited. This hole was nine inches in diameter and one foot deep. This hole was the result of the fire, magnificently precise, of a Chinese machine-gunner the night of the attack on the neighbouring RCR position. Is it necessary to add that our Browning machine gun was rendered perfectly useless on the unique occasion during the preceding year and a half that its fire was essential?

In essence, in Korea we made war as though the good times would never end – as though the enemy would never mount a serious attack.

All right, then, how should we have defended our positions *taking account of the fact that the enemy had reacted against our initial methods of occupation* and was mounting raids against us from time to time? In the first place, the first factor to note was that we had decided to occupy our positions until the end of the war. Therefore, we should have prepared our positions for permanent occupancy.

It was necessary that our defences remain based on hills. But every hill occupied by a platoon or more must be encircled with two, and preferably, three lines of trenches. The rows should be so developed that an attacking enemy can always be engaged by fire from at least two rows regardless of his line of approach. Each of our circular defence lines must be connected underground by tunnels. These tunnels must be adequate to shelter the entire force and proof, except at their entrances, against 1,000 lb bombs.

Additional depth should be given to the whole line by developing hills in the rear in the same manner as the forward hills. Inevitably, however, the three-circle method of hill defence requires more men on any given hill. This leaves fewer men for reserve hills. That is acceptable. If the enemy was capable of breaking through a three-circle-defence hill, they would certainly have been able to break through two or three one-circle hills one after the other – as they did, in fact, on 2-3 May 1953.

The company command posts (CP) should be deeply dug in just behind the crest of the hill-top. It should be impervious to the heaviest bombardment. The CP, by the way, is not necessarily where the company commander sleeps: it is the place from which the company HQ wireless sets and telephone exchange as well as the FOO's communications operate. Upstairs from the CP and just on the forward slope is the company commander's observation post. This is his (and his FOO's) battle station by day and by night. From it should radiate tunnels leading to the top circle of trenches (from whence, of course, access can be gained by other tunnels to the lower circles). The whole plan of defence revolves around the company commander's OP. From here he observes and fights the battle. The OP occupies the vital ground. It is the place of no retreat and no surrender. It is the keep.

If we, for some reason, are willing to surrender the initiative to the enemy (as we did during the last 18 months before the Korean armistice) then we must expect them to raid our positions. To prevent surprise we must patrol no-man's-land. This is best done by highly mobile one or two-man roving patrols armed with sub-machine guns. However, even if we do not use these mobile outposts, it will be obvious that the enemy cannot over-run a triple-circle hill in a surprise raid in the same way they did our single-circle hills. Even if the artillery and mortar DFs do come down late, the enemy will certainly be engaged by the centre and top circles before his bombardiers have finished grenading the bottom circle.

The company's four 60 mm mortars – beautiful weapons – are the company commander's most useful arm. They must be meticulously registered on every avenue of enemy approach – and the DFs should be close-in, 35 yards from the forward trenches. Each mortar should have a separate DF/SOS (target on which the mortar is ready to fire instantly when it is not engaged in firing on another target). Within 30 seconds of a platoon commander calling for a DF/SOS, the bombs should start falling full on the enemy.

The mortars must be sited on the reverse slope as close to the CP as possible. The other considerations regarding their siting are: a) far enough down from the crest so that their flash will not be seen from the front by night; b) within the defensive perimeter; c) as close to the administrative road as possible for ease of ammunition re-supply.

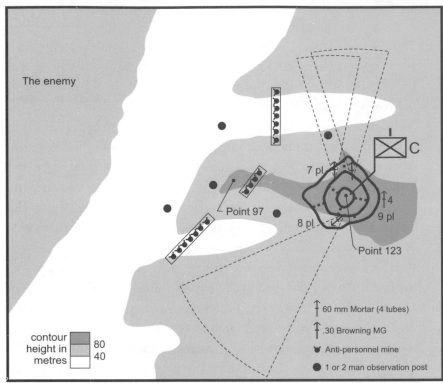

Fig. 1 – A Company Position in Korea, Nov 1951-Jul 1953

Fig. 2 – A Company Position, 1952-53 Reacting to the Enemy

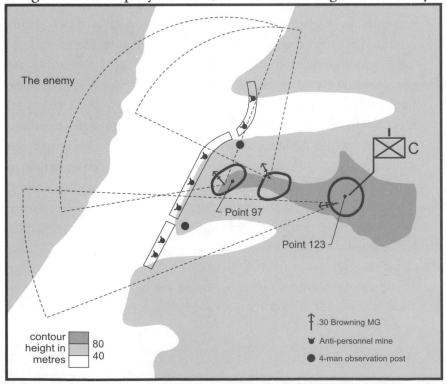

Notes for Figure 1

Figure 1 shows how a Commonwealth Division company occupied a defensive position from November 1951 (when the static phase of the war started) until 27 July 1953 (when the armistice was signed). In fact, this figure is an exact reproduction of the position that my company ("C" Company, 1R22eR) occupied between 8 and 20 April 1953 and was occupied by "C" Company, 3RCR, on 2-3 May 1953 when a Chinese raid on the two forward platoons cost them 26 killed, 27 wounded, and 7 prisoners of war.

1. Each platoon occupies a hill, with a single circle of trenches
2. No platoon can fire in support in front of another.
3. Each .30 Browning is on the forward slope and has an enormous arc of fire. In theory, these MGs fire in support of the neighbouring companies, whose Brownings, sited in the same way, fire in support of "C" Company – still in theory.
4. The minefield, over a year old and composed of one mine for every seven yards of front, covers the whole front except for two narrow gaps, clearly marked, and visible both by us and the enemy at a distance of at least a mile (especially in winter, when the paths made by our patrols in the snow are even more visible).
5. The static outposts, each of four men, are always situated in the same permanent positions immediately on our side of the minefield gaps.

Notes for Figure 2

Figure 2 shows how we should have occupied the same position long before 2-3 May 1953 – in reaction to the enemy raids.

1. The whole company is positioned in three rows of trenches encircling a single hill. The company HQ is in the top row. The platoons occupy the two bottom rows. The two forward platoons (7 and 8) each occupy a quarter of the two lower circles, while the reserve platoon (9) occupies the rear half of the two bottom circles.
2. The three rows are joined by several tunnels.
3. The top circles can fire in support of the lower circles.
4. The .30 Browning MGs are defiladed from the front (being either on the reverse slope or because they are in concrete bunkers). They fire only in support of the neighbouring companies. The Brownings in the neighbouring companies do the same for "C" Company.
5. The high-density minefields hardly cover more than half the front. The gaps are far too large to serve as sites for enemy ambushes.
6. The outposts are each composed of one or two men. They never occupy the same position on two successive nights.
7. If the enemy raids a neighbouring company, tanks supported by infantry will come down at least as far as point 123, and maybe as far as the minefield, to attack the enemy in a flank.
8. The four 60 mm mortars are in the lowest line of trenches on the reverse slope.

The mortars must fire as a battery; farming them out to the platoons is not necessary because of their two thousand yard maximum HE range. When companies replace each other in the line, the mortar positions and the base plates should be handed over to the incoming company.

The mortar positions, designed as they are for permanent occupancy, should be made of reinforced concrete to make them as protected against counter-battery fire as possible. Also, with the base plates solidly anchored in concrete, it would not be necessary to re-register the DF/SOSs when companies succeed each other in the line.

Each rifle company should be allotted a minimum of three .30 Browning MGs – but in the case of the forward companies, *not* to fire to the front; nor should they be sited so that they can be engaged by the enemy from the front. Their task is to fire in enfilade across the front and on the flanks of the neighbouring companies. They should either be sited on reverse slopes or on forward slopes. In either case, they should occupy permanent positions in bunkers made of reinforced concrete, completely proof against enemy machine gun fire as well as enemy shells and bombs.

They should be manned by men of Support Company. Their DFs and DF/SOSs should be allotted in the same manner as mortar and artillery tasks and for which the neighbouring companies should be able to call as readily. For this reason, each .30 Browning must have a wireless set on the battalion net. In short, the .30 Brownings in a company position must have nothing to do with that company: it is "in locality" only. It is a serious error to employ the Brownings on the tasks of the Bren LMGs. The Bren LMG provides the high volume of direct automatic fire to the front to defend its own position, NOT the .30 Browning.

Minefields should never be laid covering the whole front of a battalion, a brigade, or a division, for their effect is to restrict the movement of our patrols. In fact, such minefields canalize their movement while rendering them very susceptible to ambush in the minefield gaps. Also, such large-scale minefields hinder the movement of our infantry and our tanks during our counter-attack. They give us a false sense of security while the enemy is quietly making unauthorized gaps prior to his raid or attack. Finally, most of our year-old minefields appear to be effective only against our own patrols that have strayed from their course.

Generally speaking, the positions prepared for our tanks on the crest of our hills were good. The ideal was to have our tanks able to fire directly on the enemy in front, while also being able to fire in enfilade in front of the neighbouring companies – certainly their primary task. Because of their armour, one could intelligently give this double task to the tanks – something impossible for the medium MGs.

However, the tank's mobility must never be forgotten again. If the enemy is raiding an infantry locality, tanks supported by infantry should go down into the valley (if the ground permits this) in an attempt to take the enemy in the rear or at least in a flank.

During the last year and a half of the Korean War, we were dealing with an enemy that was courageous, well-trained, and led by competent officers. However, the enemy faced serious disadvantages: inadequate communications, lack of all sorts of materiel because of our air attacks and their own poverty, bad roads, few tanks compared to us and no air power in support of their forward positions. For these reasons, the enemy could only attack us at night and only after a very careful preparation.

The enemy accepted their disadvantages and then set about discovering how we defended our positions. That done, the enemy developed a technique to mount raids against us. Our reaction should have been as I've described it above. No doubt, the enemy would have found weaknesses in the defensive methods I've described: we would have to react again.

Chapter Ten

Returning to Canada

There were three majors due to return to Canada at the end of September 1953. Two were staff officers who had had a pleasant, shell- and bomb-free year in comfortable quarters well behind the lines. The other was I. The staff officers flew home. I was put in command of 250 men, not one of whom was from R22eR, to take home in an American troop ship. We did not start off well. When I arrived at railhead, I was met by a flustered British railroad transport officer (RTO), who told me that the whole bloody lot, my new command, had arrived drunk and that I should refuse to accept the draft. I told him: "Load your train." Which he did.

I got the drunken mob to Pusan. Next morning, early, I had them all on parade. I told them what the RTO had recommended. I told them that I had not accepted the RTO's recommendation because I had been given the job of getting the whole lot home and I was going to do it, even if they were to spend the next two weeks under close arrest. "Yesterday's drunk," I went on, "was understandable: you were celebrating having survived the war and the end of your tour in Korea. But that's the last drunk you'll have. You are still soldiers. You have served honourably in Korea. Continue to serve honourably for another month or so. Do not disgrace yourselves, and your country, by acting stupidly while on board an American troop ship."

On 3 October, while at Kure, Japan, with my draft, a couple of days before we boarded the SS *General M.M. Patrick*, I wrote my mother, in part concerning what uniforms I would need in Brussels:

> …Ask Papa if he believes I'll need my sword (or rather, his [for he had given it to me]). I suppose I'll only need it in case of marriage to cut the wedding cake! I brought it to Korea with me – I was going to wear it if ever we attacked the Chinese, but as you know, I never had that chance. Maybe it was just as well, for I always preferred a Tommygun or a rifle in the attack; the sword, I'd have had it in my legs for nothing!

Apart from a typhoon – the captain told me that he had never seen the glass so low – that forced the ship to anchor in lee of the Aleutians, the voyage was uneventful. The typhoon hit when I was involved in a game of bridge in the captain's cabin. Despite a truly impressive roll of the ship, I was not seasick. It is remarkable what being responsible for 250 proven drunks will do to calm one's stomach. Hell, I did not even throw up on my daily walk-through of the hold where my poor bastards were crammed. My losing my breakfast there would have been discouraging to the inmates, especially to those who had already lost theirs, and would have been a case of carrying coals to Newcastle with a vengeance.

After a couple of months leave at my father's embassies in Brussels and Madrid, I arrived in Kingston in January for the 1954 Staff Course. Here, at the end of the course, as at RMC in 1942, the next College publication was graced with a sketch on each student written by the student following him alphabetically. Mine started:

> A true individualist and the only 'Van Doo' among a host of RCR, PPCLI and Guards, Harry carried on his own private war against students and DS [Directing Staff] alike. He could always be counted upon to produce the unusual and his searching questioning of guest lecturers often left both audience and speaker speechless....

My first posting after Staff College was, at the end of October 1954, to be Deputy Assistant Adjutant-General (DAAG) at HQ Quebec Command in Montreal. Fortunately, Lieutenant-Colonel Dextraze was to become GSO 1 and he wrote me as follows (in English) on 22 October 1954:

Dear Harry:

I must apologize for not having written to you sooner. Of course, I received your post card from Italy [where I was on leave after Korea] and was very pleased to know you were in good health and unfortunately coming back to civilization. Anyway, as usual, I am quite busy hence will get down to brass tacks.

I have heard through the grape-vine that you are being posted to Montreal as DAAG; knowing you as well as I do, with your lack of tact and ability to settle problems "*à l'amiable*" [amicably] with people usually of senior rank to you, I have decided to get this posting canceled if possible and get you appointed as GSO 2, Quebec Command.

The following is to show you consideration; incidentally, I don't see why I should have any for you, but nevertheless having been a staff officer for the past two years, I have somewhat amended my ways of dealing with people; I would like to know if you are interested in coming to work for me as GSO 2. Should you not be interested, please make no bones about it and tell me honestly. For my part, I'd very much like to have you as I would relish the opportunity to whip you properly, as I believe from what I heard, you still need it.

I am sorry to have missed you when you came to Quebec City some three weeks ago and I hope I shall see you in the near future; incidentally, I am taking over my duties of GSO 1 on 22 Nov 54. As there is an awful lot of work to do here, I urge you to carefully consider the above suggestion.

Friendly yours,

Jimmy

I replied the next day, 23 October 1954: "*Oui.*" ("Yes.") And one of the first things I did when I was in his office and saw him ending another letter "Friendly yours," was to tell him that while "*Amicalement vôtre*" was fine in French, the phrase's literal translation into English was not. Colonel Dextraze told me to go to hell. But eventually, "Friendly yours" no longer ended his letters.

After about a couple of months of my one-step-up-from-my-six-times-repeated adjutant's job, I started 1955 as GSO 2(SD) (Staff Duties). This job had been created by my predecessor to make room for another major on the General Staff. The job consisted of getting pieces of paper from GSO 2 (Training) asking me to order Ordnance to release to a Militia unit the equipment the unit required for an exercise. I certainly did not require a week's worth of such pieces of paper from my GSO 2 (Training) colleague to realize that I was utterly useless in the scheme of things. Colonel Dextraze immediately agreed with me that GSO 2 (Training) could pass his requisitions directly to the Ordnance. And so I became GSO 2 (Officer Training) and spent the next two years not as a staff officer but in fact as a training officer responsible for preparing all the Regular Force officers in the province for their captain-to-major promotion exams and staff college entrance exams. Also, I headed the Militia Staff Course (MSC) for Militia captains and majors.

This led Lieutenant-Colonel Dextraze to include the following in my 1956 confidential report:

> For the past eight months, this officer has, apart from his numerous duties, been in charge of Militia and Regular Force Officer Training. He has had to spend many nights and weekends working on either the preparation or correction of assignments. This additional task has always been undertaken freely and without any prompting on my part. Since 1 Sep 56, he has been entirely divorced from any work other than Officer Training. He is indeed doing a fine job of it. Last year, I mentioned in his confidential report that he was studying for his BA. He has since obtained it and is now studying for a Ph.D [actually, an MA]. At the same time, he is taking a course in Atomic Physics at Sir George Williams College. I have been told that AHQ is considering posting him to Regimental Duty. If such is the plan, it should not take place before the end of Apr 57, as this would completely disrupt the Officer Training programme in the whole of Quebec Command.

Quebec Command had had the lowest exam passing rate in Canada. All the exams and training were in English. The French-speaking officers, who, of course, were the majority, had the option of writing their exams in French. But this meant that they would have to translate what they had learnt in English into French. Whatever language they wrote in, they were at a disadvantage. Moreover, and this applied across Canada, the whole system was atrocious. To take infantry officers only, they received some training and passed a company commanders' course at the Royal Canadian School of Infantry (RCS of I) at Camp Borden. A completely different group of officers in the Directorate of Military Training (DMT) in Ottawa would set the papers. Some time later, marking guides would be prepared for the officers at AHQ detailed to mark the papers. The only qualification these markers needed was to have passed staff college. Thus an Ordnance officer could find himself marking a paper on infantry tactics.

I decided the only way to beat the system was to get permission to spend a couple of days in Ottawa with a staff-sergeant who was bloody good at shorthand to copy every marking guide of previous years we could get our hands on. Every so often a worried looking DMT officer would look in and ask, "You're only taking notes, aren't you?" Between the two of us we took very good notes!

Back in Montreal, based on the previous years' marking guides, I prepared four "tactical exercises without troops" (TEWTs), one for each phase of war: advance, attack, defence, and withdrawal. Colonel J.A. Dextraze decided they would be called Exercise Jadex, which was fine with me: "Popex" wouldn't have sounded well anyway. I also drew up a booklet giving the outline for complete operation orders for the four phases of war. Finally, I drew up a booklet giving sample "appreciations of the situation." It had been said it couldn't be done: each appreciation had to start completely from scratch, no model was possible. What gave the lie to this ridiculous notion were the marking guides. If a marking guide could set out a model appreciation for those that had to mark exam papers, why couldn't model appreciations for attack and defence be studied before the exam by those that had to write them?

The results of all this were summarized by Colonel Dextraze in the confidential report he prepared on me in 1957:

Major Pope has an extensive knowledge of his Corps and a sound knowledge of the capabilities of other Corps and Arms. He is a very good instructor which is further evidenced by the much higher rates of "passed" obtained by the officers who wrote their promotion examinations this year (under the guidance of Major Pope) in comparison to previous years. Pope was employed during the period covered by this report as GSO 2 in charge of both Militia and Regular Force officer training. This officer writes well thought out and prepared letters in a firm and strong style. When called upon to present his viewpoints, he does so in a logical and frank manner which does not leave his listeners in any doubt as to what his opinion is. When preparing a report to be delivered either in writing or verbally, the information given is accurate and shows that attention to details has not been overlooked. Pope's capacity seems to know no bounds and is definitely a challenge to his superiors. This officer has the ability to adapt himself to changing conditions without losing his efficiency. In the absence of orders, he is able to act on his own responsibility. In the evaluation of facts to arrive at a logical conclusion, Pope shows judgement and common sense. I must add, to clarify the above statement, that logical conclusions reached by an individual in the study of facts affecting a particular problem are always coloured by the moral standards of the individual concerned. I would like to state here that Pope's moral standards are very high. It may be appropriate, for the sake of clarity in this instance, to bring to light some of Pope's characteristics. He is somewhat austere, no doubt by nature. He lives by a rigorous code of discipline which is evidenced by his conduct either at work, in the Service, study at the University, or play, which is beyond reproach. Socially, in the mess, he is not liked by some, and this may be with reason. Pope has no time to devote to people who, in his own mind, do not intellectually or in their conduct measure up to his ideals. However, I must say he has become much more tolerant of them. As a matter of fact, many officers have frankly mentioned to me that Pope was surprisingly more co-operative now than they have ever known him to be. In conclusion, I would like to say that this officer's conduct is beyond reproach. He dresses meticulously at all times. In particular, he is respected by his subordinates for his ability, knowledge, sympathy and efficiency in dealing with their personal problems.

To all this, Major-General Bernatchez, GOC Quebec Command, as reviewing officer, added, "I concur in this report. I am of the opinion that Pope's attitude has greatly improved in recent years."

In 1958 I was GSO 2 in HQ Eastern Quebec Area in Quebec City but went back to the Montreal area to take part in the pre-Staff College entrance and pre-Militia Staff Course exam study course given in late winter at Ste-Thérèse. This resulted in a letter dated 21 March 1958 from the new GSO 1 at HQ Quebec Command, Lieutenant-Colonel J.H.J Gauthier:

Dear Harry,

I would not miss the opportunity to express my appreciation for the part you played during the last pre-staff concentration in STE-THERESE.

I am aware of the amount of personal preparation and extra work it has entailed and I am deeply indebted to you for the graceful manner in which you made your services available.

Although the results of the examinations will not be known for a good while yet, I feel confident that your co-operation in this endeavour will have contributed substantially to whatever success we may expect.

May I convey once more on behalf of the candidates and myself my sincere thanks for a job extremely well done.

Three months later I received a letter dated 19 June 1958 from Major J.H. (Howie) Langstaff, one of the half-dozen Militia officers who had served in 1956 and 1957 in Montreal in the "College of Cardinals" – as this cadre of instructors for the Militia Staff Course, headed by a Pope, were pleased to call themselves. Major Langstaff wrote:

People around Quebec Command are extremely happy with the MSC results this year. The ground work obviously paid dividends.

On 10 July 1957, I wrote my father in part as follows:

As you may recall, a couple of years ago I told you I was writing an essay on the unification of the armed forces. You advised against it at the time on the grounds that my military superiors would not take kindly to the idea. [Always the *last* thing that would discourage me from doing something!] In any event, I was not happy with my first draft and because of lack of time I let the essay lie dormant.

The April 57 issue of the *Canadian Army Journal* gives the following as the subject of the 1957 Conference of Defence Associations Prize Essay Competition: 'Eminent authorities have suggested that the three fighting services can be replaced by a single unified fighting service. Discuss the desirability of such unification. What do you think should be the preliminary steps in this conversion?'

I enclose a copy of my revised essay which I intend sending the *Journal* by mid-October, in time to collect the $200.00 first prize. Since I refer to the views of Generals Simonds and Macklin, I have sent each of them a copy for their comments. In General Macklin's case, I also request his permission to quote him...

As usual not taking my father's advice and wishing, as always, to get as much mileage as possible out of anything I wrote, I also sent a copy to the Suggestion Award Committee of the Department of

National Defence, stating, "I believe it comes under the terms of reference of suggestions from members of the Regular Forces dealing with improvements of methods, procedures and systems."

R. Lavergne, Chairman of the Committee, writing from the office of the Deputy Minister, thanked me on 15 July and wrote: "The details of your idea are being examined by specialist officers of the Department in order to determine its applicability and usefulness." Mr. Lavergne wrote me again on 11 December 1957:

> Your essay on Unification of the Armed Forces has been carefully studied by the Chairman of the Chiefs of Staff.
>
> Unfortunately, this is a matter of higher government policy and cannot be considered for an award under the Suggestion Award Plan. However, you are to be complimented on your excellent discussion of a complicated subject. It has been suggested that you put forward this material to the *United Services Journal* or some other military journal which offers prizes for essays on military subjects.
>
> Your interest in the Suggestion Award Plan is appreciated and you are encouraged to forward any ideas which you may develop.

So, for once, not taking my father's advice did *not* get me into trouble with other generals!

But to go back to 10 July 1957. At that time, Major-General Macklin, now retired, was publicly strongly advocating the unification of the armed forces. In my letter to him I wrote: "I have been much influenced in rewriting my essay by your own article in the 22 September 1956 issue of *Week-End Magazine*.... I would greatly appreciate any comments you may have on my essay. If you think that it might be useful to you in your own efforts to achieve unification of our Services, I would be delighted and flattered by any use you would care to make of it..."

On 12 July 1957 (*two* days later), General Macklin answered in a two-page full-length foolscap letter of detailed advice and criticism: "It was very good of you to send me a copy of your draft essay on unification.... if I were attempting a scholarly essay on the subject I would start with ... Man is a land animal...." I took General Macklin's advice (at last!): the essay started: "Man is a land animal."

General Macklin also included much historical background:

There was a time when the roles of the navy and army appeared to be and actually were, to a large extent, separate. But the Spanish Armada carried far more soldiers than sailors, and the Navy invented the Marines a long time ago.

Certainly, under modern conditions it is impossible to carry out any operation of war bigger than a dog fight without at least two of these three forms of so-called 'Power.'

The Americans....produced, back in 1942, the most common-sense description of a military force that I have ever heard. They began to speak of a 'Task Force.' When you get down to facts, any military force that is going to be of any use whatever has to be a task force, designed for the job, and including every form of force needed to do the job. Whether you are capturing an island, or a fortified hen coop, or driving the enemy out of the Sinai desert, any other kind of an armed force is just plain useless.

The complete separation of the services never worked well in British history. Cromwell sent along a civilian to the West Indies to make the Admiral and the General co-operate. It didn't work. Nelson and Wellington never even met each other. Nelson once said of [the Army's general in Spain] Sir John Moore that he wished Moore was a thousand leagues away. There was endless bickering on every joint campaign. The Admiralty gummed up the Dardanelles before the army was sent there.

I don't think the development of air power was much accelerated by separation. The R.A.F. was created in 1917 because there was no co-operation between Admiralty and War Office [Army]. The Navy had cornered all the aircraft production while the R.F.C. was being shot out of the sky by German Fokkers. So they solved this by creating a new Ministry and a new Service. It only made things worse. It took the powerful Admiralty 15 years to get back control of its own aircraft.

The trouble with the air force from the beginning is that it has treated the aircraft as an end, instead of a means to an end. The army made the same blunder when they created the Royal Tank Corps. These birds concentrated on the tank as a TANK – an armoured box. If the armoured box and its engine had been given to the Artillery in 1916, the gunners would have thought of the thing as a gun in a box, which is what it should be. The result of letting Tankers develop the thing was that the British in 1940 had tanks that weighed 40 tons and mounted a 2-pounder pop gun. Germans had no such inhibitions and came along with an 88 [mm] in a tank that blew ours off the battlefield. Canada has spent at least 350 million developing planes when the same money spent on missiles would perhaps have put us in the lead in missiles.

I do not agree and never did that the air force is "The dominant Service." I have listened to that song for thirty years. It is NOT air power that has produced the present situation. It is the power of atomic fission, and pretty soon the fissionable war head will be fired in a missile and the present conception of so-called 'Air Power' will disappear entirely. Aircraft will revert to their primitive role of transporters.

An 'Air' Force armed with missiles is artillery whether you dress it in blue or khaki. Just as a tank is now and always was a self-propelled gun, no matter who rides in it.

Finally, I say that the place to start integration is at the top. These Tri Services cadet colleges do NOT accomplish the purpose of educating people with tri-service minds. Let the kids be taught to fly or to shoot or to sail, and let them stick to their trades until they are 30, and then send the brainy ones to a tri-service STAFF COLLEGE, and when they get on the Staff let them be staff officers in Green hats no matter where they came from. Army has done this for generations.

I am sending back your copy with notes, but will be glad to have it to keep when you have it ready for publication.

With Kindest Regards,

Sincerely

W.H.S.Macklin

"With Kindest Regards"! What a difference from the "God dammit Pope" of six years earlier! But then, in these six years, he had not heard of any bonehead plays.

On 17 July 1957, I thanked General Macklin, ending my letter with: "The full extent of my indebtedness to you will be apparent when I am able to send you the essay in its final form." I won the Conference of Defence Associations 1957 Prize Essay Contest (*Canadian Army Journal*, July 1958). I then wrote General Macklin again, apologizing for my plagiarism. He replied on 10 July 1958:

My dear Pope:-

I am very delighted that you picked up the prize in the Essay Competition. I have read your paper and will be reading it again.

The immense labour of producing a really good book on Defence Strategy rather appalls me though. As you say, there is some need of it. I will give the matter some thought.

I do not think that anybody who aspires to write should be ashamed of plagiarism. After all, Shakespeare stole practically all his plots....

The Army may be in for a lean time as we blow our money on jets and electronic gadgetry but its time will come again.

Regards,
W.H.S. Macklin

On 25 September 1958, the "Father of the Armoured Corps," retired Major-General F.F. Worthington, CB, MC, MM, CD, wrote me in his own hand from the Rideau Club in Ottawa:

> I have just finished reading your prize essay in the Army Journal and wish to express my congratulations for a well thought out and progressive exposition on a very important subject.
>
> Your thinking indicates a great deal of careful research to garner the truth. Many of the things you say I could match from practical experience.
>
> In my opinion, for what it is worth, you have put your finger on the exact spot that matters.
>
> The reason I write you, other than to commend your work, is that you would appear to be one of the younger thinkers. As such you must not be destroyed as was my old friend British Major-General J.F.C. Fuller. You will stir up a hornets' nest with your essay therefore I would like you to know there are others who believe as you do.
>
> I do not know where you are stationed but if you do come to Ottawa it would be a privilege to meet and talk with you.
>
> Yours sincerely.

Of course I answered and General Worthington wrote me again in his own hand on 14 October 1958:

> Thank you for your note of the 2nd. I am glad to note that you are to speak to the U.S.I. of Quebec which shows you have created interest. [Not quite! As a director of the Institute, I selected the speakers: I selected myself and *required* the attendance of Regular Force officers.] My old friend J.F.C. Fuller said to me once that by stretching the point almost until it seemed nonsense it would arouse the complacent into a fit of rage. Thus they would 'think' up rebuttals; any thinking was better than none.
>
> The fact that you have been awarded the prize is a good omen and that your thoughts have not fallen on barren ground. I have just returned

from the Armoured Corps Association Conference and was most pleasantly surprised to hear some of the thoughts expressed by our Brass....

My best wishes

On 24 September 1958, Colonel Jim Tedlie, who had been my second commandant at Fort Churchill eleven years earlier and was now commandant of the Royal Canadian Armoured Corps School in Camp Borden, wrote me:

> I received my issue of the *Canadian Army Journal* only yesterday and last night read with great interest your prize essay. Although, as ever, I cannot agree with everything you say, I must state that it is one of the best reasoned and comprehensive military essays I have ever read, and you are to be warmly congratulated. Marg too, read it with great interest and she joins me in sending congratulations.

> I also wish to acknowledge your kindness in sending me the third edition of *Operation Orders and Appreciations.* I have not as yet had a chance to read through it, but a quick glance at the format would indicate that it will be of great interest to us here at the school.

> If the luck of the draw should ever bring you to Camp Borden, do not fail to look us up.

Paul Hellyer, as Minister of National Defence, brought in unification of the armed forces in the sixties, quoting, according to Southam News, everyone from Sir Winston Churchill to Major W.H. Pope – an Irish compliment if ever I heard one! But despite this appeal to authority, unification was not well done. For instance, whereas before there had been three separate Chaplain Services (one Catholic and one Protestant) for each service each headed by a colonel, now two brigadier-generals (one Catholic, one Protestant) were placed over the lot, with no further substantive change. That's not unification; that's empire building! And putting everyone in green uniforms simply helps destroy regimental spirit, *esprit de corps*. As General Macklin makes clear, it is at the *headquarters* level that unification was – and is – needed. And thus avoid the "cascade of committees" which filled NDHQ in pre-unification days. Where things really did go wrong with unification was when, in the early seventies, the military and civilian sides of NDHQ were amalgamated. Sheer stupidity – as the confusion at NDHQ during the Somalia affair surely shows. But Hellyer had nothing to do with this military-civilian amalgamation: he was out of government by then.

My last military posting was to Quebec City, where I headed the General Staff of Eastern Quebec Area as GSO 2 from mid-1957 to August 1959. Having spent two years in Montreal qualifying officers, both Regular and Militia, for promotion, I continued my efforts in this direction in Quebec City. Once a week in the evening, I would lecture on military subjects in a Laval University classroom in Ste. Foy to Regular Army officers – mostly from the two battalions of R22eR then in Valcartier. Attendance was always excellent, if for no better reason than that I had the Area Commander sign a letter to COs telling them that if their officers did not attend my lectures, they, the COs, would be responsible for qualifying them for promotion and for the Staff College entrance exams.

I soon noted that in most Militia units there were lieutenants and captains that had not attempted to increase their military qualifications since the war: 12 years of enjoying the privileges and comforts of a fine club – the officers' mess – without having done a damn thing to earn them. Retirement of useless people is not a General Staff responsibility. It's the job of the "A" Branch. However, the General Staff is responsible for a unit's efficiency, its preparedness for war.

So, drawing the files of all the junior Militia officers in Eastern Quebec Area, I decided which of them appeared useless. I then wrote a "General Staff Efficiency Report" on each of these and sent the Reports to their COs, ending with a General Staff recommendation that they be transferred to the Supplementary Reserve. In a word: out.

It seems the COs were delighted with my recommendations. They were probably fed up having people hanging around purely for the social benefits of being a Militia officer. I do not recall one officer being retained when I had recommended his dismissal. Naturally, I had not told the "A" Branch of what I was doing. Had he known, Lieutenant-Colonel Henri Tellier, DSO, the AA&QMG,

would have, quite rightly, pointed out to me that while *unit* efficiency reports were the responsibility of the General Staff, *personnel* efficiency reports were the responsibility of the "A" Branch, which came under him, Tellier. In any event, when a year later orders came down from the Adjutant-General to do in effect what I had done a year earlier, our Area "A" Branch must have been surprised and gratified at what a clean slate of officers each unit had.

Shortly after I had initiated the clean sweep of inefficient Militia officers, a large-scale officers' ball was held in Quebec City. I went alone. At that time, I was unhappily girlless – my own fault, of course: if you so mess up your life (and that of the 20-year-old girl who loved you) that you reach the age of 34 unmarried, you'll find that all the current sweet young debutantes consider you too old (or their mothers won't let you in the house regardless of what their daughters may think), while all the beautiful post-debutantes will be married (and quite often faithful to their husbands). A Militia captain – one of those that had unexpectedly found himself in the Supplementary Reserve – came up to me and said, in a *not* unfriendly manner, "*Vous êtes le bourreau.*" ("You are the executioner.") But he didn't quite have it right. According to my *Larousse*, *le bourreau* is he who is charged to execute corporal punishment pronounced by a criminal court, especially the death penalty. But I was acting under my own authority; indeed, as Henri Tellier would have told me, beyond my authority.

Quite contrary to Army regulations, I had been active in the CCF/PSD (Co-operative Commonwealth Federation/*Parti Social Démocratique*) since arriving in Montreal in late 1954. The GOC Quebec Command, Major-General Bernatchez, knew I was a member of the PSD. We would sometimes talk about Quebec politics in the mess. The General's own brother was a member of the provincial assembly. But the General never gave me the slightest indication that he knew how active I was. If he had had any idea, I think he would have warned me that this was precisely the type of bonehead play that the Adjutant-General had said, in 1952, would lead to my instant dismissal from the Army. On the other hand, maybe everybody in HQ Quebec Command knew and agreed somewhat along these lines: "What the hell, Pope will always be doing something like this. But he's useful and so long as he doesn't join a union picket line in full uniform, with his medals, sword, and spurs, let's just shut up about it."

Thus, in Quebec City, I was secretary of the local PSD club (calling myself "Jean Dumonceau," part of my Belgian grandfather's name), and as secretary, I invited the CCF leader, Mr. Coldwell, to address our club. He did so, with great gusto and in as partisan a manner as anyone could have desired. This got a good play in the press. Unfortunately, no distinction was made between the completely non-partisan talk to the United Services Institute and the highly partisan one to the Social Democrats. Premier Duplessis ran a tight ship and he was not at all pleased that a damned Socialist should, apparently, have said all those rude things about him to the United Services Institute right across the street from his office. One of my co-directors in the Institute was a distant cousin, Colonel Taschereau. Since he was also ADC to the Lieutenant-Governor, he did his best to avoid the Premier for the next week or two – not entirely successfully, as he told me with a pained look on his face.

On 22 October 1958, I wrote the Commander Eastern Quebec Area, Brigadier Ménard, as follows:

> 1. Yesterday morning, I received a phone call from Mr. Jean Pellerin of *Radio-Canada*, Montreal, asking me to take part in the television programme '*Les Idées en Marche*' at 2000 hrs 7 November 1958. Apparently, this will be a one half-hour panel discussion on conscription.
>
> 2. I asked Mr. Pellerin how it came about that I was being considered for such a programme. Mr. Pellerin replied that it had been decided that among French-speaking officers I would be suitable. It is possible that my recent article in the *Canadian Army Journal* has drawn attention to my name. Also, I know Mr. André Laurendeau [publisher of *Le Devoir*] who, I believe, often takes part in these panel discussions on '*Les Idées en Marche*.' [Not having a TV, I couldn't be sure!]
>
> 3. In accordance with QR (Army) 19.37(4), I request permission to accept this invitation.

Brigadier Ménard passed my letter to the GOC Quebec Command in Montreal, Major-General J.M. Rockingham, who replied to the Brigadier on 29 October 1958:

> First of all, let me assure you that I think that Major Pope would do a very good job of this subject and would be nothing but a credit to the Army, even when he declared that he was not speaking for the Army and was in civilian clothes etc. But, I must say that I cannot see how he could possibly keep away from answers which would involve him in a political controversy. As you know, serving soldiers are expressly forbidden to discuss in public matters of policy. Conscription is a matter of government policy and a subject on which a serving officer should not express his opinion.
>
> Were he to head off numerous embarrassing questions, which would be bound to be directed at him, by a statement to the effect he could not enter into this discussion because a policy matter, then there would be no point in being on the discussion at all. Obviously, the promoters of the programme are hoping for a sensational discussion, and, in my opinion, the only people who are in any way permitted to deal with this subject are a cabinet minister or somebody appointed by them to take part in this discussion.
>
> Throughout history conscription has been an explosive and dangerous football in Canada, and I can't think of a subject which could do more damage to a serving officer were he to discuss it.
>
> Would you convey this information to Major Pope and tell him that if he is not satisfied with my decision, that he is to say so without hesitation and I will take the matter up with the CGS.
>
> Actually, apart from the display of intelligence which, I am sure, would emanate from Major Pope in his public discussion, I think that the rest of the effect would be detrimental to the Canadian Army and perhaps to the whole Department of National Defence. I certainly would refuse such an invitation if it were given to me.

Naturally, I disregarded General Rockingham's obvious horror at the whole idea and took another kick at the can by writing Brigadier Ménard on 3 November 1958, but I was rejected again.

In early 1958, Brigadier Allard told me to give a lecture on patrolling in the next war to the scouts and snipers platoons of the two R22eR battalions then in Valcartier. I decided *not* to make the mistake that others had made in Korea; that is, blithely assume that one's past experience of war was all that was needed to prepare for the next one. I therefore studied many accounts of war, leading to my "Problems of Future War: The Tactical Doctrine and Organization Required by Land Forces" (*Canadian Army Journal*, April 1959, and republished in the military journals of Australia, Belgium, and India. And maybe also, I like to think, somewhere in the Kremlin – though the Red Army, like the Americans, might well have considered me "tainted" by the Trotskyist-Colleen episode of eight years earlier!).

My study may have led to a more useful lecture but that's not certain. The first question asked by one of the scouts was: "Why doesn't the married men's bus stop at Ancienne Lorette anymore?" *All* that the man had got from my lecture was that I was from the Area HQ in Quebec City and therefore should know something about transportation arrangements from Quebec City.

But the study of the next war also led to my resignation. I was told in mid-1959 that I would be returning to 1R22eR in September as second-in-command. Certainly, this meant that my army career was going well and that I had, in effect, overcome the 14 months loss of seniority that I had visited on myself in 1951-52 by upsetting the Adjutant-General once too often. But, by now, my disagreement with NATO's strategy and my interest in politics had become overwhelming. I told Major-General Allard, now Vice-Chief of the General Staff, of my intention to resign. He wrote me on 9 June 1959 (translated):

> My dear Harry:
>
> I was very surprised to learn of your decision to quit the Army for a civilian position and I hope that this decision is not irrevocable. I easily sympathise with your feelings of frustration; if you had an idea of the situation here, no doubt these feelings would be intensified. Nevertheless, after the rain comes fine weather and I am firmly convinced that the balance is now starting to shift and is moving away from the aerian philosophy and the principle of the thirty day war. "I think if I were in your place I would wait approximately another year before definitely quitting the profession that you have followed for seventeen years with considerable success.
>
> Sincerely yours,
>
> Jean V. Allard

Once again, I did not take a General's advice. Thus on 30 June 1959 I presented the following letter to Brigadier Dollard Ménard, DSO (who had taken over as Area Commander from Brigadier Allard, on the latter going to Ottawa as VCGS on promotion to major-general):

1.   For a long time I have been interested in political questions and in strategy and higher tactics. I have come to the conclusion that our foreign policy under both the Liberal and Progressive-Conservative Administrations does not reflect the true interests of the Canadian people and that it will lead to disaster. I am further convinced that the organization of our armed forces is faulty, that the emphasis on the employment of nuclear weapons by NATO is suicidal, that our adherence to NORAD is wrong, and that the nuclear tactics devised by our army are inadequate.

2.   As a member of the regular army there is very little I can do to change these conditions. I am therefore compelled to resign from the regular army, which I now do.

3.   I regret having thus to break my service with the Royal 22e Régiment, whose troops I have been honoured to command in two wars. So that I may again be able to serve with the Royal 22e Régiment in any future conflict, I request that upon my release I be transferred to the supplementary reserve under QR(Army) 10.04(1).

4. Mr. Hazen Argue, Parliamentary Leader of the Co-operative Commonwealth Federation/*Parti Social Démocratique* has asked me to become his executive assistant on or about 15 Aug 59. So that I may have a short time to take over from the present executive assistant I request that my release be completed by 10 Aug 59.

5. Since my employment with Mr. Argue will be in the Civil Service, I think release under QR(Army) 15.01(4)(a) is appropriate. If higher authority does not agree, then I request I be released under QR(Army) 15.01(4)(d).

6. I am aware that my release from the regular army is not to my advantage in regard to pension rights or in regard to my salary in the new position. My reasons for resigning are given in paragraph 1. They are not related to my pending appointment as second in command of the 1st Battalion of my Regiment, which appointment I regard as a compliment. My decision is irrevocable.

I was right about my salary: a cut from $7,500 to $4,100. I was equally right about the "pension rights:" I got back (without interest), as I had expected, only what I had contributed myself since 1942 –

around $6,000. A friend was executive assistant to the Minister of National Defence of the time, Major-General George Pearkes, VC. When my resignation landed on the General's desk, he is reported to have said: "Good God, what about his pension? Do you think I should talk to his father?" However, old Pearkes got over his initial impulse: his was the last minute on the memorandum of the CGS to the Minister: "This officer's resignation may be accepted but he is not entitled to a pension."

Major-General J.M. Rockingham, as GOC Quebec Command, in a sense gave me my last army confidential report in forwarding my letter of resignation to Ottawa on 2 July 1959:

> Major Pope, in my opinion, is a very able and efficient officer and I feel will be a great loss to the Canadian Army. However, I see no choice but to recommend that his resignation be accepted. In view of his statement in paragraph 1 of his letter, it would seem to me that it would be impossible to keep him serving in the army when his views are contrary to established policies.

I had, of course, sent a copy of my letter of resignation to the Honorary Colonel of the Regiment, General Georges P. Vanier. He replied, in his own hand in French, on 3 July 1959:

> My dear Harry,
>
> I deeply regret your departure from the Royal 22e Régiment, where you fought in such a way as to bring us honour. We are suffering a heavy loss and deplore your resignation.
>
> On the other hand you are master of your destiny. You feel a call to a very different field of action.
>
> Be assured that your Colonel who is also your friend offers you his warm and affectionate wishes for a successful and happy future.
>
> I hope we will have the occasion to see each other again before long.
>
> Cordially yours
>
> Georges P. Vanier

Epilogue

Since this is a book of military history with emphasis, naturally, on service in action in both Italy and Korea, it ends, appropriately, with the letter from General Vanier deploring my resignation. But my life didn't end 40 years ago.

I resigned from the Regular Army in August 1959 to become openly active in politics – having been active, but not *openly* active, for some years previously. For the first four and a half years after my resignation, I was executive assistant to the leaders of the CCF/NDP in the House of Commons – in succession Hazen Argue (who quit us on the way to becoming a Liberal Senator), Bert Herridge (the Squire of the Kootenays), and Tommy Douglas. I finally ended my support of the NDP in 1975 when it showed it knew no more about achieving full employment without inflation than the others.

But to go back to 1962. For that year's federal election the New Democrats of Calgary North wanted Bertrand Russell as their candidate in the hope of winning against the Minister of National Defence, Douglas Harkness, on the issue of the nuclear-armed Bomarc. While Lord Russell had better things to do, I didn't. While I was thus losing my first election (of a total of five), the Créditistes were winning some 25 or so seats in Quebec with such simple and sensible slogans as "What is physically possible must be made financially possible."

So on returning to Ottawa I began studying economics. Early on I was fortunate in having a professor who knew his Maynard Keynes but couldn't teach it. Thus he had his students read aloud *The General Theory* by the hour. Ever since, I can find such good bits as these with ease:

"....one can almost hope....the technique of the bank rate will never be used again to protect the foreign balance in conditions in which it is likely to cause unemployment at home." [Translation: The central bank forcing up interest rates to bring in foreign loans that will force up the external price of our dollar, thus reducing exports and increasing imports, causing increased unemployment.]

Keynes looked forward to "the euthanasia of the rentier, and consequently, the euthanasia of the cumulative oppressive power of the capitalist to exploit the scarcity-value of capital [money]. Interest to-day rewards no genuine sacrifice....The owner of capital can obtain interest because capital is scarce....there are no intrinsic reasons for the scarcity of capital." [Translation: *Never* allow the central bank to force up interest rates: there are other, far better, ways to prevent inflation. Interest rates must be kept low *permanently*.]

These ideas are not hard to grasp, though the thinking behind them does require somewhat more effort. Because this effort has not been forthcoming for more than 30 years either from governors of the Bank of Canada or from officials of the Department of Finance, about a dozen of us formed the Cartier Circle in mid-1982 in the hope of influencing government policy in a direction more favourable to Canada. With not the slightest success.

Fourteen years ago we expanded the Cartier Circle into the Committee on Monetary and Economic Reform (COMER) with about 20 times as many members mostly in Canada and the United States.

In 1971 McClelland and Stewart published my *The Elephant and the Mouse: A Handbook on Regaining Control of Canada's Economy*, an out-growth of the work I did as a research assistant in the mid-sixties for the Task Force set up by Walter Gordon on Foreign Ownership and the Structure of Canadian Industry ("The Watkins Report"). Though the print run of 5,000 copies of my book was eventually sold out, no one got rich on the deal. But my now being a published author induced McGraw-Hill Ryerson to ask me to take on the Canadianizing of Campbell R. McConnell's *Economics*. Thus between 1978 and 1990 I co-authored the first five Canadian editions of McConnell/Pope *Economics*. While setting out conventional economics, I also happily set about analysing the errors of Ottawa's economic policies – those of Finance and the Bank of Canada.

When I retired early from 20 years of teaching economics at Ryerson to give me more time to write, the publishers seem to have decided that going to a thoroughly non-controversial text was worth a try. So the 6th (1993), the 7th (1996), and the 8th (1999) editions came out without my name on them and, so far as I could see, not a controversial word left in them.

Thus I was delighted when, in the summer of 1995, COMER decided to begin a series of short books on aspects of economic policy and asked me to write the first one. The first edition of *All you MUST know about economics* came out in 1996. The first printing quickly sold out. Sheila Kathleen, my wife, and I then established our own publishing company – Bergendal – to handle the second printing. In 1997 Bergendal published our second edition, now also in its second printing.

Both editions cover all the essentials of economics. They are distinguished from the mainstream principles of economics textbooks first by their brevity; secondly, by their analysis and subsequent criticism of the policies of the Government and Bank of Canada; and thirdly, by their chapter showing how foreign investment in Canada is *not* an unmitigated, costless benefit. The emphasis on *MUST* in the title of both editions simply means that in a little over a hundred pages enough is written for the reader to understand what Ottawa is doing wrong and what it must do to do it right.

I cannot deny that when I went back to university full-time in the mid-sixties to get down to serious study of my new trade of economics, I often enough felt a bit of an ass. There I was, well into my forties, a student again almost 25 years after marching off the square at RMC. I occasionally had a dream, a nightmare really, of being back in the army in my old rank of major – sometimes even as a captain if my subconscious believed I was again getting the Adjutant-General upset – while all my equals of 1959 were brigadier-generals, at least. In short, it was a feeling of failure.

I've long since got over all that (otherwise I wouldn't talk about it!).

My Regiment has not been to war since I left and so I've missed nothing that, in my view, would have compelled me to return – or at least try to. On the other hand, I am still being useful – at least trying to be – by writing and advocating economic policies that would bring us back to the full employment without inflation that existed after the war for ten full years from 1945 to 1956.

Finally, had I not become an economist and taught what I knew, I never would have met Sheila Kathleen. And she is worth incomparably more than crossed sword and baton and as many maple leaves as Ottawa might have cared to add to my epaulettes.

William Henry Pope
Uxbridge, Ontario, 2000

Index